LEGENDS OF WRESTLING

"CLASSY"
FREDDIE BLASSIE

World Wrestling
Entertainment™

LEGENDS OF
WRESTLING

"CLASSY" FREDDIE BLASSIE

LISTEN, YOU PENCIL NECK GEEKS

FREDDIE BLASSIE

with

KEITH ELLIOT GREENBERG

POCKET BOOKS

New York   London   Toronto   Sydney

World Wrestling
Entertainment™

First Pocket Books trade paperback printing February 2004

10 9 8 7 6 5 4 3 2 1

Visit us on the World Wide Web
http://simonsays.com
http://www.wwe.com

Manufactured in the United States of America

For information regarding special discounts for bulk purchases,
please contact Simon & Schuster Special Sales at 1-800-456-6798 or
business@simonandschuster.com

To Miyako,

I can't
imagine life
without you

ACKNOWLEDGMENTS

Aside from the people quoted in this book, the co-author wishes to thank the following people.

From World Wrestling Entertainment: Barry Werner, Stacey Pascarella, Mike Faziolli, Frank Vitucci, Jayson Bernstein, John Arnold.

From Pocket Books: Margaret Clark and Dave Stevenson.

Dr. Mike Lano was a constant resource, providing background about Freddie Blassie's years in the ring, as well as pro wrestling's old "territory" system. Jeff Steinmark recalled Blassie career highlights, and even accompanied me to Freddie's home to help us reminisce. Keith Schildroth of the *St. Louis Post Dispatch* and Tom Raber helped paint a vivid image of old St. Louis for me. Cage Nakayama and I discussed Blassie's Japanese tours, and WWE career. Shun and Wally Yamaguchi, as well as Hisatune Shimma, assisted me in Japan, while Yoshimi Homma translated. Jessica Dymczyk transcribed interviews, as did my wife, Jennifer Berton Greenberg, who also offered useful insights about the manuscript. Ed Ricciuti helped orchestrate my long relationship with WWE in 1985, and conveyed valuable writing tenets back when I was impressionable enough to absorb them.

I also relied on Dave Meltzer's *Wrestling Observer Newsletter* and Steve Yohe's vital Freddie Blassie record book to maintain historical accuracy.

INTRODUCTION

This book is very special to me because Freddie Blassie is very special to me. He's a unique, charismatic individual who can tell great tales, and his story is very important.

Freddie Blassie is a foundation of our business. Before there was World Wrestling Entertainment, Freddie was out there. Freddie has transcended so many different eras. He worked for my grandfather, he worked for my dad, he's worked with my wife, Linda, and me, and he's worked with our children, Stephanie and Shane. We're deep in terms of our roots. And no one feels greater loyalty to Freddie Blassie than I do.

This is Freddie's story, but, to a degree, it's also my family's story.

To a certain extent, Freddie represents my father to me, the era that my father came from. Every time I'm with Freddie, I think of my dad. I remember how much my father admired Freddie because he was a ballsy son of a bitch who gave so much. He had a very strict way of looking at the world. Either he was on your team or he wasn't. And when he was on your team, there wasn't anything he wouldn't do for you. It's a quality a lot of people lack, and I'm honored that my family meant so much to this exceptional man.

To me, Freddie Blassie is an entertainer, and that's what our business is about. Whether it was Gorgeous George headlining the show or The Rock or Stone Cold Steve Austin or Undertaker, it's always been about entertainment. Freddie understood that. He was a pioneer who knew—whether it was 1942 or 2002—how to use psychology to get a boo or get a cheer.

INTRODUCTION

This book is a testament to the phenomenon that we sometimes called The Hollywood Fashion Plate.

As Freddie gets on in his years, I think about the days when he won't be here anymore, what a loss it will be to our company, and to me personally. I love Freddie very much, and it touches me to think that now millions of readers will know him the way I have.

—Vince McMahon

ONE:
IT HAPPENED IN ST. LOUIS

"Blassie, you ain't worth a bucket of cold piss!"

I scowled at the crowd squeezed into Jersey City's Roosevelt Stadium, a decaying ballpark in a grimy city. Once, the Brooklyn Dodgers used to come across the Hudson River and play a couple of home games here every year. But that was a long time ago. Now, it was 1964, the Dodgers were in sunny California, and everything about Jersey City seemed hopeless. Unless you were Italian, and loved Bruno Sammartino.

"Go back to California, you bleached blond piece of shit!"

Bruno was a bear of a man with a busted nose and cauliflower ears. Like a lot of the crowd, he was from Italy, and even worked the same lousy jobs they did when he came to America. But Bruno wasn't hauling bricks or pouring concrete anymore. He was the champion of the World Wide Wrestling Federation (WWWF), the company that later became World Wrestling Federation and then World Wrestling Entertainment (WWE). When Bruno won a match, the people in Roosevelt Stadium felt like champions, too. And when someone like me beat the shit out of him, they wanted to hang me upside down from a gas station, just like the Italian partisans did when they finally got their hands on Mussolini.

"You're a no-good bastard, Blassie!"

I kicked at the ropes, and waved my arms forward, dismissing the crowd and everything they believed in.

"Sit down, spaghetti bender!" I yelled at the entire front section.

I was the heel, the bad guy in the match, and I was doing what a heel was supposed to do, "get heat" from the fans. Good heat was when they got engaged in the action, jumping up and booing. This was bad heat, the kind that could get you killed.

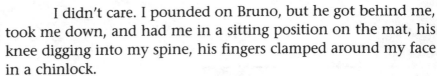
I didn't care. I pounded on Bruno, but he got behind me, took me down, and had me in a sitting position on the mat, his knee digging into my spine, his fingers clamped around my face in a chinlock.

Garbage was flying around everywhere, and there was no security that I could see. Fourteen thousand people swarmed forward, like the mosquitoes coming off Newark Bay. Then, some big fat Italian woman—who was probably fifty but looked like she was eighty—came running all the way up to the edge of the ring. She was straight off the boat, wearing a dress they wouldn't even sell you in America.

"Bruno!" she yelled, beating on the ring apron. *"Kill-a the son of a bitch! Kill-a the son of a bitch!"*

Sammartino was pulling my head back, but I looked down, over Bruno's stubby fingers, and blurted out the two words that summed up my attitude about her, and my philosophy about everything else in life.

"Fuck you!"

2

I had to wait eighty-five years before someone asked me to write a book, which is really incredible, since I've done things that no ordinary human would do. I was the most obnoxious wrestler who ever lived. That's why I was stabbed twenty-one times by crazy fans, and had acid thrown on me in Los Angeles. I used to bite my opponents 'til they bled, and file my teeth on interviews. When my knees gave out on me, and I began a second career as a manager in the World Wrestling Federation, I'd regularly break my cane over the head of whomever my protégé was wrestling.

During my first tour of Japan, twenty-five people dropped dead from heart attacks, just watching me on TV. Over my entire career, ninety-two people died because of "Classy" Freddie Blassie. But I've always said that was a disappointment. My ambition in life was to get one hundred.

Even now, women do a double-take when they walk by me on the street. And you should have seen me fifty years ago! I had thirty different ring robes, with sequins and everything. That's why

I was called The Hollywood Fashion Plate. Even when I wasn't dressed up, I looked like I stepped out of the pages of *Esquire.*

Women used to drag their pencil-neck husbands to the arena just to see what I'd be wearing that night. I used to enjoy teasing these women, calling them frustrated housewives, and reminding them that one second with Blassie was equivalent to two hours with an ordinary layman.

I remember taking my mother to the arena once, after I'd become one of the most notorious heels in the business.

"They hate you like this all over?" she asked me.

"Yeah."

"I don't understand it. Why do you have to call the fans names? Why don't you be nice like you used to be?"

I told my mother to look at the kind of people sitting in the audience. "As far as these idiots are concerned, I'm not nice and I don't want to be nice. Do you see anybody with any intelligence, any brains? They're not fit to travel in Freddie Blassie's company."

My mother stared at me, a little bewildered. She wasn't sure if I was being myself, or living my gimmick.

To tell you the truth, neither was I.

In the town where my mother, Anna Sind, came from in what was then Austro-Hungary, you measured a person's wealth by how many geese he owned. Her father had a big flock of geese, but this one mischievous kid, this rotten bastard, would always trespass on the property. He'd run at the geese and chase them toward the edge of this cliff. Some of them couldn't stay airborne, and they'd hit the ground and die.

Nobody could do anything to stop this kid. His father would beat his brains out, but the kid kept coming back and killing those geese. He was a mean son of a bitch.

Looking back on it, I'd say my mother wasn't dealing with a full deck because she married this ding-a-ling. His name was Jacob Blassie—or *Yacob,* as they said in German—and he moved her across the Atlantic Ocean, from her little village to south St. Louis, Missouri.

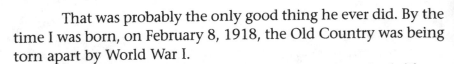

That was probably the only good thing he ever did. By the time I was born, on February 8, 1918, the Old Country was being torn apart by World War I.

I didn't come into the world lightly. I weighed fifteen pounds. My mother would have had an easier time giving birth to an elephant, and she never had another kid again. I don't know if that was because her labor was so difficult or she simply realized that once you have a Freddie Blassie, there's no point in trying again.

My mother had been a frail woman, but, once I was born, she began putting on weight. She got heavier and heavier until she hit the two-hundred-pound mark. Still, her bulk didn't slow her down. She worked in a cotton mill when I was a kid, operating a machine. I remember my grandmother taking me to visit her at the mill at lunchtime, and knowing that I was the reason she got up and worked so hard every day. If there ever was a god on earth, it was my mother. She was a magnificent woman.

My father—who was called "Jake" in America—was a completely different story. He was a big, sturdy bastard who worked as a hod carrier, hauling around buckets of cement dangling from a stick over his shoulders, at construction sites. He did his job well enough. But when he got paid on Friday, he'd start drinking, and sometimes wouldn't come out of his idiotic stupor until Monday afternoon.

What was even worse was the way he'd mistreat my mother. He'd call her terrible names, slap his hand across her flesh, and pound on her with his fists. I still hate him for doing that, and when the fighting started, I'd run a mile and a half to his parents' house, and tell them, "Dad hit Mom again."

My grandfather would tell my grandmother to get dressed, and then they'd hurry to my parents' house, raging the whole way. "You're a bum," my grandfather would scream at my father. "You have a wonderful wife, and this is how you treat her? You don't deserve your wife and son! You don't deserve anything." But my father didn't care.

My parents were always breaking up, and getting back together, and I'd stay with my grandparents for long periods of time. Even when I was away from my father, I'd hear about his drunken calamities. He had this feud going with this other

An undated family photo of Freddie.

moron, a saloon owner, and they'd beat the hell out of each other whenever they could. Unfortunately for my family, and the rest of the city of St. Louis, they never killed each other. The police would come and lock them both up, and then they'd meet somewhere else the next week for a rematch.

When I was about thirteen, I reached my limit. My father hit my mother, and I picked up a baseball bat, got behind him,

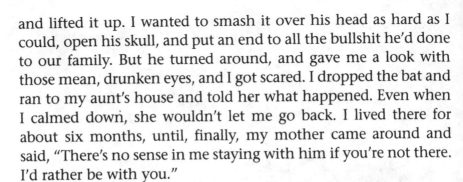

and lifted it up. I wanted to smash it over his head as hard as I could, open his skull, and put an end to all the bullshit he'd done to our family. But he turned around, and gave me a look with those mean, drunken eyes, and I got scared. I dropped the bat and ran to my aunt's house and told her what happened. Even when I calmed down, she wouldn't let me go back. I lived there for about six months, until, finally, my mother came around and said, "There's no sense in me staying with him if you're not there. I'd rather be with you."

Somewhere in the back of her mind, she'd thought that I would come home because I wanted to have a father. But he wasn't worth a damn.

My mother and I now struggled together. At one point, we were living over a store, and felt so hungry that my mother rigged up some apparatus so she could pull potatoes into our apartment through a hole in the floor. No matter how bad it was, though, my grandparents always came through for us.

Like my parents, my grandparents were named Anna and Jacob Blassie. They were decent, proud, honest people who would have gone to war for me. I remember when I first started wrestling, my grandfather came to the arena, and grabbed a chair when he saw my opponent torturing me on the mat. He was moving toward the ring when the security people grabbed him and threw him out into the street. My mother was there, and explained that the old man's grandson was one of the wrestlers. But when the security guards invited him back in, my grandfather said in his German accent, "The hell with you. You put me out, and I'm going to stay out."

Once, while I was attending St. Peter and Paul Grammar School, we were taking a test and I accidentally broke the point of my pencil. I asked the nun whether I could sharpen the pencil again and, for some reason, she refused. So I went home and told my grandmother about it, and she flew into a frenzy. She was a stocky woman, built more or less like a man, and the next morning, she put on her shawls from the Old Country and marched into the school.

"That's my number-one grandson," she told the nun. "The next time you don't let him sharpen his pencil, I'll pull your arms out of their sockets."

Believe it or not, I sang in the church choir as a kid, and enjoyed it very much. I guess the priests saw something in me because they asked if I wanted to become an altar boy. That was a little too much for me, waking up earlier than everyone else, putting on a black cassock, getting the holy water and the wine ready, and standing there, looking serious, as I handed the chalices to the priest during mass. I guess I didn't want to make that much of a commitment to my Catholic faith.

I remember before I had my First Holy Communion, I was told to go up to the front of the church, kneel down, stick my tongue out, and receive the host. Now, the nuns impressed upon me that I couldn't touch the wafer with my fingers. But how the hell could I stop it from falling out of my mouth if I couldn't touch it? I felt like a jackass, with the priest standing in front of me while I stuck my tongue in and out to keep the host from falling, lapping at it like a fuckin' cat.

At Christmastime, at St. Peter and Paul, they'd have St. Nicholas visit the school. But instead of giving out presents like a regular Santa Claus, this guy—probably a demented priest in a costume—would pick out all the boys who'd done something wrong—playing hookey, hitting other kids—and whip their asses.

One year, I heard him coming up the stairs, in his red suit and fake beard, screaming, "Blassie! Blassie!" And I said, "Fuck, I don't have to put up with this," and darted out of the classroom. Then, he told the kids to run into the hall after me.

"Get him! Get him!" St. Nicholas hollered.

Swinging his strap, he chased after my so-called buddies, urging them to block my escape.

"Watch the steps! Don't let him get down the steps! Or you'll receive his punishment instead!"

Everyone was screaming and running and bumping into each other, and my friends grabbed me and threw me back at St. Nicholas. And he had a merry fuckin' Christmas that year, slapping my daylights out with his big strap.

Occasionally, during my wrestling career, I told people that I'd graduated high school in St. Louis, and attended two years of college. I always made an effort to stay well read, so nobody really questioned me; it's not like I claimed to have a doctorate from Oxford or anything. But I was just blowing hot air. I

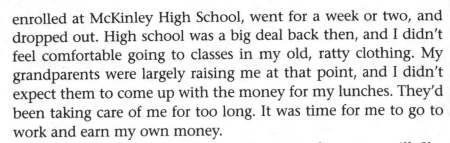

enrolled at McKinley High School, went for a week or two, and dropped out. High school was a big deal back then, and I didn't feel comfortable going to classes in my old, ratty clothing. My grandparents were largely raising me at that point, and I didn't expect them to come up with the money for my lunches. They'd been taking care of me for too long. It was time for me to go to work and earn my own money.

By then, my mother was no longer in the cotton mill. She was working in a restaurant, where she asked around to see if anyone could find me a job. The woman who ran the restaurant bought her meat from this place called the Lynn Meat Company, and she talked to the owner and found out that they needed a kid to help out. I'd clean up, trim all the bones, and do anything else the meatcutters wanted. I wasn't a cutter, though—that's a trade in itself. At the end of the week, my salary was eight dollars.

St. Louis was a wild town back then, full of pool halls and speakeasies and mayhem. In the north side, there were shoe factories. The south side was loaded with breweries. The biggest was Griesedieck Brothers, and it remained that way until the 1960s, when Anheuser-Busch overtook them. The kids played "bottle caps," a form of baseball with bottle caps and broomsticks, and a game called "cork ball" with barrel corks from the breweries.

The St. Louis Browns didn't make it to the World Series until 1944, so the city's motto for a long time was, "First in booze. First in shoes. Last in the American League."

Criminals ran the show in the neighborhoods where I traveled. I remember walking to the movies with my mother, and seeing glass all over the place because some gangsters had pulled up in front of a saloon with machine guns blasting.

If you drifted a few blocks in the wrong direction, you were in a fight. There were Italian gangs, German gangs, Irish gangs, Hungarian gangs, fighting with knives, brass knuckles, and, occasionally, guns.

Because my father was so violent, I knew how to handle myself with my fists, and there were few fights I remember losing. My father saw me punching it out with some kid one time, then beat me up for fighting. I thought that was pretty strange, since he was getting locked up for doing the same thing almost every Saturday night.

After a while, I got tired of fighting in the street, and thought about making a career out of it. I began boxing at the Seward Community Center, and earned a bit of a reputation for myself, even winning the Heavyweight Championship in one tournament there.

But as natural as the sweet science came to me, wrestling was really my calling. I'd been sneaking into the matches since I was allowed to cross the street. It didn't matter if it was a big show at the Peerless Theatre or a rinky-dink card in a carnival tent. I couldn't get enough of the squared circle, and, by my teens, had seen some of the best wrestlers ever to pass through St. Louis.

Ed "Strangler" Lewis held a version of the world championship four times, sometimes using a headlock as his finishing hold. Back then, most fans believed that wrestling was pure sport, and when Lewis clamped on a headlock, they thought the other guy's skull was going to crack. Lewis claimed that he'd perfected his headlock by practicing with a wooden head, squeezing until the thing burst.

What I didn't know, of course, was how much clout Lewis enjoyed behind the scenes. He, his manager Billy Sandow, and Toots Mondt—a sadistic wrestler, as well as a promoter who'd team up with WWE owner Vince McMahon's father, Vince, Sr., in the WWWF decades later—were called the Goldust Trio. Lewis was the one who kept them in power. He didn't mind losing his championship when it was good for the promotion. But he was also a legitimate shooter—a wrestler who could go at it for real when the situation warranted. If an opponent who was scheduled to lose tried going into business for himself and turning the match into a shoot—or real contest—the Strangler would stretch him until he repented.

There was also Joe Stecher, Hook Nose Nelson, Joe Sanderson, and my idol, George Tragos. I never saw the tough Greek lose, and there was good reason for that. He was one of the most vicious "hookers" of all time. A hook was an excruciating, potentially crippling hold that could be applied when a match turned into a shoot. There were very few real hookers in the business, capable of positioning an opponent's body to break bones or cut off his breathing, and guys like Tragos were treated like grand masters in the dressing room. In one match, he supposedly ripped an opponent's muscles, tendons, and ligaments with a top wristlock. Later on, the story goes, the separated bone became infected, and the poor guy had to have his arm amputated.

It was Tragos who trained Lou Thesz, the son of a Hungarian shoemaker from another St. Louis neighborhood, into possibly the most respected hooker of the twentieth century, a six-time World Heavyweight Champion, and the Babe Ruth of the squared circle.

Every time the bigger names visited St. Louis, they worked out at Harry Cook's Gym, at Sixth and Pine. The place would usually be packed with people, watching the guys spar on the mat. At first, I was a member of the peanut gallery, too. Eventually, though, I got up the nerve to ask some of the wrestlers to teach me a few moves.

Today, there are wrestling schools all over North America, where students are taught how to take a bump—or fall—properly, deliver a moonsault off the top rope onto a crash mat, and cut a promo—or interview. But in the 1930s, no one was that forthcoming about pro wrestling's show business aspect. You trained like you were training for the Olympics.

10

If a guy was in a good mood at Harry Cook's, he'd show me a half nelson or an armbar. But usually, the experienced wrestlers just wanted to practice on you. They'd grind you into the mat and then, when you got up and couldn't move your neck, laugh about it to each other.

After a while, I got to know some of the wrestlers, and when I went to the Wednesday night matches at St. Paul's Social Center in East St. Louis, the ticket taker would wave me in. One night in 1935, when I was seventeen years old, I was there with a girl, and someone came out and said that one of the wrestlers didn't show up. Well, I'd already told this girl I was a wrestler, so I kept up the act.

"I'll take his place," I said. "The only problem is I didn't bring any gear."

The promoter was willing to provide the ring attire for me. He gave me a pair of trunks, and shoes that were about two sizes too large. He also offered to lend me a jock strap—*someone else's* jock strap—but I passed. I was told my payoff was going to be a dollar, but I couldn't get into the ring until I paid five dollars for a wrestling license. So right away, I was four dollars in the hole.

If anyone had asked me about the sport's authenticity, I would have argued its virtues with all my heart and soul. There was no meeting ahead of time to discuss the match's highlights—or "high spots," as the wrestlers call them—with my opponent, or arrange the finish. This was going to be a legitimate wrestling match, and I came to the ring to shoot.

The ring was like a boxing ring, only smaller, and from the dressing room, the thing looked pretty frightening. I remember walking through the crowd, and having my name announced: *"From South St. Louis—Fred-die Bla-asie!"* It was a moment I'd anticipated for a long time, but now I was too nervous to feel any excitement.

My opponent's name was Bill Scharbet, a curtain raiser who worked the second or third match every Wednesday at St. Paul's. There was nothing special about him; he had no color. But he still knew enough to batter me.

Almost immediately after the bell rang, Scharbet put me down on the mat. That's where I remained, while he tried out his arsenal: a wristlock, an armlock, a full nelson. I can't recall delivering any offense. I just tried to stay in the match, and make a respectable showing. After seven or eight minutes, I finally gave up.

Scharbet got some polite applause from the crowd, and I walked back to the dressing room, almost invisible, got dressed, and tried to slink out of the building. Then, I remembered my date. I went back into the arena, and there she was, waiting for me.

"You didn't do too good," she kind of mumbled.

But she didn't say it in a haughty way. In fact, she was pretty impressed. After all, how many girls from the neighborhood could tell their friends that they went out on a date with a bona fide professional wrestler? She thought I was something.

When I was nineteen, my mother remarried. Her husband, a steel foundry inspector, was a wonderful Croatian guy named Ilya Miletic, but we called him Eli. As soon as we met, I thought of him as a father; it was like he carried my mother in the palm of one hand, and me in the other. I sometimes wonder about the childhood I would have had if he'd come into my life earlier.

Anna and Freddie's stepfather, Eli.

12

Eli had a sickly daughter named Antoinette. She had terrible eyes, and would tilt her head back and peek up at me when we were talking. The time we decorated the Christmas tree together still stands out as one of my happiest memories. I bought these bulbs and ornaments and had them spread out all over the house. I was standing on a chair, and saying, "Okay, Antoinette, bring me those lights, bring me that tinsel." And she was running all over the place, with a big smile on her face. My mother was watching the whole thing, saying, "See how she listens to you. There's nobody like her brother, Fred. She thinks the sun rises and sets on you."

After being an only child my entire life, I loved having a sister, particularly one as kindhearted as Antoinette. Then, before she was out of her teens, this frail, gentle girl died, and I lost the only sibling I ever had.

I had graduated to working as a meatcutter at the A&P supermarket, while wrestling whenever I could. My mother was hoping I would get the wrestling out of my system, and pursue a dependable livelihood. See, we already had a star in my family, my cousin, Nick Blassie. He was president of the Meatcutters

Union, Local 88 for twenty-five years, and a real political power-house. Later on, there were stories that he gave President Harry Truman the Oval Office plaque that said, THE BUCK STOPS HERE—I know Nick had the same one in *his* office—and coined the phrase, "Give 'em hell, Harry."

The people called Nick "Colonel" because, somewhere along the line, he'd been made a Kentucky Colonel. He drove around the city in a brand-new Cadillac Coupe de Ville, to the Elks Club, the Variety Club, the Democratic Club, and started an organization called the Backstoppers of St. Louis, which ensured that cops and firemen killed in the line of duty went to their graves debt-free. In 1949, he tried running for mayor, but couldn't command the support he did at the union hall.

When Nick campaigned for reelection at the Meatcutters Union, he called the other Blassie cousins to collect the votes. We were all a bunch of roughnecks, and I guess that was pretty intimidating to anyone harboring thoughts of voting in the other direction.

One night, I was driving past the Jefferson Hotel, when I saw this commotion spilling out into the street. It was Nick and another union guy, fighting some scabs. Well, I couldn't resist pulling over and joining in. The fight had been two against six. Now, it was three against six. And we gave those scabs a hell of a beating.

I have to admit that I took great pleasure in participating in these kinds of after-hours union activities. But that didn't mean that I wanted to spend the rest of my life as a meatcutter. My family was bewildered, and had regular discussions about changing my mind.

"Do something, Nick," my mother would yell at my cousin. "This wrestling is nothing but foolishness."

"I don't know what's wrong with the guy," Nick used to answer. "If he listens to me, he'll have money in his pocket all the time. I can fix it so he'll be at the A&P for maybe a few more months. Then, he'll become manager of the meat market."

But I didn't want to become manager of the meat market. I wanted to become a wrestler. I was starting to work the wrestling shows at the carnivals, walking past the hootchie-kootchie tent, the fortune-tellers, the fire eaters, carrying my little bag with my

trunks and gym shoes and towel. I could see the way people looked at me, knowing that I was one of the performers. If anybody doubted who I was, I'd say, "Why, shit, watch me. I'm going to wrestle."

The whole point of any carnival is keeping the "marks" in the dark about the techniques being used to separate them from their money. And I was as big a mark as anyone else there.

Whenever I participated in a match in those days, I wrestled legit. Of course, my matches weren't the ones the people came to see. Every carnival had a routine that involved some kind of champ taking on all comers. The first couple of volunteers would be plants, dressed like housepainters or construction workers. The champ would beat them, but they'd get in enough offense for him to look vulnerable. Finally, some musclehead in the audience would take the bait, step forward, and say he'd like to try out the champion. Everyone in the tent would put up their money, sure the local yokel had what it took to get the victory. This match would be a shoot, and really challenge the champ's abilities. He had to have the skill to carry his opponent to an exciting contest—you didn't want the fans to leave, feeling flimflammed— but know enough secret torture holds to, ultimately, make the challenger submit.

Some really strange things happened in the carnival. I was told that when Bruno Sammartino came over from the Old Country, he went to the carnival with a bunch of other Italian immigrants, all stonemasons and builders. One of his friends said, "Hey Bruno, I hear they'll give you a hundred bucks if you can stay in a cage five minutes with a monkey."

"A monkey for a hundred dollars?" Bruno said. "What the hell can a monkey do? I'll kill him."

Well, Bruno was as strong as they came, but he didn't know the difference between a monkey and an orangutan. When they faced off, the orangutan started ripping off Bruno's clothes. Bruno was going bar to bar, with the orangutan grabbing his neck, hitting him in the balls. But he couldn't go anywhere because they were in a goddamn cage. By the time he got out, Bruno was practically naked.

At one of the carnivals I worked, we had a guy named Toughy Trusdale, who'd wrestle an alligator. When the creature died, they didn't have a replacement, so Toughy went into the tank with the dead alligator to give the people their money's worth. He was rolling around, twisting the alligator's arms and head, and pretending that it was fighting back. It wasn't a spectacular performance by any means; there isn't too much you can do with a dead alligator. But Toughy is the only one who really knew the difference.

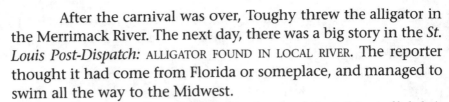

After the carnival was over, Toughy threw the alligator in the Merrimack River. The next day, there was a big story in the *St. Louis Post-Dispatch:* ALLIGATOR FOUND IN LOCAL RIVER. The reporter thought it had come from Florida or someplace, and managed to swim all the way to the Midwest.

I may have been a mark, but I sensed that this stuff didn't go on in other professional sports. Yet, none of the older wrestlers was willing to smarten me up. In fact, they went out of their way to keep me confused. When they were talking to each other, they'd speak this language I'd never heard before, a kind of pig Latin punctuated by Zs. It wasn't until years later that I figured out that they were speaking "carny." This particular dialect was known as Z-talk. There was also a variety called bell talk, that involved peppering your words with "bees" and "bells" instead of "eez" and "zeez." I knew better than to ask anyone to translate; when the other wrestlers trusted me, I figured they'd tell me.

Amazingly, some wrestlers continue to use Z-talk in the WWE dressing room today. And I still can't speak it. Despite all my years in the business, nobody ever bothered to teach me this mysterious vernacular.

In the carnival, when I'd walk into a room where a bunch of older wrestlers were talking, they'd all say, "Kay fabe. Kay fabe." It meant, "Shut up. There's a mark listening." I've heard a couple of theories about the origin of the term. Some people say that there was a deaf and dumb wrestler named Kay Fabian, so "kay fabe" implied, "Go mute." There's another story that Kay Fabian could hear and speak, but he was a real gossip and pain in the ass, so nobody told him anything.

Over the years, wrestlers would not only use "kay fabe" in front of outsiders, but "kay fabe" each other about news that wasn't meant to be shared. My friend Gorilla Monsoon, the late World Wrestling Entertainment Hall of Famer, had a New Jersey license plate "K-Fabe" on his Lincoln Continental.

Other carny elements have also carried over. The insider terms *heel* for villain, *babyface* for good guy, *juice* for blood, and *spoon* for dressing room instigator, all originated in the carnival. When I meet a wrestler married to a stripper—and that's a pretty common combination—I think about the hootchie-kootchie girls who hung around the wrestling tent, watching their husbands' matches.

* * *

One afternoon, before I was scheduled to wrestle, the guy who ran the tent suggested, "Why don't you go next door and watch the geek?"

"What's so special about the geek?"

"Oh, he's great. He bites the heads off chickens. He bites the heads off snakes."

"Jesus Christ, that's fuckin' horrible," I said. But who wouldn't be curious? So I went into the geek's tent, and not only was he decapitating animals, but sticking pins in himself and driving nails through his hand.

When I got back to the wrestling tent, my friend wanted to know what I thought of the show. I told him, "Did you see what that guy looks like? He's got a neck like a stack of dimes. He's what you'd call a real pencil neck geek."

And that's how my most famous catchphrase originated.

17

From time to time, when the carnival went on the road, I traveled along. The money was almost nonexistent. But I got laid so much, I could have contributed some of the pussy to charity.

In a lot of ways, the carnival was the perfect place for a kid who barely knew a wristlock from a wristwatch. If you screwed up in the ring, it didn't make that much of a difference. The people who came to carnivals weren't all that versed in the fine points of wrestling. So I wasn't too concerned about them. I was concerned about myself. Would I succeed or wouldn't I?

Even when I got out of the carnival, the venues weren't much more glamorous. A lot of the wrestlers had other jobs, and got in the ring for extra pocket money, and it showed in the way they performed. At different towns around Missouri, I'd occasionally wrestle in burlesque houses. A stripper would take her clothes off, before the wrestlers came out and twisted each other's bones out of joint.

The mats in these places were filthy—they hadn't been cleaned in years—and guys would walk around with skin infections and eye diseases. If you came down with trachoma, something that could be contracted through having your face rubbed in another guy's armpit and wiping your eyes with a dirty towel, you could go blind.

In time, I started working for the more established promoters, Tom Packs in St. Louis and George Simpson in Kansas City. I was still losing most of my matches, getting tiny payoffs, and sleeping in the car on road trips. If I had to use the bath-

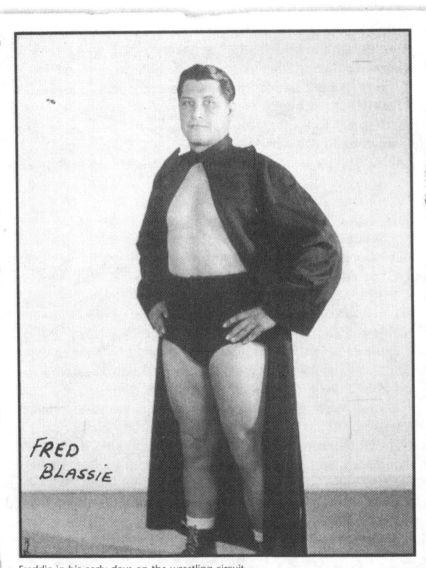

FRED
BLASSIE

Freddie in his early days on the wrestling circuit.

room, I went to the service station. My meals were a loaf of bread and fifteen cents of bologna. But I was no longer fearful when I stepped into the ring. I'd learned to ignore my feelings when the bell rang, and concentrate on what I needed to do to get ahead.

The more time I spent hanging around, the more the older guys were willing to show me little tricks to use in the ring. That didn't mean that they gave away the true nature of the business. Everything was still "kay fabe." The veterans thought that if I knew that their matches were "worked"—or predetermined—I'd tell my neighbors, and they'd stop believing. And if they stopped believing, the logic went, they'd stop coming to the matches and paying their money.

But the guys were enlightening me in other ways. If I had someone in a hammerlock, he'd reverse it on me and then let loose. I'd slip out, and shoulder block him, and he'd take a big bump on the canvas. No one sat me down and said, "Hey, Freddie, this is how the business works." But you'd have to be an idiot not to start figuring it out.

Then, one night in St. Louis, the booker—the guy who matched you up with the other wrestlers—came over to me and said, "Your opponent's going over tonight."

I couldn't believe my ears. The booker was asking me to lose! In my wildest dreams, I never imagined holding back and letting another guy win. Then again, I'd never been all that capable of winning before. I guess I'd improved to the point where the booker had to guarantee that I wouldn't disrupt his long-term plans. So in a backhanded way, the request was a compliment.

After working so hard to get established in the business, I wasn't about to do anything to set myself back. So I "did the job," just like I was supposed to.

Now, I had another concern. I didn't want to get a reputation as a "jobber," or someone whose only purpose was losing week after week. As a result, I began to travel, hoping that I'd catch on in another part of the country.

I went up to Nebraska to work for the Dusek Brothers. They were billed as Wrestling's Riot Squad, and were well respected throughout the business. Rudy, the promoter in Omaha, had

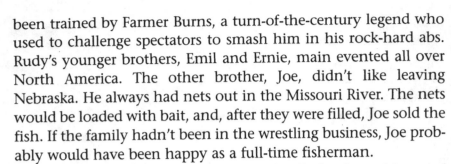
been trained by Farmer Burns, a turn-of-the-century legend who used to challenge spectators to smash him in his rock-hard abs. Rudy's younger brothers, Emil and Ernie, main evented all over North America. The other brother, Joe, didn't like leaving Nebraska. He always had nets out in the Missouri River. The nets would be loaded with bait, and, after they were filled, Joe sold the fish. If the family hadn't been in the wrestling business, Joe probably would have been happy as a full-time fisherman.

I think it was Emil Dusek who finally let down his guard and agreed to work out a match with me. He said, "This is what I'll do. This is what you'll do. I won't hurt you, and you won't hurt me. And this is what this game's about."

From Nebraska, I stayed on the road. In Minnesota, the promoter Tony Stecher—brother of former World Champion Joe Stecher—took me out to a Greek restaurant. I'd never tried Greek food before, and couldn't believe anything tasted that good. I started to fall in love with Minnesota—until I wrestled there in the winter. All my life, I hated cold weather, and in Minnesota, you had months and months of it. Maybe the Swedes, Danes, and Norwegians who live there like it because it makes them nostalgic for home. But not me.

Over the years, Minnesota became one of the country's most successful wrestling territories. Former NCAA Heavyweight Champion Verne Gagne would start American Wrestling Association (AWA) there and—like many promoters who also wrestled—award himself the championship. A lot of big names— Reggie "Crusher" Lisowski, Maurice "Mad Dog" Vachon, Nick Bockwinkle, Hulk Hogan, Jesse Ventura—would get some of their best exposure in Minnesota. But I avoided it as much as I could. I'd rather work someplace where the snow melts once in a while.

New York seemed like a great location to wrestle. St. Louis was a backwater compared to it. You had large, lively crowds, and decent payoffs. And when the matches ended, you could stay out 'til five in the morning, living it up. But one night after I wrestled, the promoter asked to have a talk with me in the dressing room.

"Can I be honest with you?"

I nodded.

"I'm sure one of these days you're going to develop into a top talent. But this is a pretty big territory, and you're not qualified to work here yet. Keep traveling, learn the ropes, and come back when you're ready to be a star in New York."

What could I say? I wasn't happy with his advice, but I couldn't take issue with the guy for telling me the truth.

The promoter was Jess McMahon. If you're reading this book, I think you can guess the name of his grandson.

TWO:
LOVE AND WAR

On December 7, 1941, Japanese pilots attacked the U.S. Naval Base at Pearl Harbor, killing some twenty-three hundred Americans, capsizing the USS *Oklahoma*, demolishing the USS *Arizona*, sinking three other ships, and destroying more than one hundred eighty aircraft.

At the time, I was a member of the Emmets Athletic Club in St. Louis. We staged boxing and wrestling matches, played poker, and, on Saturday nights when I was in town, went to dances together. On December 8, when President Franklin Delano Roosevelt declared war, all sixteen of us volunteered for service.

I picked the Navy. I already had a couple of cousins in the military, and they told me that, in the Army, you were likely to get stuck out in a tent in a muddy field somewhere, with bombs dropping all around you. At least in the Navy, you had a place to eat and sleep.

I was stationed in St. Louis at first, then shipped out to California. Pretty quickly, I made contact with the other boxers and wrestlers—I'd heard of some of them; none had ever heard of me—and we started putting on exhibition matches for the enlisted men. Once in a while, I'd go AWOL to wrestle at a little show in a small town.

Because we were also at war with Germany, my relatives in St. Louis weren't always treated too hot. One time, my grandfather was watching a parade, and forgot to salute the flag when it passed by. Some soldiers must have overheard his accent, and accused him of being some kind of spy. He really didn't understand what the hell they were talking about, and as he argued, he became more and more frustrated. This seemed to get the soldiers

even more riled up. They ran him inside his house, barring him from watching the rest of the parade. If I had been there, we would have had our own Battle of the Bulge right on the street. But because I was away, my grandfather had to do as he was told.

We still had family over in Austria, and, at the beginning of the conflict at least, there was contact. I can't remember any discussions about Hitler; nobody was sophisticated enough to

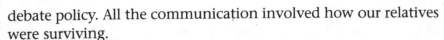

debate policy. All the communication involved how our relatives were surviving.

The fact that no one in my family cared one way or another about the Nazis made another part of my life less complicated. I had fallen in love with a pretty, black-haired Jewish girl named Nettie Needles. We'd met a few years earlier, when we were both working at the Lynn Meat Company. The night I won the Heavyweight Boxing Championship at the community center, Nettie was there with about fifteen other people we knew, cheering me on. She was a real sweetheart, but we were kids. We'd go out for a few months, break up, then go out again.

Nettie's family had come over from Russia. Her father owned a pretty successful moving company, and the other relatives were also in the trucking business. They had a pretty big influence over her, and she insisted on getting married by a rabbi. I didn't give a damn; after getting chased by that crazy priest in the St. Nicholas outfit, I wasn't particularly insistent that my children be raised Catholic. My mother thought that Nettie was a nice girl, and didn't care either.

We got married while I was on leave. The rabbi showed up, but her parents didn't. Maybe it was because I was German, and it was World War II. Maybe it was because I was a wrestler. Maybe they just didn't want her to marry me.

I spent a total of forty-two months in the Navy, fourteen of them in the Pacific Theater. When I was stationed in the Philippines, we had a huge gasoline tank on our base. It seemed like every day, the Marines would come and load up on gasoline, and every night, the Japanese would fly over and bomb the thing. We'd patch it up, and then the Japanese would come and bomb it again.

But I had an easier time, compared to most of the enlisted men. The word had gotten around that I was a wrestler, and I was put in charge of the athletic department on the base. I didn't have to sleep in the barracks with the other guys. Instead, I had my own Quonset hut with two Ping-Pong tables, side by side, and softball, basketball, and boxing equipment.

Everything was going fine, until a lieutenant, a guy from the Philadelphia area I didn't know that well, decided to pull rank on me and take the Quonset hut for himself. I asked my officer,

who was a pretty good friend of mine, what I should do, and he said, "Fuck him. When he tries to move in, just throw his shit out."

I took that as a license to punish the guy my own way. I was out when he finally turned up, but when I came back, I took all his gear and tossed it into the rain.

The lieutenant returned about an hour later. By then, everything he owned was soaked and muddy, and he stomped up to me, and said, "You son of a bitch. Do you know who I am?"

"Fuck you," I said, and hit him with a straight jab, knocking him on his ass. Then, I took the guy's jeep, drove over to my officer's quarters, and told him the whole story.

He was shocked. "You hit him?" he asked. "Why the fuck did you hit him? I didn't tell you to hit him. I told you to take his shit and throw it out."

"I did take his shit and throw it. But then he cursed at me. What the fuck did you expect me to do?"

Well, they made me go in front of a tribunal, and busted

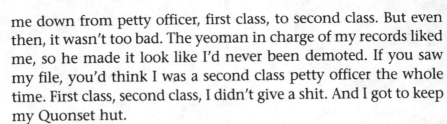

me down from petty officer, first class, to second class. But even then, it wasn't too bad. The yeoman in charge of my records liked me, so he made it look like I'd never been demoted. If you saw my file, you'd think I was a second class petty officer the whole time. First class, second class, I didn't give a shit. And I got to keep my Quonset hut.

As far as the war went, there was always the feeling that we were on the verge of jumping into something deadly. One New Year's Eve, we were called out on duty because we heard that the Japanese were in the area. We brought extra ammunition, and positioned ourselves near some shrubbery and trees. It was pitch-black outside, and we waited and waited, until finally we heard footsteps marching in unison. We stiffened up with our hands on our weapons, as these soldiers passed right by us. We couldn't see their uniforms, but we could make out their shapes.

We'd been warned not to fire a shot. Our instructions were only to observe. But we were nervous, and trigger happy—we wanted them bad. Still, nobody went against orders. We held our breath and watched, then reported back to the base the next morning.

That's when we found out that the soldiers weren't Japanese. They were American. If someone had started firing, we would have annihilated each other.

Before the war ended, I also ended up in New Guinea. I'm not really sure why I was sent there. I guess they figured that if the fighting escalated, they could stick me on a ship and send me into battle. But I was bored out of my mind. There were thousands of men there, wandering around in uniform, wondering what the hell their next assignment was going to be. A friend of mine was so stir-crazy that he stole a jeep from one of the officers, and took it for a joyride. While he was speeding around the island, the thing flipped over, and he died.

I'm happy to say that I was nowhere near Hiroshima or Nagasaki when the United States put an end to our adventure in the Far East. In fact, I survived World War II without ever shooting at another human being.

From the South Pacific, I was shipped to Washington State, then shuttled back to St. Louis so I could be discharged. The train was freezing, going up and down over mountains, all the way to the Midwest. At each stop, the doors would open and we'd see these old women from the Salvation Army, their skin red from the icy air, holding pots of warm coffee. I never forgot that and told myself that, if I ever made it big, I'd find a way to show my appreciation.

Nettie liked the way I looked in my uniform. But I'd been wearing that monkey suit for three and a half years, and couldn't wait to buy a new wardrobe of street clothes. My mother hoped that now that I'd had a few years to think about it, I'd put my wrestling behind me, and dedicate myself to becoming the best meatcutter in Missouri. And now, she had a new ally in her campaign: my wife. But neither of them could change my mind. As soon as I settled in, I called a couple of promoters and went back out on the road.

Things weren't much different than before I left. I was still losing almost every match. The only difference was that I had come up with my first gimmick: "Sailor" Fred Blassie. The wrestling programs printed photos of me in my uniform, while I was in the Navy. The plan, of course, was that the fans would associate me with the patriotism they'd built up during the war. It didn't really work.

2 7

Fortunately, St. Louis had pretty much become America's wrestling capital. Between 1939 and 1947, there were eight world-title changes in the city. In all honesty, there were other promotions around the country with their own world champions. But I was crossing paths with some of the best wrestlers in the game, including Babe Sharkey, Orville Brown, and Wild Bill Longson.

Somehow, the promoters seemed to make money, even when I left the arena broke. If a thousand dollars in tickets were sold, the promoter would end up with nine hundred. The rest of us split the remaining hundred. And not only would he fleece us, he'd often blame us for our own predicament, saying things like, "We would have made money if all the boys didn't want free tickets for their friends. You guys are bankrupting me."

Surprisingly, the wrestlers would grumble about this to each other, but rarely say anything to a promoter's face. Today, a lot of the guys performing for WWE are college-educated. They have lawyers and agents and friends in financial fields to advise them on business decisions. If wrestling hadn't worked out, Kurt Angle and Edge and Chris Jericho would have probably ended up in white-collar careers. Among my friends, it was either wrestling or the pick and shovel. And some guys were so excited just seeing their names listed in a newspaper advertisement or wrestling program that they'd keep quiet.

I know that this doesn't make sense to some people, but even during the worst times, I never wanted to do anything else. I enjoyed the camaraderie of the dressing room, and the feeling that—at least to the small segment of the population who lived and died by wrestling—you were a celebrity. Sure, it was a given that the promoter was going to cheat you. But at least you weren't in it alone. Just about every other guy on the card was going through the same thing. So we put up with getting swindled because this was the life we wanted—and always found a way to make our own fun.

28

Walter "Killer" Kowalski: I'm a couple of years younger than Freddie. But he'd always tell people, "Oh, I remember Kowalski. I used to carry his bag when I was a young kid."

There was a time we went to Japan to wrestle, and I brought my camera to take pictures of the trip. We were on a boat going from one island to another island. And I'm walking down a hallway, past the men's room, and the door was open. And I look in there, and here's Freddie Blassie, taking a leak in the urinal. So I put up my camera, and said, "Fred!" And he turned his body toward me and I took a picture of him peeing, showing his penis.

I had an eight-by-ten made, and gave him the picture. He took it home, and mixed it in with a lot of other pictures. But he always kept this picture at the bottom. Then, he'd ask people, "Do you want to see my pictures?" And they'd look—at Freddie wrestling, at Freddie traveling—then come to the very bottom, to Freddie taking a leak with his penis showing there. And he'd go, "Oh, sorry. I don't know how that got in there." And he'd do it every time.

Dick "The Destroyer" Beyer: In 1958, we were working together in Nashville, Tennessee, staying at the Maxwell House Hotel.

A group of strippers also had rooms there, and we found out that they had a lot in common with the wrestlers. They lived at night, like we did. Some of them would go out with the wrestlers, and do their wash for them and everything.

Freddie and I used to go to the strip club after our matches, to get something to eat, relax, and enjoy the show. Freddie had this spray gun, like a thing for nasal spray, with hot mustard in it. When the stripper walked by us on the way to the stage, he'd spray it on her legs and her ass.

The girl would get up onstage, and not feel anything at first. She'd start dancing, then get all hot. She wouldn't know what was happening. She'd be rubbing her ass, and moving from leg to leg, doing all kinds of movements. Freddie did it a bunch of times, until the guy who owned the place said that wrestlers were no longer welcome.

Every night, you had to be ready for a shoot. Even when guys were friendly in the dressing room, we all wanted to build a reputation. If that meant taking advantage of someone when his defenses were down, so be it. No one called himself an entertainer back then. We thought of ourselves as pure wrestlers, tough guys who could beat the shit out of any boxer or football player who made the mistake of taking us lightly.

Whatever went on behind closed doors—working out finishes and so forth—was our business and nobody else's. We were a family, and these were intimate, family secrets.

I sometimes wished that the fans knew how much we sacrificed for them. We were constantly getting hurt, and—instead of taking time off like other athletes—took pride in ignoring our injuries and limping on to the next town. If the fans paid to see you, we told ourselves, you gave them a great show. No self-pitying excuses were accepted. So it pissed me off when fans we killed ourselves to satisfy had the balls to look me in the face and ask, "Is it fake?"

There was no need to give them a detailed response. I'd usually just answer the "fake" question with one of my own: "When your father fucks your mother, is *that* fake?"

*   *   *

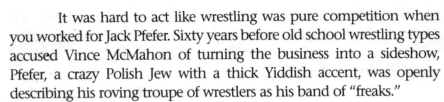

It was hard to act like wrestling was pure competition when you worked for Jack Pfefer. Sixty years before old school wrestling types accused Vince McMahon of turning the business into a sideshow, Pfefer, a crazy Polish Jew with a thick Yiddish accent, was openly describing his roving troupe of wrestlers as his band of "freaks."

"Freaks I love and they're my specialty," he said in a 1938 edition of *Collier's* magazine. "I am very proud of some of my monstrosities. You can't get a dollar with a normal-looking guy, no matter how good he can wrestle. Those birds with shaved, egg-shaped heads, handlebar mustaches, tattooed bodies, big stomachs—that's for me."

At one time, Pfefer was actually taken seriously—as one of a group of partners working with Jack Curley, the influential New York promoter whose cards regularly featured the original "Golden Greek" Jim Londos. But then he tried to stage a coup, and replace Curley himself. Instead, Pfefer was banished—not only in New York, but everyplace else where Curley had sway.

Pfefer was feeling desperate, so he did something so stupid, he was fortunate not to be murdered. In 1933, he went to Dan Parker, the *New York Daily Mirror's* sports editor, and exposed the business. Now, everyone knew about what Pfefer described as "fakery" in our profession.

"I've never seen an honest wrestling bout in my twenty years in the game," he said. "Maybe there was one, but I wasn't there."

This created quite a commotion. But—as in other periods, when someone violated "kay fabe" to the press—it blew over. People forgot about the story. And fans wanted to believe anyway. In 1937, after Curley died, Pfefer started promoting again in New York. Still, he was never an insider after the scandal. He freelanced around the country, using Toledo, Boston, and Nashville, among other places, as a base of operations before moving on. Sometimes, he hired himself out as a "consultant."

When Pfefer couldn't afford to book a certain wrestler, he faked it, telling fans that Lou Kez, Bummy Rogers, and Bruno Zagurski were coming to town—as opposed to Lou Thesz, Buddy Rogers, and Bronko Nagurski. There's a story that when the real Lou Thesz called up and complained, Pfefer said, "You can come here and I'll give you the same money he's getting."

"How much is that?"

"Fifteen bucks."

Because most of the big talent was off-limits to Pfefer, he thought of every wrestler as a vaudeville act. Pfefer was one of the first promoters to offer "characters" on his cards, men hired solely on account of their malformations. He'd give you a Leather Man, a Lion Man, a Blimp, a No-Neck, and so many other types of oddities, I've lost track.

The French Angel, Maurice Tillet, had a distorted head and amazing strength. Pfefer even managed to get him publicity outside the wrestling world when he pulled some subway cars in New York City. He was a nice enough guy, but it was hard to have a conversation with him. Besides his French accent, his vocal cords sounded like they were stretched—a little bit like Andre the Giant a few decades later—and he bumbled when he talked. People have asked me what kind of condition he had, but, to tell you the truth, I never thought to ask. The wrestlers would just say, "He was born that way," and that was that. Plus, he was growing money, and you couldn't knock the pocketbook.

The Swedish Angel, Phil Olafsson, had a similar look. We called him Popeye because he resembled the cartoon character, but with a huge head. Aside from that, he was no different than you and me. He had a friendly wife who was a great cook, and all the wrestlers looked forward to an invitation to their home. He was a good-hearted fella, just very grotesque.

There was another Swedish Angel, the Super Swedish Angel, who was a bit of a movie star as well as a wrestler. Tor Johnson also had a big head, and you could barely understand him. So in the movies, he usually played a monster who did little more than growl. In total, he made more than thirty films, including Bela Lugosi's final three movies: *Bride of the Monster, The Black Sheep,* and *Grave Robbers From Outer Space.* In the last film, Tor was a murdered policeman returning as a zombie, and Lugosi played his killer, Ghoul Man. But Lugosi—who most people remember as Dracula—was a morphine addict, and died during production. So director Ed Wood had some idiot run around with a cape over his face for much of the picture, pretending to be Lugosi.

I guess you could say that Tor Johnson belonged to two bands of freaks—one with Pfefer, the other with Ed Wood.

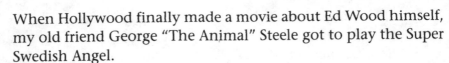

When Hollywood finally made a movie about Ed Wood himself, my old friend George "The Animal" Steele got to play the Super Swedish Angel.

Pfefer also loved booking midgets. They were purely a novelty act. During their matches, fans would hoot, like they were watching a wrestling match between babies. One midget would get down on all fours, while the other pushed the referee over him. Then, the ref would get up, grab one of the midgets, put him over a knee and spank him. The midgets went from promotion to promotion, and were treated with very little respect. After I became popular, the promoter would always arrange for my transportation when I came to town. The midgets would have to rent a car and drive together—they had extensions that went to the brake and gas—because nobody ever thought about giving them the same courtesy. I doubt that they made anything close to what the other wrestlers were getting and, a lot of times, we weren't getting that much.

Because they never spent time in one place for too long, they usually stayed apart from the rest of the boys. They had their own little clique, their own little arguments, and their own little practical jokes that they'd play on each other.

The way I figure it, Pfefer related to freaks because he was something of a freak himself. He grew his pinky nail extra long to dig snot out of his nose, and he had the stinkiest feet in the universe.

One time, we were in Nashville, and had to go to some town beyond Knoxville. He was very tight with money, so instead of paying for his own gas, he said, "Blassie, I want to ride with you."

I didn't dare say no; if you want to get a push in this business, I don't suggest declining when the promoter asks for a favor. Pfefer got in the car with me, and we started to drive. I have to admit that I didn't completely mind his company; I was kind of entertained by his bullshit stories. It was the middle of the winter, so I turned on the heater, and started to get comfortable. But I noticed something. The longer we rode, the worse the car smelled. I couldn't figure out what the hell was wrong. I thought the odor might be coming through the vent or something, so I turned the heater off. When the car got cold again, the smell began to fade. That's when I realized that his feet were causing the stench. I don't know if this guy ever bathed or changed socks. I know he didn't change shoes.

It made perfect sense that Pfefer used girl wrestlers whenever he could get his hands on them. They were curiosities, like midgets and freaks. Some men get sexually excited from watching women fight, and a guy like Pfefer enjoyed appealing to that kind of sick, deviant taste. Despite this, a lot of these women were good athletes.

Pfefer renamed Lillian Ellison "the Fabulous Moolah" because he said he understood why she was in the business—"for the moolah." She first won the Women's World Championship in 1956, in a thirteen girl "Wrestle-Royal" in Baltimore, and didn't lose it for nearly thirty years. In 1999, when she was more than seventy years old, she won her last title, defeating Ivory at a World Wrestling Federation show in Cleveland.

Like the midgets, the girl wrestlers didn't stay in one area for long. They'd come in for a show, wrestle each other, and work for another promoter the next night. So I didn't get to know too many of them. Mae Young was an exception. She'd play poker with the boys, and lift up her leg and let out a big fart. If a guy

did something to piss her off, she'd try to provoke him into a fight. She knew how to take a punch from a man, then kick his ass. When she was around eighty years old, she did an angle in World Wrestling Federation involving Bubba Ray and D-Von Dudley picking her up on the entrance ramp, tossing her off, and smashing her through two tables. I heard that the Dudleyz were nervous the whole time, but Mae was as happy as she'd ever been in her life. In fact, as she was lying there, with wood splintered all around her, she squeezed Bubba's hand to let him know she wasn't dead.

From the 1930s through the '50s, though, when Mae and Moolah were coming up, the queen of women's wrestling was Mildred Burke. She could blow up inner tubes until they burst, and made it into *Ripley's Believe It or Not* by doing one hundred body bridges on the editor's desk. When she was in the carnival, wrestling men, one guy—a short-order cook from Bethany, Missouri—had second thoughts about shooting with her. The guy fled, and the promoter sent the sheriff to get him. Back in the tent, Mildred's opponent said he couldn't wrestle because he

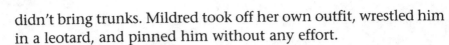
didn't bring trunks. Mildred took off her own outfit, wrestled him in a leotard, and pinned him without any effort.

Mildred was working at her mother's diner in Kansas City in 1932, pregnant with her first child, and abandoned by her first husband, when she met this scumbag named Billy Wolfe, an older wrestler who was always looking for his next meal ticket. Mildred told him that she wanted to be a wrestler, and, after the baby was born, he began training her. Pretty soon, he realized that she was tougher than most guys, and took her to carnivals to wrestle men. Mildred was only five-foot-two, and when she was all dressed up, looked pretty harmless. But when the guys got in the ring with her, they didn't stand a chance.

Wolfe married Mildred, had her train other girls, and began selling promoters on including women's wrestling on their shows. In 1938, *Life* Magazine ran a picture of her participating in the first mud-wrestling match ever held. Another time, she wrestled in a mixture of swamp mud and melted lard, picking up an ear infection that damaged her hearing for the rest of her life. But she was a star. When the average Major League Baseball player was earning six thousand dollars a year, Mildred took home more than eight times as much.

Of course, Mildred didn't get to keep the money. Wolfe grabbed every penny. He took his group of lady wrestlers from place to place, fucked as many as he could, and tried to control everything they did. If one of them dated a male wrestler, he fined her one hundred dollars. Someone once told me that the fee was two hundred dollars if that wrestler was Freddie Blassie.

Even though Billy had been a wrestler, he kept away from us, and we kept away from him. He wasn't one of the boys, as far as we were concerned. We thought of him as a pimp.

Mildred was billed as the women's world champion, but it seemed like Wolfe was always looking for a replacement for her. Sometimes, he'd tell a girl to double-cross Mildred, begin shooting on her, and take her title. But Mildred had trained most of her opponents, and could shoot better than any of them. In a match with June Byers in 1954, Mildred's knee popped out of its socket. She pushed it back in and wrestled for another forty-seven minutes to retain the championship.

Mildred claimed that Billy tried to have her drowned, and

removed parts from her car so she'd die in some unfortunate accident. Things got even more complicated when she fell in love with Wolfe's son from another marriage, G. Bill. There was something wrong with the kid, though, and the father got into his son's mind, and had him turn against Mildred. Then, the two of them beat her up outside a liquor store in Los Angeles.

Mildred survived this beating, like she did every other one she received in her life. When she died in 1989, she had trained more than two thousand women, and more than earned her reputation as the first goddess of the ring. Meanwhile, both Wolfes were dead by 1962, largely forgotten, like the crumbs that they were.

On July 14, 1948, a group of promoters met at the President Hotel in Waterloo, Iowa, to start the National Wrestling Alliance (NWA). Sam Muchnick came from St. Louis, Orville Brown from Kansas City, Tony Stecher from Minneapolis, Max Clayton from Omaha, Pinky George from Des Moines, and Al Haft from Columbus, Ohio. The system of different promotions recognizing different world champions wasn't helping anyone, they said. It only caused confusion for the fans, and cheapened the credibility of the various titles. Instead, these guys would crown one champion, who would go from territory to territory defending the crown against the local favorite.

Like mob bosses, each promoter would respect the other's boundaries—Muchnick wouldn't promote in Des Moines; Stecher would stay away from Kansas City. If someone tried to come into any of those cities and start his own league, the other promoters would send in their top talent so the guy couldn't compete. Even when there wasn't a crisis, the promoters would trade wrestlers back and forth to make their cards more interesting. If one of those wrestlers refused to play ball with a certain promoter, everyone agreed to blacklist him until he had a change of attitude.

By the mid-1950s, the NWA was the most powerful organization in professional wrestling, with about forty promotions represented around the world. Every year, they held a convention, where they voted on whether to renew or end the champion's reign. From 1949 to 1957, Lou Thesz wore the belt for all but eight months.

Thesz was the wonder of St. Louis. He was a tough son of a bitch, and a smart technical wrestler. He surrounded himself with great teachers—George Tragos, Ed "Strangler" Lewis—and picked up on everything they taught him. I would have to say that he was one of the best of all time.

He won his first version of the world championship when he was twenty-one in 1937, and held the title for a competing promotion when the NWA was formed. He was supposed to meet the NWA's first champion, Kansas City promoter Orville Brown, in a unification match in 1949 in St. Louis. But when Brown was injured in a car wreck three weeks beforehand, the NWA decided to crown Thesz anyway. Not only that, they linked their history to the promotion he'd represented. Now, the NWA claimed that their championship lineage extended all the way back to 1904, when "The Russian Lion" George Hackenschmidt defeated Tom Jenkins in New York.

Sam Muchnick, the promoter in St. Louis and president of the NWA, was a former sportswriter, and marketed wrestling like it was serious business. In fact, in his territory, he didn't allow a manager to accompany his protégé to ringside until 1969; that was too flashy for Muchnick. Thesz was also very protective of his championship, and even resented having female wrestlers work the undercard when he appeared in the main event. To Thesz, the girls were there for sex appeal only, and belittled the overall presentation.

3 7

Today, the few of us who are still alive from that era debate over whether wrestling was better back then. Some give you this bullshit speech, "In my day . . ." But when they look back, they're only remembering guys like Lou Thesz. They forget about all the boring matches they had to watch, and the shitty wrestlers who never drew a nickel. And they ignore people on today's WWE roster. I'm convinced that, in a shoot, Chris Benoit would beat 90 percent of the guys I've ever seen. Brock Lesnar was the NCAA Heavyweight Champion in 2000, and Kurt Angle a gold medalist in the 1996 Olympics. How much better can you get than that? Angle also respects our business, and, after starting in World Wrestling Federation, went to Thesz himself to learn about our traditions. With all deference to Lou, if Kurt had been around in 1948, he might have been the one who held the NWA title for all those years.

*   *   *

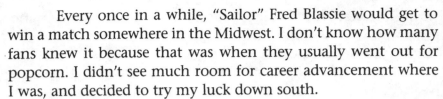

Every once in a while, "Sailor" Fred Blassie would get to win a match somewhere in the Midwest. I don't know how many fans knew it because that was when they usually went out for popcorn. I didn't see much room for career advancement where I was, and decided to try my luck down south.

I'd never seen a place so segregated. The black fans had to sit up in the balcony, and the black wrestlers could only work against each other. In the dressing room, it was southerners on one side, Yankees on the other. At first, I questioned my decision to come to Dixie. It didn't seem like a Yankee could get a push. To the promoters, I was just a body they used to build up their big boys.

Then, one night in Charlotte, the promoter, Jim Crockett, Sr., told me, "You're doing double duty tonight."

"What do you mean?"

"You're working twice."

I wondered if that meant I was also going to get paid twice, but I didn't say a word. He had this guy, the Masked Marvel or some bullshit, who'd been on a winning streak for the past year. His opponent, Larry Villmer, hadn't shown up, and Crockett wanted me to be the surprise substitute in the main event.

"And you're going over," he added.

This was the chance I'd been looking for, an opportunity not only to work a main event, but win it. It was like something was handed to me out of nowhere. We had a good, solid match, ending when I bodyslammed the Marvel, tore off his mask, and exposed him as Larry Blaine.

After that, everything changed. Instead of working as a curtain raiser, I was higher up on the card, playing the babyface, even though I was born in the north. Once in a while, I got into a main event again. On August 29, 1950, in Louisville, I wrestled Lou Thesz for the NWA Championship. I lost, of course. But the promoters had elevated me into Thesz's stratosphere.

Sometimes, a guy gets a break and squanders it away. Either, he can't hold his own with the elite of this business, keep the fans interested, or behave himself in the dressing room. A year or two later, he's a jobber again, losing every match, and when he walks into a restaurant, everyone thinks he works in the kitchen. I told myself over and over again that I wasn't going to turn into one of those guys. As far as I was concerned, there was no stopping me.

I once asked Crockett, "Why did you decide to give me a push?"

"I just saw something in you that I didn't see in the other fellas."

"What's that?"

"Conceit."

Before the late 1940s, wrestling had a hard time attracting new fans. How would you even know who the wrestlers were if you had to go to the arena to see them? Then, television started. Stations needed programs to fill the air space, and promoters were happy to send over footage of the matches. Soon, wrestling was on all the time, and people who'd written it off became interested. Guys who ten years earlier would have been working on the assembly line during the week, and wrestling opening matches in the prairie on the weekends, became stars overnight.

3 9

None of them were bigger than Gorgeous George.

Through the years, a lot of guys—including myself, and even nonwrestling personalities like James Brown—imitated Gorgeous George. But he was the one and only.

George's real name was George Wagner, and he wanted to be a heel in the worst way. He wore spats and a fancy hat to the ring, carrying around a walking stick. But, at first, the fans didn't care one way or another.

Then, he made his wife, Betty, pro wrestling's first female valet. Once, somewhere in Oregon, when she took too long to fold his robe, the fans started jeering, and saying the lewdest things. Betty left the ring and slapped one of them. After that, George went out and punched the guy. If this happened now at a WWE show, they'd both get fired, and Vince McMahon would have a multimillion-dollar lawsuit to worry about. But times were different then. Now, Gorgeous George had a routine that worked.

"The more spectators hate me," he'd later say, "the more they will be free to love one another."

Once television came into the picture, George really went overboard. He even legally changed his name to Gorgeous George. He dyed his brown hair blond—the first guy I remember ever doing so—and held his long locks in place with golden bobby pins he called Georgie Pins.

George claimed that he gave his very special friends 14-karat Georgie Pins, but only after they said, "I do solemnly swear and promise to never confuse this gold Georgie Pin with a common, ordinary bobby pin, so help me Gorgeous George."

It was a gimmick even Jack Pfefer couldn't have come up with, the beginning of what WWE would later bill as "sports-entertainment."

George came to the ring to entrance music—something that wasn't really incorporated into wrestling until the 1980s—the song "Pomp and Circumstance." After Betty, he had other valets, both male and female. They'd spray the ring with perfume, held in a jar called The Atomizer. He also brought a candelabra to the ring, using his pinkies to extinguish the flames.

As the fans shouted for George's execution, the ring announcer took the microphone and declared that "the Human Orchid, the Sensation of the Nation, and the Toast of the Coast" had arrived.

Once the bell rang, George made a big production out of acting finicky about touching his opponent's "dirty" body. When the referee searched him for hidden weapons in his trunks or boots, he'd scream, "Take your filthy hands off me," and instruct his valet to spray the official's hands with The Atomizer.

After such a buildup, everything George did in his match got heat. Thanks to television, he was one of those characters even nonwrestling fans wanted to see, and he knew it. If a promoter wanted to bring him in, he asked for—and received—an incredible one-third of the gate.

The rest of us could only watch with astonishment. I can't tell you how many wrestlers attempted to copy Gorgeous George over the years—Gorgeous George, Jr., Beautiful Bobby, Exotic Adrian Street, "Adorable" Adrian Adonis. But Gorgeous George was the originator, and everyone knew it. While we were driving Fords and Chevrolets, he had a brand-new Cadillac. If you were invited into his car, he had a chauffeur and about a dozen bottles of liquor for himself. Later on, his taste for alcohol would destroy him. But at his peak, a lot of the wrestlers thought that Gorgeous George was a pretty classy guy.

In 1952, Jules Strongbow, the booker in Los Angeles, was looking for two brothers to form a tag team. They didn't really have to be brothers, of course. Strongbow didn't give a shit if you were from different solar systems. It only mattered that the fans bought your relationship. A kid I knew from St. Louis named Billy McDaniels happened to be wrestling out there, and he recommended me for the role of his sibling, Fred McDaniels. The arrangement made sense for both of us: he had more polish in the ring, but I had more color.

To this day, I'm grateful. I never would have become The Hollywood Fashion Plate if Billy McDaniels didn't sell the Los Angeles promotion on taking a chance with me.

I loved wrestling in California. The TV show out of Los Angeles had national exposure. I stayed on Santa Monica Beach, and spent every day in the sun—rotating my body on my blanket until every part was bronzed, and lying on my stomach and spreading my hands apart so I even tanned the spaces between my fingers. L.A.'s Olympic Auditorium was a majestic place, built in 1927 for the 1932 Olympic Games. There was a lot of boxing and wrestling history in that building, and when you walked through the door and saw pictures of all the greats in the lobby, you couldn't help but feel like you were part of that tradition. Any fan interested in buying tickets didn't have to call Information or search for the Yellow Pages. A giant sign with the arena's phone number—Richmond 9-5171—loomed on a wall behind the ring, and added to the Olympic's charm.

Billy and I clicked pretty well in L.A. Wrestlers rarely settled themselves into one territory back then; you didn't want to get stale. So after a few months, we went to Louisville and did our brother routine there. Except now, we were Billy and Fred *Blassie*.

Even though we were babyfaces, we were still Yankees, and the fans tried to fuck with us from time to time. One night in Kentucky, some drunken asshole was mouthing off from ringside, so I said, "Why don't you come up here, you dim-witted motherfucker?"

To my surprise, the jerk got out of his seat and stumbled up to the ring. He was so far gone, he nearly fell off the apron. But once he got his bearings, he was ready to fight.

Billy looked at me and said, "Get away, Fred. I'll take care of him."

I stepped in front of Billy. "No, let me have him."

Just as I was pushing Billy away, the fan swung at me from the other side of the ropes. I leaned back, and he missed by about two feet. The other fans let out a howl, as I stepped forward and coldcocked that son of a bitch so hard, he collapsed on the apron, and fell onto the floor.

"See how easy that was?" I said to Billy.

Then, with the rest of the crowd all wound up, we continued our match.

I was having the time of my life, but now I'd had a taste of Los Angeles, and wanted to get back there. In 1953, I returned. After paying my dues for so many years, I could finally draw a crowd by using the name Freddie Blassie.

There were some great characters working in L.A. Baron Michel Leone was billed as a European nobleman, and I think he kind of believed it. He had shoulder-length hair, a pencil mustache, and walked to the ring in a short tunic lined with Greek patterns and tied with a thin belt. I guess that was okay, considering his gimmick, but I thought it was kind of strange the first time I saw him dressed like that on the fuckin' street. After a couple of years of decent payoffs, he bought a three-story house in Santa Monica and named it Leone Castle. There was a turret on the top floor, and he'd stand up there at night, with a serious look on his face, gazing through a telescope.

"Did your brain malfunction?" I asked him once. "What do you think you're gonna find—gold?"

My friend Charlie Iwamoto was billed as Mr. Moto, a crew-cutted Asian heel who wore spectacles to the ring, like Hideki Tojo, the Japanese prime minister executed for war crimes after

World War II. Moto's gimmick involved playing off the anti-Japanese anger still lingering from the war. He'd slap his opponent with an Oriental fan during the referee's instructions, choke the guy once the bell rang, sneak in an "illegal" karate chop when the referee wasn't looking, then break into an exaggerated smile and bow to the crowd. Like so many Japanese villains later on, Moto conducted a salt ceremony before his matches, only to secretly stash the substance and toss it into his adversary's eyes.

"Look at this," the announcers would yell, raising heat. "Mr. Moto just Pearl Harbored his opponent."

It's ironic that Charlie had the same patriotic loyalties as the people calling him a "nip" and a "gook." He'd been born in Okinawa—where the U.S. maintained military bases—and would have given his life for this country. I guess that was a pattern with so-called Japanese villains. My future protégés, Professor Toro Tanaka and Mr. Fuji, were really from Hawaii, and Yokozuna, the massive World Wrestling Federation champion billed as a former sumo star in the 1990s, actually hailed from American Samoa. Every single one of them would have identified himself as American.

One of the funniest things I remember about Moto was the time we were wrestling each other, and got too close to the ropes. Some girl who was hot for Freddie Blassie walked right up to the ring, pulled out her nail file, and slashed Moto with it. It wasn't a very deep cut, but Charlie went nuts.

"Shit, shit, shit," he yelled, jumping up and down. "Fuck this shit!" Then, he ran through the ropes and into the aisle, leading to the dressing room. I thought he was just getting his bearings straight before we could continue, but he kept going, and didn't come back. That was it—the match was over! He was scared to death.

I later told him, "Charlie, if I did that every time some idiot cut me, I'd have to retire."

It was around this time that I also met John Tolos. Like Jim Londos, he was called "The Golden Greek." He and his brother, Chris, had come down from Canada, where they'd been raised, and were blazing a path as a tag team. I respected them in the ring, and I liked them as people. I wrestled John, one on one, a few times, and had some pretty good matches with him. One day, I figured, we'd do big box office together. I didn't realize that I'd have to wait until 1971, when we had the hottest rivalry in the country.

After coming from a family of meatcutters, I can't describe the thrill of walking to the ring, and seeing movie stars cheering for me. Someone told me at the time that 50 percent of the guys working at the movie studios were gay. So the girls came to the wrestling matches 'cause they wanted to have a man once in a while. That was okay with Freddie Blassie. I did my best to make sure they didn't leave empty-handed.

Anna, Freddie's mother, with his children, Ron, Gary, and Cheryl.

Needless to say, that wasn't the best thing for my marriage. Nettie and I eventually ended up having three kids—two boys, Ron and Gary, and a girl, Cheryl—and there was already tension in the house because their father was away all the time.

Nettie never caught me in the act, but she was a pretty sharp woman, and I can't imagine that she didn't know that whatever I was doing on the road wasn't legit. But she didn't bring it up, and I wasn't about to either.

I still regret what I did to Nettie. But I'd finally hit the top echelon of wrestlers, and women were a dime a dozen. I'd check into my hotel and—I'm not exaggerating—within an hour, fifteen different girls would call me on the phone, inviting themselves up. I don't recall anyone else saying no, and neither did I.

After spending so much time in dressing rooms, I—like so many others in our profession—had begun to think of the wrestlers as my family, and my real family as secondary. Still, during those rare times when I did manage to come off the road, I remember having a very nice time with my wife and kids. My boys would occasionally lead me to believe that they were smart to the business. But they didn't learn anything from me. Like most wrestlers who came up when I did, I always kay fabed at home. The way I figured it, the less my family was connected to wrestling, the better off everyone was.

While I was traveling, my mother and her second husband, Eli, helped out my wife, and looked after the kids. My children didn't give a damn about the fact that Eli wasn't related to them by birth. He loved my children, and was a real grandfather to them.

Eli got a kick out of having a wrestler in the family, and enjoyed watching my matches on TV. My mother would be in the kitchen, and Eli would yell, "Anna, come in here and look."

"What are they doing?" she'd yell back.

"The other guy hit Fred."

"I don't wanna see that."

"Oh, now Fred hit him."

"I like that."

I blame Eli for the fact that I'm the worst guy to have a conversation with about investments. Whenever anybody wants to talk to me about stocks, I run in the opposite direction. Eli always told me that during the Depression, when the banks closed up, he lost everything. It was just a few thousand dollars, but that was money he never recovered. So it makes

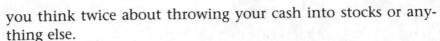
you think twice about throwing your cash into stocks or anything else.

Still, Eli took his caution to the extreme. He kept all his money in a pickle jar with a lid, and buried it in the dirt in the garage. Nettie tried to tell him that banks were safer now, but he wouldn't listen for the longest time. Finally, she convinced him to dig out the pickle jar. When they opened it up, the bills were all moldy and stuck together. Christ, he really panicked. He'd been saving that money since the banks closed, and thought it was worthless.

Well, my wife took the money to the bank anyway, and they went through everything. In the end, the only thing he lost was a twenty-dollar bill. I don't know how the hell they loosened up all the other notes. But the experience cured him of his habit of burying money in a jar.

Ron Blassie: Even if my father hadn't been a wrestler, we had a pretty unusual family. I know my mother's parents didn't approve of my father at first, but, by the time I was born, everyone seemed to get along. So you'd go to these family gatherings, and one side's speaking Yiddish, and the other side's speaking German. Yiddish and German are similar languages, so they could even speak to each other. But the whole thing was very strange to me. Had everyone stayed in the Old Country, one side would have gotten burned, and the other side would have burned them.

Even though we were raised Jewish, the one Christian holiday we celebrated was Christmas. I was the only kid who'd come out of temple, as his mother was pulling up with a big Christmas tree sticking out of the trunk.

All of us loved Eli, and considered him our real grandfather. I don't remember ever meeting my father's actual father, Jacob, even though I knew he was an asshole. But my grandmother told me that she was in the car with Eli once, and she looked out the window, and there was my grandfather, Jacob, drunk and in a fight on the street when he had to be about seventy years old.

In St. Louis, everyone knew that my father was a wrestler, but he didn't work there that often, so they weren't familiar with what he did week to week. That meant that when we were together at home, we could walk around, and do normal things. Then, we'd

go to a territory where he worked, and he was living in notoriety everywhere he went.

I thought my father was okay as a babyface, but I loved him as a villain. Everyone hated him, and it was just wonderful. I'm not sure if that was such a great lesson for me. Even now, I'd much rather be hated than loved. It's easier to keep up.

FOUR:
AMONG THE GRIT EATERS

In September 1953, I began my long relationship with the Atlanta promotion run by Paul Jones—the *original* Paul Jones, not the wrestler by the same name who worked throughout the south in the 1970s and '80s. Jones, the promoter, had been a pretty rough character in the ring himself, winning his matches with the hook scissors. What he'd do was slide in behind you when you were sitting on the mat, pull back one arm like he was applying a half nelson, tie his long legs around your midsection, and bend you sideways, until your shoulders were on the canvas. If he really clamped on the pressure, you'd be gasping for air like you had a boa constrictor wrapped around you. By the early '50s, he had one of the biggest territories in the country. Atlanta was the home base, but his wrestlers worked shows all over Dixie.

Jones paid his boys better than a lot of the other pricks in the business. So while still taking bookings around the country, I made myself a regular on the Atlanta circuit. It was there that I started relying on the spinning neckbreaker as my finisher, gripping my opponent under the chin, rotating his head around, and falling to the mat with him. When I traveled to different promotions, I called the move the *Southern* neckbreaker to make it sound exotic.

My arch nemesis was Don McIntyre. He'd first won the Southern Heavyweight Championship in 1949, beating Tom Mahoney. In 1954, McIntyre was in the middle of his ninth title reign when I took the belt from him in Birmingham, Alabama. For the next couple of years, we both made a good living, working main events, and trading the championship back and forth.

In between, I had a couple of donnybrooks with Bull Curry—a wildman who had one large eyebrow going across his head—my buddy Mr. Moto, and Dick Steinborn. Steinborn actually worked as Dick Gunkel, claiming to be the brother of Ray Gunkel, a top babyface in the south who'd been an intercollegiate wrestling champion out of Purdue University. Eventually, Gunkel became one of the owners of the Atlanta wrestling office, and, in 1972, dropped dead from a heart attack in the ring at the city's Civic Auditorium. Some people think he could have been revived, but no one had the bright idea to ask a doctor to show up at the arena that night.

The Southern Heavyweight Championship was a big deal in the '50s. Since the NWA champion only came to town sporadically, the southern title was the one usually defended in the main event. When the NWA titlist—whether it was Thesz, Whipper Billy Watson, Dick Hutton, or Pat O'Connor— did journey to our territory, he came to wrestle the number-one guy—and that was usually the Southern Champion. Between 1954 and 1960, I held the belt fourteen times, defending it in Macon, Knoxville, Chattanooga, and every-place else in our territory.

Although my family was still in St. Louis, I had my own place in Atlanta. In a way, I considered the city home, and a lot of the fans there were huge Freddie Blassie supporters.

But not all of them. Even when I wrestled clean, I'd get booed just because I wasn't a southern boy. After growing up in St. Louis, it was like I moved to a strange country. I'm telling you, these people were demented. They were still fighting the Civil War! And no matter how much I waved to the crowd when I came to the ring, or got down on the mat and wrestled a good, scientific match, there were always chants of, "Go home, Yankee!" In 1956, I finally said, "The hell with this. If these idiots want to boo, I'll give them something to boo about."

So I turned myself heel. On interviews, I'd call the fans pencil neck geeks, taunt them for not having the same physical attributes as the great Freddie Blassie, and say over and again that I was God's gift to women. I didn't have much else in my repertoire because I was still learning how to cut a good promo. But the few things I did say had the audience pretty pissed off.

FRED BLASSIE AND HIS SOUTHERN HEAVYWEIGHT CHAMPIONSHIP BELT

"Remember the name Freddie Blassie," I'd yell, "meanest man that ever stepped in the squared circle!"

When I got into the ring, I'd rile up the fans in other ways, pulling hair, gouging eyes, raking faces, and punching behind the referee's back, then strutting around with my chest out, pounding on myself like I was a fuckin' gorilla in the jungle. I'm happy to report that it didn't take long to be fairly despised.

Now, some of these fans were pretty dim, so I decided to do something to make it obvious, from the second they laid their eyes on me, that I was a heel. I went to a beauty shop and told the operator to dye my brown hair blond, the same as Gorgeous George. So she did, and I liked it. I even resembled Gorgeous George a little bit. And, just like him, I began wearing spangled jackets to the ring. To fans, who'd spent their entire lives keeping their mouths shut and doing what they were told, my new look said "arrogance."

The audience seemed to be offended just by the sight of me. They'd stand on the seats, and scream out, "Blassie, you're a fag!" But once the matches ended and I went back to the hotel, I did everything to prove I was not.

Of course, after Gorgeous George, lots of other guys also bleached their hair: "Nature Boy" Buddy Rogers, Johnny Valentine, and Gene "Mr. America" Stanlee, to name a few. But I wasn't going to allow myself to be regarded as one more imitator. Before I'd wrestle another blond, I'd get on the microphone and convince the fans that I was the innovator—and my opponent had changed his hair color to be more like me.

"You're looking at the Original Freddie Blassie," I shouted during one interview. "This guy finds his bleach in a dime store. This Johnny-come-lately is nothing. You know what I mean? Scum! As low as you can get! You have to scrape the bottom of the barrel to find the likes of this pencil neck geek!"

When you're a heel, fans like to question your toughness. So I had a surprise for them. During interviews, I'd pull out lightbulbs and chomp them into tiny shards.

It was something I'd first seen in the carnival. I remember asking the performer, "How do you do that?"

He tried to kay fabe me and say, "I just chew 'em."

I took him at his word and, initially, had an easy time getting the fans' attention with this shtick. Then, I cut the inside of my mouth, and couldn't get the bleeding to stop. So that eliminated my lightbulb chewing.

But I always had a backup routine to get heat. My Plan B involved smashing cans against my head. I'm not talking about soft aluminum cans that fold up on contact. These were hard, metal cans that were used to store coffee cream. I'd get a bunch of these things and bash them into a V shape on my forehead. And the edges would split and scrape against my skin. I always bled. But that was the point.

Now, a few promoters didn't want to see blood. If you had a reputation for adding "color" to your matches, you wouldn't get booked. But the fans went out of their minds! Some of these were people who came into the arena telling their friends, "This stuff is fake." Then, when the blood poured out, they'd change their opinion. How could it *not* be on the up-and-up? If you were bleeding, they figured, everything else you were doing had to be legit.

I also started biting in my matches. I don't know exactly how it began. I just found this guy on the other side of my fangs. I enjoyed seeing the blood flowing out because it antagonized the crowd. If an opponent had some scar tissue over his eye, it was even easier to get him to juice. When I saw how fans responded to my biting, I made it one of my trademarks; later I'd wear the word BITE on the back of my ring jackets. Soon, the same promoters who were afraid of blood were billing me as "The Vampire—Freddie Blassie."

Still, there were a few guys left over from the old days—when wrestling was covered in the papers as serious sport—who didn't like what I was doing. These were the same ding-a-lings who complained the first time they saw a flying dropkick because they thought it hurt the business—after all, no one would leave their feet and deliver a dropkick in a real fight. Too many dropkicks, they reasoned, and the fans would desert in droves. Sometimes, when I'd come back into the dressing room with blood all over my mouth, a joker would pass a comment like, "That's not wrestling."

"I don't give a fuck what you call it," I'd say. "I'm doing it."

Every time I walked to and from the dressing room, I was fighting for my life. People swung sticks, clubs, anything they could get their hands on. In the ring, I'd have to keep one eye on my opponent, and the other on all the debris that was being tossed in my direction. I'd get hit with beer bottles, rotten apples, oranges, even bags of shit. Imagine that—keeping a bag of shit in your pocket all night so you can throw it at a wrestler. I like to think that these birdbrains scooped up dog shit before they came to the arena. But when you got a look at some of these half-wits, you had to wonder.

I never backed down. In fact, the angrier the fans got, the more I egged them on, daring them to come up to the ring and challenge me. Most of the time, they'd walk about halfway down, then pause long enough for one of their friends to catch up to them and hold them back. But once in a while, someone actually got up the nerve to put their hands on me.

Rome, Georgia, was the first place where I ever got cut. This son of a bitch got up to the apron, reached through the ropes, and stuck a knife in my calf. I was walking around the ring, and saw that knife jutting up, and kind of shook my leg, hoping the damn thing would fall out. Nothing happened.

"Oh, fuck," I said, jumping off the apron and storming back to the dressing room. I pulled out the knife—and a big hunk of meat with it—poured some peroxide on the wound, put on a little Band-Aid and walked back out into the crowd.

It was a stupid thing to do. Aroused by the blood, it seemed like the whole town had come off the streets and joined the crackers in the arena, hoping to finish the job and lynch me from some oak tree. I don't know how many people were there—maybe a thousand, maybe two—but I pushed my way past them and got back in the ring.

"You gutless, no-good motherfuckers!" I screamed. *"Which one of you wants to come in here now and get his fuckin' head handed to him? You pencil neck geeks! There's not a man among you! You let your women do your fighting!"*

The cops were there by now, trying to get me to leave so they could restore order. But I didn't give a damn about the police; one of them would have probably knifed me himself if he'd been out of uniform with a couple of shots of Wild Turkey in him. I wanted to grab one of these bastards out of the crowd, and beat him into unconsciousness.

"Use me for a pin cushion, you redneck motherfuckers! I'll fuckin' kill all of you!"

I guess someone in the audience must have had a conscience, and pointed out my attacker. The cops cuffed him, and rushed him out of the building.

That seemed to calm everyone down. I went back to the dressing room, and the crowd headed home. When the case finally went to court, I expected nothing less than an attempted-murder conviction. But I didn't understand southern justice. The judge listened to the details, then fined the guy a hundred fifteen dollars.

"If I'd known it was gonna be that cheap," the imbecile said, "I would have cut him again."

Ray "Big Boss Man" Traylor: Freddie used to like to mess with the crowds in Georgia. He'd walk through the audience and call people names, right to their faces, and the whole arena would get hot. Freddie's favorite insult was "pencil neck geek." But in Georgia, he changed it a little. He called people "pencil neck grit eaters." Nobody thought that was witty or funny. The people hated it.

My mother told me that, before I was born, she was at the Armory in Douglasville, Georgia, and Freddie was doing what he did, and my grandfather, Alfred Traylor, folded up a steel chair and whacked it over his head. My mother says that Blassie was laid out cold, and had to be carted to the hospital.

It's pretty amazing to my mother that she had a son who grew up to be exactly what Freddie Blassie was—a wrestling heel. I walk into the ring now, and the people holler, "Boss Man sucks! Boss Man sucks!" But when I look into their faces, they're doing it with a gleam in their eyes. It's a different world today. Back then, as far as the fans were concerned, it was real.

Because of our age difference, I never got to really hang out with Freddie. I would have loved to—and remind him of the time my grandpa busted him in the head. And let me tell you, those steel chairs really do hurt.

I traveled mostly by myself. Other wrestlers used to pack themselves into a car, four or five at a time, to save money, but I was too much of a loner to take part in any of that shit. It was probably better for everyone. If some asshole fan saw me coming out of a vehicle, he'd try to break the windshield while I was in the arena. People were real brave when you were nowhere in sight. They would bang sticks against the sides of your car, and try to kick in the doors. You'd come back, tired after wrestling a long match, and there'd be a big ding in it.

I had purchased a baby-blue Cadillac sedan, and drove it proudly from booking to booking, the way my cousin, Nick, maneuvered his Coupe de Ville around St. Louis. There was an American Indian wrestler named Chief Little Eagle working around the south, and one night, he heard me talking about my new car in the dressing room, and decided to buy one himself. He went down to the dealership, but they were out of baby-blue Cadillacs. So Little Eagle bought an aqua car, since it looked almost exactly the same as the one I owned.

Not long afterwards, we were wrestling in Hogansville, Georgia. Now, I understood the risks of being Freddie Blassie, and always parked about two blocks away from the arena, in the dark, so no one could identify my vehicle. But Little Eagle didn't know any better, and parked his brand-new car right next to the building. I think he wanted the people to notice him and think, "Wow, look at that fuckin' Cadillac. Those wrestlers must be loaded." But he fucked up. Apparently, some fans had seen me driving through town, and when they spotted Little Eagle's Cadillac, they thought it was mine.

At the end of the night, when Little Eagle left the arena, his car was the only one left on the block—with four flat tires.

"You taught me a lesson," he told me later on. "Never buy a car like Blassie."

I should have known what I was getting myself into when I interrupted the ring announcer in a little building, outside of Mobile, Alabama, and told him, "Step aside, white trash. I'm here to talk to my fans." I pointed at the balcony. "All my *Negro* fans."

A few minutes into the match, the security guards pulled out knives, and dared me to come out of the ring.

"I'll cut you up, you Yankee son of a bitch!"

Now, I wasn't really in the mood for a knife fight—I was there to wrestle, not disarm a group of morons, who some other moron hired to work security—but once I had the audience going, I didn't know how to rein it in.

"Fuck you, you pencil-neck, grit-eating motherfucker! Fuck you, and fuck your mother, too!"

I won my match, and bailed out of the ring real fast. As crazy as I was, I recognized that this building didn't put a high premium on crowd control. I walked briskly through the dressing room, grabbed my clothes off the hook, threw them on, got in my car, and took off.

I headed back to my motel in Mobile, driving eighty to eighty-five miles per hour on country roads. It was pitch-black, and I was hoping that a cow or a pig wouldn't step into the road and cause an accident. Then, I noticed a set of headlights a few car lengths behind me.

It didn't concern me at first. You generally didn't see too many people driving around in the middle of the country at that hour, but you never knew. Still, this car didn't turn off, onto a farm or another road. Wherever I went, those headlights followed.

Somewhere along the way, I lost the other car, and began to think that I was just feeling paranoid about being tailed. I pulled into the motel, went to sleep, and got up in the morning to check if anyone had scratched the car while I'd been in the arena. There was a hole in the rearview mirror, a perfectly circular hole. When I went around and looked in the car itself, I found a bullet lying on the backseat.

I had been followed after all. And whoever was driving behind me shot into my car, hoping to blow off my head on that dark country road.

I have to admit that I was a little bit shaken. But not surprised. Everyone understood the wrath I provoked, particularly my so-called brothers in the wrestling fraternity. When I'd walk into a restaurant after a show, and two or three of them were enjoying a meal together, they'd look down into their soup. "Keep going, Blassie," they'd mumble. "Don't sit here."

Their worst fear was that someone would associate them with Freddie Blassie, and they'd get tarred and feathered one night by some deranged mob in the backwoods of Mississippi.

The situation got so ridiculous that, one night in the dressing room, I held a little meeting. "Look, you motherfuckers think you're smart," I began, "telling me, 'Don't sit here. Keep moving.' Well, rest assured, you don't have to worry about me sitting at your table. You're about the lowest scumbags I ever met. It's all right if I sell out the arena, and you all get a good payday out of it. That's something you like. But you don't want my company. Hell, don't worry. I don't want yours."

In all honesty, I would have been tickled to death to have a couple of friends. Fortunately, the women in the different towns were more courageous than the wrestlers. In fact, they were thrilled to be seen with me. They couldn't wait to divulge to their friends, "Guess what? I fucked Freddie Blassie last night. Don't tell anyone." Which meant, of course, "Please tell everybody."

I was still married, and didn't have a mistress of any sort. I just went from woman to woman in every town, like a butterfly going from flower to flower.

Somewhere along my travels, I'd discovered this stuff called Lubricane. It was like a gift from heaven, and reinforced my claims about being God's gift to women. You'd rub it on the head of your dick, and you'd get a hard-on you could keep for an hour. All you felt was numbness. You couldn't even tell if you popped your nuts. It was that good.

Unfortunately, there was another side to this miracle cream. You couldn't feel a fuckin' thing. I remember banging this broad once, and slipping out of her. But I didn't know it, and kept pumping and pumping. She finally said, "Freddie, what are you doing?" I'd been screwing the pillow that she had under her ass.

No matter where I went, I always loaded my tool with Lubricane. I even told my son Ron about it. Maybe it's not something the average father would discuss with his kid but, hell, I had to pass the knowledge down to somebody.

Dick Steinborn, a.k.a. Dick Gunkel: Freddie sold me a cock-stretcher one time. It's a tube, about two inches in circumference and about six inches long, made of plastic. And then what you do is you

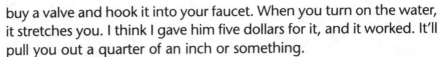

buy a valve and hook it into your faucet. When you turn on the water, it stretches you. I think I gave him five dollars for it, and it worked. It'll pull you out a quarter of an inch or something.

In the ring, Freddie was a worker's dream. It would look like he was killing you, but he was really loose as a goose. When Freddie got a headlock on you, it was so loose that you could slip out. But, because of his facial expressions and the way he held his body, you'd think he was going to pop your head off. Here's the way Freddie worked—if I shook your hand hard, or I shook your hand like a girl, that would be the difference.

He'd always apply a headlock on the left-hand side. And what I would do was reach around his waist with my right hand, grab his wrist, and tighten the grip. That way, I could shove him all over the ring, or grab on to him, pick him up, and let him drop.

When I first got started in the business, my Dad (veteran Milo Steinborn) told me, "The one thing you gotta learn is take care of your opponent. He's putting his trust in your hands. Your job is to protect him. His job is to protect you." That was Freddie. He was a marshmallow on you. He was a gentleman worker, I would say that.

When I was leaving the territory to work in Indianapolis, we came up with a great angle. Blassie took a Coca-Cola bottle and came out for an interview with Ed Cappral, the announcer we had on Channel Eleven in Atlanta. Freddie says, "Here, Ed. I bought you a Coca-Cola." And Cappral goes, "Well, thank you very much. I'll drink it later."

So now, another match goes in the ring, and I come out as a guest commentator. I'm sitting behind the desk with Ed Cappral, and I start coughing. And I say, "Ed, is this yours?" And he goes, "Yeah, sure, you can have it." And I gulp the Coca-Cola down a little bit.

We put the bottle down, we have intermission, and then I go out to the ring to wrestle Blassie. I'm about halfway through with the match, and all of the sudden, I start stumbling around and around, then fall to the canvas. I'm on all fours. I try to get up, and I fall again. And Freddie's standing back, laughing.

Believe me, these people sitting in the front in that TV studio came running to the ring, beating their hands on the mat, saying, "Oh my God. He put something in that drink and doped him." Then, Blassie gives me four neckbreakers—neckbreaker, neckbreaker, neckbreaker—and pins me, one-two-three.

Now, Ray Gunkel, this hero in Atlanta who's supposed to be my brother, comes running out to Cappral and says, "Get Paul Jones out here. I want to wrestle Blassie. Look what he did to my brother. I don't even care if you pay me. I'll wrestle him for nothing."

After I finally left for Indianapolis, the Atlanta office arranged to fly me in for the match between Ray Gunkel and Blassie. I didn't even wrestle. I just went out, and sat at ringside in a neckbrace. When I disappeared after that, no one questioned it. If you saw what happened on TV, you'd think Blassie ended my career.

You couldn't believe the effect Freddie had on people. There was a girl who used to go to the matches in Athens, Georgia. I liked her, and kind of messed around with her a little bit. Well, this girl told me that she went out of her way to play up to Freddie one time, and told him, "Why don't you come to my house?" Freddie drives up to the house, a little wooden house in the middle of the country, and the girl's mother is there. She says, "Freddie, would you sign this picture?" Freddie signs the picture. "Freddie, can I have a lock of your hair?" She takes a little scissors and cuts his hair. "Do you have a souvenir I can get?" He gives her a handkerchief.

Well, this is a very superstitious family. They take all this stuff they got from Blassie, and the mother chants over it, saying, "Freddie Blassie. I put a hex on you. And you'll be gone out of Atlanta in two weeks."

I never learned how to save money. You see, I came from a poor family. Once I got some money in my hands, I couldn't stop buying, making up for those days when my mother and I had to steal potatoes for dinner.

The way I figured it, money was there to be spent. I'd buy three or four automobiles a year—I didn't give a damn. When I'd talk to my mother about it, she'd raise holy hell. But the money kept coming in, and I wasn't too concerned about the future.

At one point, I began to think that I'd overstayed my usefulness in Atlanta, and started talking about going back to L.A. or some other territory. I was the star attraction, but how long could it last? Paul Jones, the promoter, didn't want to see me go. So he made me a proposition that meant I'd have even more cash to throw around.

"How would you like to be a partner in Atlanta?" he said.

I wasn't the first wrestler he'd approached with that offer.

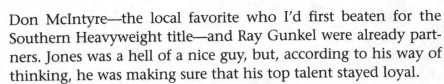

Don McIntyre—the local favorite who I'd first beaten for the Southern Heavyweight title—and Ray Gunkel were already partners. Jones was a hell of a nice guy, but, according to his way of thinking, he was making sure that his top talent stayed loyal.

It was a great deal. I received a larger percentage of the gate, and didn't have to invest a thing. But when I traveled around North America, working in different territories, I'd talk to the other wrestlers. If I saw somebody good, I invited him to work in the Atlanta promotion.

Of course, Jones was still the majority owner. But I was saving him a huge headache. With all his business interests in Atlanta, he couldn't really take the time to recruit talent in dressing rooms in Chicago, Dallas, and Montreal. And I'm not sure the promoters there would have necessarily welcomed him. If I had one thing going for me, it was credibility. The boys all knew that I didn't shoot any bullshit. When I promised something, it happened—even if the money had to come out of my pocket to make good on a pledge.

I'd always gotten along with the Fabulous Moolah. She'd been one of Jack Pfefer's "band of freaks," so we understood each other. Back in her youth, she was a very attractive woman, and Pfefer put her in a skimpy outfit, and had her accompany "Nature Boy" Buddy Rogers and this hairy, mean-looking guy called the Elephant Boy to the ring. But Moolah wasn't the type to stand in the corner and let someone else do the work. She had to have the spotlight, just like Freddie Blassie.

Moolah was married to this wrestler called Buddy Lee, an Italian guy from the Bronx who became a converted southerner and, later on in life, a prominent Country and Western promoter in Nashville. The two of them trained girls for the wrestling business, booked them all over the country, and, for a time, had a small promotion based in Moolah's hometown of Columbia, South Carolina.

Technically, Columbia belonged to Jim Crockett, Sr., the promoter in Charlotte who'd given me my first push. He saw Moolah as an outlaw who was hurting his business, and told the other NWA promoters not to cooperate with her when she tried booking talent for her cards. So Moolah and Buddy Lee contacted me up in Atlanta. Could I come down and work a few shows for them? I said, "Hell, why not?" I liked Moolah personally, and didn't give a flying fuck about NWA bullshit politics.

Christ, you would have thought the world was coming to an end. Crockett booked me to work in Charlotte and, without smartening me up, put me in the ring with George Becker. You see, every promoter had an enforcer, a bona fide tough guy who could step through the ropes with a troublemaker and make him pay for his sins. In fact, not too long ago, WWE had the APA—Faarooq and Bradshaw—in that role. If some other tag team began mouthing off or projecting the wrong attitude, they'd get their lights punched out by the APA—legitimately, on national television. Well, unbeknownst to me, this was George Becker's position with my old friend Crockett.

Becker and I locked up, and I thought we'd have a regular wrestling match. The next thing I knew, he was throwing potatoes—or hard punches—at my head.

"What the hell's going on here?" I demanded.

George answered with another punch.

Screw him. If he wanted to fight, I could throw potatoes right back. And that's what happened. After I hit him with a few jabs, George hooked himself on to my body, pulled my arm back, and tried to snap it—a special request, I heard later, from the old man. But I wouldn't let Becker get a grip, and kicked him in the balls. The match ended up as a "Broadway"—an indecisive finish—with the two of us tangled together on the mat, trying, unsuccessfully, to pin one another's shoulders. The ring announcer had no choice but to tell the crowd that we'd fought to a "no contest."

The funny thing is that I liked George. He was a good kid, only doing what the boss had told him. And I wasn't mad at Crockett, either. I mean, this was the guy who'd given me my break, and I could see where he felt betrayed. So once the match was over, and he decided that I'd been taught a lesson, we let bygones be bygones. Moolah made peace with him, too; in fact, she attended his funeral. There was no need to hold a grudge over something like this. It was just the way the business worked.

* * *

"Guess what?" Ray Gunkel said to me one day in the wrestling office in Atlanta. "I booked a bear."

"What kind of a fuckin' bear? You mean a wrestling bear?"

"Yeah."

"Well, don't put me with that son of a bitch. I don't want to wrestle no fuckin' bear."

"I wouldn't do that to you, Freddie," Gunkel said, smiling and looking into my eyes like he was my best friend. "You're too big an attraction. I'll get one of the preliminary boys. He'll be happy just to be on the card and make some money."

A couple of weeks went by, and I didn't hear anything. I was standing by myself in the dressing room, minding my own business, when Gunkel approached me again.

"Freddie, you have to wrestle the bear."

"What do you mean, I have to wrestle the bear? I told you, I don't want to wrestle that goddamn bear."

"Well, I ain't got nobody else who wants to do it. We already paid for the bear to come in. And shit, I don't want to give all the money back."

"Fuck you, Gunkel. This wasn't even my idea. You like the bear so fuckin' much, you wrestle him."

"The people don't want to see me wrestle the bear. *You're* the heel. They want to see you get killed."

"See me get killed, huh? I bet that's exactly what's gonna happen, thanks to you, you scumbag."

I was scared to death of that bear. But I did what was good for business. Gunkel booked a bear, and I got in the ring and wrestled it.

You know, when you pull a bear, he pulls away from you. But when you push a bear, he pushes you back. And this bear was fuckin' disgusting. He stunk. His hair was all molted. I'm telling you, that bear was diseased.

After a few minutes, I had hair all over my body, and couldn't take it. So I kicked the bear, and he ran out of the ring. His trainer tried to bring him back, but he stiffened up and wouldn't budge. The match was over.

"Thank God," I spat, wiping the hair off my body.

Furman Bisher, the great Atlanta sports reporter, wrote a story about the episode, claiming that I was such a terrifying character that the bear was afraid of me. I liked the article a lot. Unfortunately, so did hundreds of other people. Fans who hadn't been at the arena now wanted to see Freddie Blassie wrestle a bear. Of course, Gunkel didn't hesitate before booking a rematch.

This time, the bear practically ate me alive. He had on a muzzle, but I'd heard that it wasn't enough to protect you. During a previous match with a wrestling bear, another guy had accidentally slipped the muzzle down. Once the bear was able to use his teeth, he bit the wrestler's thumb off. I was thinking about this when the bear sat on me—eight hundred pounds of dead weight. I was convinced that he was going to push me through the mat, and the ring would collapse, with ropes and turnbuckles and ring posts falling on top of us.

The referee got down on the canvas, and went to count a pinfall. But even though my chest was being crushed, and I was dizzy from the stench of that repulsive animal, I knew that it wouldn't help my career to get pinned by a bear. So I kept my shoulder up, and the bear was too stupid to try to push it down.

63

When the referee saw that I wasn't going to quit, he called for the bell, and declared the match a stalemate. The trainer pulled the bear away, and I stood up, trying to rub that vile bear slobber off my face, and regain the Freddie Blassie swagger as I returned to the dressing room.

I tried putting the incident out of my mind. Then, about three weeks later, Gunkel told me some interesting news. The trainer had brought that bear up to North Carolina to wrestle for Jim Crockett, Sr., and the animal dropped dead.

"Good," I told Gunkel. "That son of a bitching creature should have died before he met me."

Thinking back, it was obvious that the bear was sickly. But that rotten trainer didn't tell a fuckin' soul. I wanted to kill the bastard, and probably would have introduced him to the Freddie Blassie bite if I'd seen him on the road. But the man vanished from the wrestling circuit, now that his meal ticket had passed into the next life. My only hope is that he caught something from his animal, and ended up getting buried, right next to him, in some mosquito-ridden pet cemetery.

* * *

Once in a while, I'd encounter what wrestlers called a "smart" fan, someone who admired me not because he believed my gimmick, but because he understood that wrestlers helped people escape from their jobs and mortgages and family problems—and Freddie Blassie did a better job at it than mostly everyone else. My other supporters, though, were mostly misfits and maniacs. They'd follow me around, when I went out to eat after the shows, when I stopped at the gas station, when I was chatting up a girl. And no matter how hard I worked at it, I couldn't lose them. It wasn't even worth my time to tell these ding-a-lings to respect my privacy—they were too far gone. I just tried my best not to monkey with them. I had enough of my own problems without cultivating new ones.

Some of these guys were convinced that if they lived to serve me, I'd grow to like them. Wrestlers had a word for these characters: *marks,* the carny term for "suckers." Unfortunately, too many of the boys used the expression to characterize everybody who liked wrestling. That wasn't me. To this day, some of my most loyal friends are people who started out as my fans. If it wasn't for them, what the hell would I be? But when people made complete morons of themselves, there was no other label that fit. I mean, you should have seen these jerks. They did things that an ordinary human with common sense couldn't even dream about.

"The Golden Boy" Arnold Skaaland: Freddie really was like the king of Atlanta. And he had all these crazy marks running errands for him and driving him places. I remember one time, two of these guys drove him to the arena. Freddie got out of the car, but he didn't invite them in. He just said, "Wait out here 'til I'm done."

It was a small building, like a gymnasium. And I'm in the ring, wrestling, and, for some reason, I happen to look at one of the windows. And there are these two marks, standing on their tiptoes, peeking in, waiting for Freddie to be done with his match so they could drive him somewhere else.

There was another guy named Hymie who used to hang around. He owned a shop that recharged car batteries or something like that. But he was a total idiot, and would do anything that Freddie Blassie said.

He couldn't understand how Blassie could be so good with the women. He'd go, "Freddie, you get laid all the time. How do you do it? I want to get laid, too."

Finally, Freddie convinced him that he got laid so much because he bleached his hair blond.

"Is that it?" Hymie said. "All I have to do is bleach my hair, and I'll get laid, just like you?"

"That's about it," Freddie told him. "Look, I'll even do you a favor. If you want, I can bring you up to the hotel room, and bleach your hair for you."

So Hymie goes up to the room, and Freddie puts this stuff in his hair. But what Freddie doesn't say is he isn't putting bleach in Hymie's hair—he's using hair remover, like the stuff the women use to shave their legs. Blassie finishes up, and says, "Now, wait a half hour and wash it off." Hymie does everything he's told. And when we all saw him next, he was bald.

No matter what I did to him, Hymie wouldn't go away. This guy was as nutty as a fruitcake. He bought a new car, and I put water in his oil. After that, I switched the tires on him. While the car was parked, I put on smaller tires. He was driving around, and his automobile was lower to the ground. But he didn't know what the hell was wrong with it.

He asked me, "Freddie, does something about this car seem strange to you?"

"It looks okay to me."

"No, no. When I bought it, it wasn't like this."

It seemed like he didn't really understand. But who the hell knows? Maybe he knew I was ribbing him, but didn't care. Nobody else paid any attention to him anyway. At least I thought about him enough to play all these practical jokes.

I don't want anyone to think that I only ribbed fans. The other wrestlers got it the worst. Tom Drake was a kid from Cullman, Alabama, who briefly played football with the Pittsburgh Steelers. He'd just started wrestling when I met him, and was doing pretty well. But he was an innocent country boy, completely vulnerable for a practical joke. We were in a restaurant one night, and he introduced me to his wife, and bragged, "Hey, Freddie, guess what? I just bought my first Cadillac."

"Is that so, Tom? Which model? What color?"

"Go outside and see it for yourself," he said, gushing with pride. "It's parked under the light on the corner."

Now, here's what a degenerate ribber I was. I carried around this stuff called mustard oil that you could buy at the drugstore. After I left the restaurant, I went over to Drake's car and poured it in—on the seats and on the carpet. Then, I rolled up all the windows. When Tom and his wife finished their meal and got into the car, they were gagging. Mustard oil burns your eyes. Obviously, Tom couldn't drive home that night, and had to get a ride from someone else. A day or so later, he took his new car to get fumigated.

"Blassie, you're a son of a bitch," he told me when he saw me in the dressing room. I was ready to get into a fight, but Tom had a big smile on his face. Shit, if someone had done the same thing to me, I'd want to kill him. Not Drake. He was nice and calm. I guess, as a football player, he understood that, no matter which sport you choose, there's a rough initiation to go through. And he was an easygoing guy by nature, and didn't seem to let anything get to him.

Maybe there's another reason why Tom Drake kept his temper. While I was pissing away my money on clothes and jewelry and broads, he was using his payoffs to fund his way through law school. During his last semester, he was elected to the Alabama House of Representatives. Even when he was practicing law and running for reelection, he continued wrestling on a part-time basis. Then, in 1982, he became speaker of the Alabama House.

So what—Freddie Blassie threw some shit in his car? If you look back on the way things turned out, who was laughing at the end of the day? Probably both of us.

FIVE:
TINSELTOWN

Even when I was main eventing in Atlanta, I constantly thought about my time in Los Angeles. I couldn't get the city out of my mind: the way you could wake up in Santa Monica, walk out your door and spend all day tanning and body surfing and looking at the characters on the beach; the grand feeling you had just walking the corridors of the Olympic Auditorium; getting dressed after a match and a messenger running up to say that some celebrity was outside and wanted to meet you. So when Jules Strongbow, the booker in L.A., called me in 1960 and asked me to come in, I was ready to say good-bye to Dixie.

I still kept my apartment in Atlanta, and continued appearing on cards there for the rest of my career. As late as 1970, I was involved in the territory's key story lines, trading the NWA Georgia title back and forth with Buddy Colt. But, eventually, I gave up my percentage of the promotion because I was no longer committed. Just like I needed to leave the meat markets of St. Louis, I had to be where life was more glamorous.

Strongbow was a large, distinguished man of Cherokee ancestry. Although no one's verified this, I'd bet my life that his name was the inspiration for Joe Scarpa, an Italian-American who turned himself into Indian Chief Jay Strongbow in the WWWF. Jules remembered me from my days wrestling in Los Angeles as Fred McDaniels, and must have seen something in me. I was a major star in the business now, and Strongbow assured me that I'd be just as big on the west coast.

Here's how I endeared myself to the people of L.A. Strongbow, who doubled as an announcer for the promotion, was interviewing me in the dressing room. I had my hair brushed

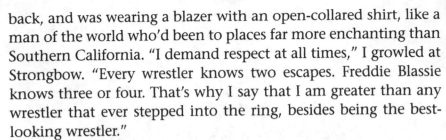

back, and was wearing a blazer with an open-collared shirt, like a man of the world who'd been to places far more enchanting than Southern California. "I demand respect at all times," I growled at Strongbow. "Every wrestler knows two escapes. Freddie Blassie knows three or four. That's why I say that I am greater than any wrestler that ever stepped into the ring, besides being the best-looking wrestler."

So far, it was a standard heel interview. But I was just getting warmed up:

"The women may swoon over me. But it doesn't do 'em any good. Because the people that I've seen so far, the women down here, the way they dress, it looks like they're all dressed in potato sacks. The women where I come from, they dress like women, and they want the fellas to appreciate them. . . . But the women that I've seen out here, believe me, they're nothing but pigs."

Strongbow, of course, acted outraged. But now that I was rolling, I decided to deliver a sermon on how I expected the women of Los Angeles to dress for Freddie Blassie: "They should wear formfitting clothes. Something that," I cupped my hands in front of my chest, spreading my fingers apart, "well, that the people can see what they look like. I hate these things where they wear padding and falsies and things of that sort."

I was pretty satisfied with myself. But the television station, KTLA, was flooded with phone calls. A few of the messages were from cranks who complained whenever they saw a heel on TV, but the most vociferous protests were from people objecting to my use of the word *pigs*. The women were furious, and their husbands were so irate that they demanded I be taken off the air.

Strongbow told me, "Some of the station executives don't want us to use you."

"Fuck them. What the hell do they think this is—a gardening show? This is wrestling. You draw money by raising heat. I guess the people must be watching, or the station wouldn't have gotten so many phone calls. Besides, Strongbow, you can't keep the greatest athlete in the world out of the ring."

I had whipped myself up into such a frenzy that I was mixing logic with my wrestling persona. In reality, I understood Strongbow's position. As the booker, he was the one who had to deal with those morons in management. But he didn't bring me to L.A. to water down my gimmick. He knew that Freddie Blassie never played by the rules—and if you asked me not to conduct myself a certain way, I'd act even worse.

Wisely, Strongbow just let me be. It led to sellouts all over the territory, and some of the most entertaining television that fans had ever seen. Honestly, I don't know where I came up with some of the stuff I blurted out. When the camera was on, I opened my mouth and made up things as I went along.

"These pencil neck geeks are very stupid because if they had any intelligence at all, they wouldn't have signed on the dotted line," I shouted before a Tag Team match. "And after we're through with them, they're not gonna walk out, they're gonna be drug out. They're gonna be vacuumed up. They look like blippets. And you know what a blippet is? That's when you take five pounds of drek and put it in a two-pound bag. And that's what they are, fifteen pounds of blippets."

Before that day, I'd never heard of a "blippet." *Drek* is the Yiddish word for "shit." I didn't realize that I knew any Yiddish. I guess when other people marry into a Jewish family, they pick up expressions describing joy and success. I retained the word *drek*.

6 9

Maybe it was because I was in Tinseltown, but sometimes when I worked the crowd, a number of people laughed, like they were watching a comedy show. During a lull in a match, for example, I'd point at my opponent, and shout, *"I understand he delivers telegrams in his spare time!"* I'm not sure what was so funny about the line. Maybe it was my delivery. A few fans would chuckle, and then some buffoon in the tenth row would scream, *"Go to hell, Blassie!"*

"Go home and wash your stinking feet!" I'd yell back. *"I can smell 'em up here!"*

Elderly people seemed to get particularly caught up in whatever I was doing. When I'd spot an old man, tapping his cane and breathing heavily, as he hurled insults my way, I'd lean on the ropes and tell him, *"Your grinders—you left them in a glass on the dresser at home!"* Then, pulling in the rest of the audience, I'd add, *"That's Old Gummy!"*

Once, a white-haired woman hobbled behind me as I was leaving the ring, doing everything she could to get my attention.

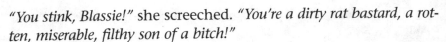

"You stink, Blassie!" she screeched. *"You're a dirty rat bastard, a rotten, miserable, filthy son of a bitch!"*

I stopped, made eye contact with her, and paused. The crowd began to simmer down, wondering if she hit a personal nerve with me. I waited a few seconds, just to milk the tension in the building. Then, I delivered my reply.

"Mom," I shouted, *"go home!"*

Martin Margulies, a.k.a. Johnny Legend: I think that Freddie Blassie was one of the reasons I became a songwriter, musician, and film director. His charisma, that unique Freddie Blassie thing, was just inspiring. If I couldn't become a wrestler, I wanted to entertain people the way he did.

I grew up in the city of San Fernando, in the L.A. area, and pretty much watched wrestling every week. Then, all of the sudden, when I was about twelve, Freddie Blassie turned up, and just completely floored the place. It was one of those life-altering experiences, like seeing Elvis or the Beatles on the *The Ed Sullivan Show.* My friends and I all went, like, "Wow." He had those catch phrases like "pencil neck geek." And the way he'd insult the other wrestlers and fans was just astounding. He made everything else look like it had been in a slumber.

I already had an underground sensibility. A small group of lunatic friends and I would go to Pershing Square in L.A. and hang out with the nuts all day, people standing up and talking about things like aliens coming down and taking over the White House. We'd also go to revival meetings and get healed. To us, Blassie came from that other side of the world.

We began following Blassie everywhere. Outside the arena, we'd run after his car to see which freeway ramp he'd get on, things like that. He had this friend named Max, who ran Max's Surfboards on Santa Monica beach. He was this weird, old Jewish guy who hung around and didn't say anything. When Freddie was at the beach, Max was always there. He'd come to the matches, and stand around. We'd recognize him and try to have a conversation because he was Freddie's friend. But it didn't seem like he talked to anybody.

Blassie always hung out on the beach to the right of the famous Santa Monica Pier. We'd just show up on his blanket, you know, in the middle of the afternoon. And he'd put up with us. We'd

literally stay there the whole day until he left. We'd give things to him to get autographed. We'd swim in the ocean next to him. If he was reading a paperback book and threw it away, one of us would go get it, bring it back to get autographed, and keep it, you know?

I still have 8-millimeter footage of Freddie by his car, putting on his pants after a day at the beach. He's just waving at us and being real friendly about it. I'm amazed how good-natured he was about

everything. He was the nicest guy in the world to us, and still managed not to break character.

The Los Angeles promotion was one of the few in North America to operate independently of the NWA. The company built up its own championship by exploiting an event the NWA wanted to forget. On June 14, 1957, Lou Thesz was defending his NWA belt in Chicago against Edouard Carpentier, a Frenchman known for his acrobatics in the ring. It was a two-out-of-three falls match. The first fall went to the champion after a flying body press. Carpentier won the second fall with a reverse body press. In the third fall, Thesz apparently suffered a back injury and couldn't continue. The referee ruled the match in the challenger's favor.

But did the championship change hands? At first, the NWA said yes. But then, there were problems behind the scenes between Eddie Quinn, the Montreal promoter representing Carpentier, and the rest of the NWA. Because of this, the organization erased this piece of history, pretending that the title switch never took place.

72

Still, a number of other promoters—fed up with the NWA monopolizing everything—used the incident as an excuse to break free. They billed Carpentier as a world champion, then brought him to their territories to drop his title to the wrestler of their choosing. In May 1958, Carpentier came to Boston and lost to Killer Kowalski. In August 1958, the "Flying Frenchman" surrendered the belt to Verne Gagne in Omaha. On June 12, 1961, it was my turn.

Carpentier and I split the first two falls of a two-out-of-three falls match. Then, Carpentier put me on the mat, delivering a series of somersaults onto my chest. Just when it appeared that I would choke, I reached up, snatched his arm, and upset his balance. Carpentier crashed to the canvas, his face clenched in agony, grasping his right knee. A doctor jumped into the ring, and made a big production out of checking Carpentier's purported injuries, before waving his arms at the timekeeper. To allow the titlist to continue would be criminal, the medic claimed. As a result, I became champion of the newly formed World Wrestling Association (WWA).

Olympic Auditorium WRESTLING NEWS

IT'S SIGNED!

BLASSIE vs. CARPENTIER

TITLE MATCH SET FOR FRIDAY, JULY 19 -- NO TV

We worked a busy schedule. On most weeks, it was Pasadena on Monday, Long Beach on Tuesday, Wednesday at the Olympic, Bakersfield on Thursday, San Diego on Friday, and San Bernardino on Saturday. Because we were the promotion for L.A., with all its media clout, I was taken more seriously than claimants to the crown in other parts of the United States. Promotions on the outs with the NWA exchanged talent with us, and brought

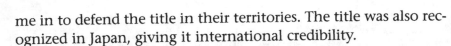

me in to defend the title in their territories. The title was also recognized in Japan, giving it international credibility.

To the people in Hollywood, I was the only world champion in the universe. Southern California was in the middle of a wrestling boom, and I was magic at the box office. I have to give some of the credit for my success to Dick Lane, the KTLA announcer who broadcast both wrestling and roller games—a Southern California offshoot of the roller derby. Whenever I'd rally in the ring, he'd scream, "Whoa, Nellie!" like the skies were parting. If you closed your eyes and listened to Dick Lane, you'd believe that the Lord himself had driven me to the Olympic Auditorium.

The Olympic was owned and operated by Aileen Eaton, a sharp businesswoman who promoted both boxing and wrestling. She didn't spend much time with the boys but, when she did, she was friendly, and from what I could tell, well liked. Her husband, Cal Eaton, acted as the buffer between Aileen and the talent, but he didn't have anyone fooled. We all knew that she'd made her reputation before they were married, and if he disappeared one day, no one would notice or care.

Cal was so skinny that he wore these padded T-shirts to make him appear bigger. Once, he came into the dressing room on a broiling hot day, took his shirt off, and sat down with the boys. He probably just wanted to fit in, but he didn't do a very good job. While the other guys were doing push-ups and flexing their biceps, Cal's bones were poking through his skin.

Aileen's son from her prior marriage, Mike LeBell, was the promoter in Los Angeles. Even during the best of times, I was always waiting for him to put a hatchet in my back. I feel pretty confident saying that every wrestler in the territory felt the same way. Because of all the publicity we got in L.A., you'd wind up with the press clippings while he wound up with the money. When the wrestlers read an interview with him in the newspaper, we'd amuse ourselves by marking it up, changing his words around so he sounded like a thief. I used to tell the boys, "When I think of Mike LeBell, I think of love. Oh, how I'd love to kill him."

Mike LeBell: Wrestlers always complain about money. You heard it before, and you still hear it. Even when "Rowdy" Roddy Piper was one of the biggest stars in World Wrestling Federation, around the time of the first *WrestleMania,* he'd call me up and bitch, "God, I got screwed. They promised me X amount and I only got this. I'm quitting."

When there's somewhere else to go, they complain. When there's no place to go, they don't complain.

My mother devised a system in L.A. that everybody uses now. They were losing money on every single show. On a boxing card, they'd give a man $10,000, another man $15,000. That's $25,000 right there. But you didn't know what your gate would be, so there was no guarantee you'd make a profit. My mother finally said, "Let's pay them on a percentage of the house."

The guys in the main event split 8 percent and got 4 percent each.

She did it with both boxers and wrestlers. They had to go to different hotels and talk to audiences. They had to make every radio show to pump up the gate. And the gates went up and they started making money.

Every single boxing promoter took after her. It wasn't until a few years ago that they started giving fighters $15 million, $20 million guarantees. The system also worked in wrestling until a couple of people got greedy and wanted to pay more in order to get a top wrestler.

Our territory extended as far as we could go south of L.A., and five miles this side of San Francisco. Along the way, we put on shows at little clubs. That was our backbone. If we drew $5,000 at a little club, my God, you could pay all the wrestlers like $75. At the end of the week, they'd wrestle at the Olympic, making $500, $800, maybe some $1,000. They were happier than hell.

The little clubs cost us nothing. In those days, it was like a joke. We paid $50 rent, and in most of the places, we built rings and left the rings there. That was about it.

One of the biggest wrestlers we had, Mil Mascaras, was a Mexican star, and he never wanted a guarantee. He'd wrestle for whatever. If we'd go to a little club, and we only had a $5,000 house, he'd take a hundred and a half and thank me for it.

I imagine that Fred was happy, too. Oh God, we were like brothers. Just tremendous. As close as you could be.

I think LeBell based his affection for people on how much money they could make him. If he was thinking that way, yeah,

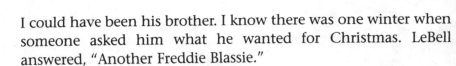
I could have been his brother. I know there was one winter when someone asked him what he wanted for Christmas. LeBell answered, "Another Freddie Blassie."

The whole idea of paying a percentage of the house was great for promoters. For wrestlers, it was bullshit. You see, there was no independent system to determine what the gate really was. That meant that you had to trust the promoter. And when you met a guy like Mike LeBell, trust wasn't one of the emotions he inspired.

Incredibly, LeBell had a brother who was the type of person you'd be proud to call a friend. "Judo" Gene LeBell was a good-hearted guy, and a tough guy, too. Gene had won the National AAU Judo Championships two years in a row—in 1954 and 1955, the second time at the Olympic Auditorium. He was a stunt man in more than one thousand movies, and occasionally put on the trunks and wrestled. Not only was he one of the top martial artists in the country, he'd trained for wrestling with some of the most vicious shooters in the business. When the family needed an enforcer to step into the ring with a wrestler who didn't want to go along with the program, all they had to do was open Gene's bedroom door and tell him to get into his wrestling gear.

It still amazes me that a guy like Gene LeBell could have a brother like Mike. There are times when I'm sure that one of them was adopted.

Gorgeous George had opened a bar called Gorgeous George's Ringside on Sepulveda Boulevard in the San Fernando Valley. It was a bad choice for a guy whose weakness in life was alcohol. I sometimes wondered if George bought the place just so he could sample the inventory. If you saw him walking down the street in the early '60s, you wouldn't realize that this was the same guy who'd been one of the first stars of American television. He didn't take care of his body anymore, and looked about twenty years older than his age.

Doctors told him that he had a serious liver ailment, and checked him into the hospital. He was released, stayed sober for a little while, then went back to his old ways.

Basically, he was living off his name. He'd call up promoters, begging for work. Because he didn't have the stamina to really have a good match anymore, he was kept out of the ring as much as possible. Instead of doing a two-minute interview and an eight-minute match, George did an eight-minute interview and a two-minute match. In Buffalo once, he was so inebriated that his seconds had to walk him up the ring steps. When he got to the top, his opponent, The Destroyer, realized that George was incapable of working a match. So he grabbed George as he was stepping through the ropes, put him in an airplane spin, slammed him on the canvas, and pinned him—one-two-three. Then, it made perfect sense when the seconds carried him back.

As far as he'd fallen, though, when you stuck that microphone in front of his mouth, he was still Gorgeous George.

His days of having a chauffeur had ended long ago. Now, he drove himself from place to place, and would sometimes have to pull over to sleep off a binge in the backseat.

I felt bad for the guy. After all, I'd admired him enough to bleach my own hair blond. But my father was a nasty alcoholic, and I had little sympathy for people who chose to drink their lives away. As cruel as it sounds, George had caused his own predicament, and it wasn't Freddie Blassie's job to throw him a life preserver.

So I was taken by surprise when I was in Las Vegas, and I stopped by this bar where Gorgeous George was a regular. "I hear you and Gorgeous George are becoming a tag team," the bartender told me.

"Is that so?"

"Yeah, two bleached blonds. It should go over pretty well. You must be pretty excited."

"Where the hell do you get your information?"

"Gorgeous George told me."

"Well, shit, you have better sources than I do."

When I saw George at the Olympic a couple of days later, he brought the subject up to me himself.

"What do you think, Blassie? We're both flamboyant. We're both heels. We're both top names. I think it's gonna work."

Generally, when somebody delivered news I didn't like, I had no hesitation about going off on a tirade. But, as pathetic as

77

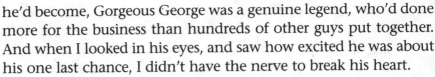
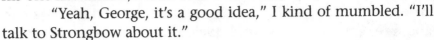

he'd become, Gorgeous George was a genuine legend, who'd done more for the business than hundreds of other guys put together. And when I looked in his eyes, and saw how excited he was about his one last chance, I didn't have the nerve to break his heart.

"Yeah, George, it's a good idea," I kind of mumbled. "I'll talk to Strongbow about it."

When I did speak to Jules, I was a little less subdued. "How long did you know about this?" I asked. "And why the fuck didn't anybody talk to me?"

"Well, think about the house we'd draw if we had Freddie Blassie and Gorgeous George in a tag team at the top of the bill."

"I have thought about it, and I'm not gonna go for it. The man's a drunk, Strongbow. You know that. He doesn't belong in the ring anymore. Look, if I needed someone to wallpaper two or three rooms, I'd call Gorgeous George. He'd do a lousy job, but at least I'd save a couple of bucks. But I'm not letting him drag me down just because he wants one more shot at glory. I don't need Gorgeous George. Gorgeous George needs Freddie Blassie. And, Jules, I can't fuckin' help him."

Strongbow understood. And George moved on, working for different promoters, and pitching them schemes he hoped would take him back to the golden days. Although I wouldn't become his tag team partner, I did agree to wrestle George again. We met in Vegas, and battled to a no-contest.

That was our final encounter.

In 1963, he was talking about opening a painting business, and had to make his son a skateboard for Christmas because he couldn't afford to buy one. On Christmas Eve, he suffered a heart attack in his Hollywood apartment. Two days later, he died at County Hospital.

The "Human Orchid" was forty-eight years old and had nothing to show for his days in the ring. The stripper he was dating took a collection for his funeral. Ring announcer Jimmy Lennon sang hymns over the coffin. Strongbow, Baron Michel Leone, and a couple of wrestlers George knew from his early days in Houston were the pallbearers. Both of his ex-wives showed up, along with a crowd of more than five hundred. Fans—who used to stand on their chairs and call for George's demise—now sent flowers from all over the country.

The Los Angeles City Council passed a resolution honoring the memory of the man who was as Hollywood as any motion picture idol. And in the dressing room, we laughed and told stories about the son of the bitch who used to walk home with one-third of the house. Yeah, the guy was a drunk who'd pissed everything away. But on the day they put him in the ground, no one forgot that he was still "The Sensation of the Nation."

Primo Carnera was another sad character. He was a giant of a man from Italy, a peasant really, who may have had a touch of the condition that affected Andre the Giant and the French Angel. He'd been a circus strongman discovered by some hustlers in Europe and put in the ring as a boxer. Once he arrived in the United States, gangsters like Dutch Schultz and Owney Madden took over his career—and his life. A number of his matches were fixes or setups against tomato cans. When he won, guess who got the purse? Certainly not Carnera. His so-called advisers squeezed every dollar they could out of the poor guy, and didn't even leave him a crumb.

In 1933, he won the World Heavyweight Boxing Championship from Jack Sharkey with a knockout punch that looked more staged than Toughy Trusdale's classic match with the dead alligator. In 1934, when he was matched up against Max Baer in a legitimate contest, Carnera got knocked down eleven times before losing the title via TKO. A year later, they put him in the ring with Joe Louis. "The Brown Bomber" pulverized the guy, and more or less confirmed everyone's suspicion that he was a fraud.

The mobsters who'd seemed so enamored with Carnera tossed him in the gutter, like the butt of an old cigar, living off the money they made from the washed-up champion. Budd Schulberg wrote a novel, *The Harder They Fall*, about a boxer like Carnera, exploited by his handlers and turned into a has-been. The book became a best-seller, and was even made into a movie with Humphrey Bogart, but it didn't do Primo Carnera any good. It's not like he got a percentage of the royalties.

I met Carnera when he was scratching out a living as a wrestler—finally saving a couple of bucks because his old cronies had taken their hands out of his pockets. I guess wrestling promoters figured that he could still draw them a good house. There was the curiosity factor—could a boxing champion make the switch to another sport?—and the fact that you could count on a couple of thousand Italians lining up at the ticket booth when Carnera was on the card. We had a WWA title match, and when we stood in the center of the ring for the referee's instructions, I noticed that Carnera was trembling.

"What's the matter with you?" I said.

"Blassie," Carnera begged in his broken English, "please don't break-a my leg."

For some ridiculous reason, Carnera had gotten it in his head that I was coming into the ring to shoot on him, and snap his leg. To this day, I don't understand why. Maybe he misunderstood something he overheard in English, or a ribber in the dressing room told the guy that I was a sadist who wanted to make a name for myself by crippling an old boxing champion.

I knew that, when the night ended, I was leaving the building with my WWA belt. If Carnera wasn't going over, I figured, there was no point in tormenting him.

"Don't worry, Primo," I responded. "I'm not going to break your fuckin' leg."

Carnera was relieved. And as we locked up and had our match, I was grateful that I'd always done things my own way, rather than letting other scumbags control my destiny.

Obviously, not everyone I wrestled had the same, tragic history as guys like Gorgeous George and Primo Carnera. It was a pleasure defending the WWA title against people like "Seaman" Art Thomas, Sandor Szabo, my friend Mr. Moto, and Nick Bockwinkle—a second-generation wrestler who'd hold the championship for Verne Gagne's AWA promotion when Hulk Hogan and Jesse Ventura were headliners there. I also enjoyed wrestling against Ricki Starr. He was a rare type of athlete who wore ballet slippers in the ring. But despite the gimmick, he wasn't gay, and often worked as a babyface. In fact, I can't think of anyone who did more to make ballet look manly. He'd do a pirouette, then fly through the air and kick you in the face.

Antonino Rocca could sell out shows just because he was an Italian from Argentina. The Italians would fill up one half of the arena, and Latins the other side. He also had a very unique style, wrestling barefoot, and wiggling his ass while jumping from leg to leg in front of his opponents. Rocca could never stand still.

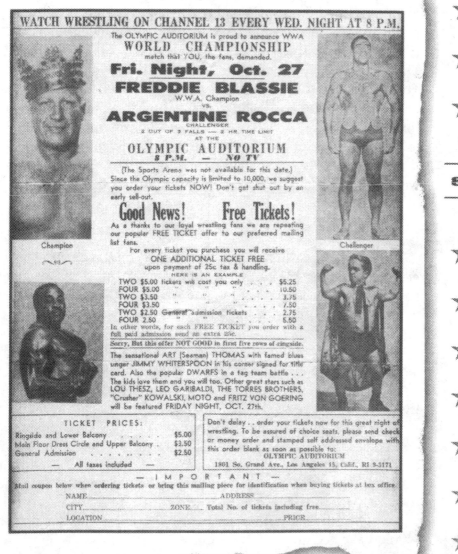

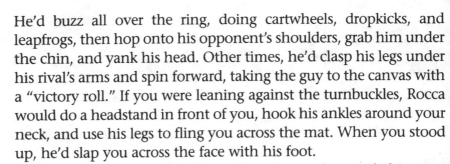

He'd buzz all over the ring, doing cartwheels, dropkicks, and leapfrogs, then hop onto his opponent's shoulders, grab him under the chin, and yank his head. Other times, he'd clasp his legs under his rival's arms and spin forward, taking the guy to the canvas with a "victory roll." If you were leaning against the turnbuckles, Rocca would do a headstand in front of you, hook his ankles around your neck, and use his legs to fling you across the mat. When you stood up, he'd slap you across the face with his foot.

There was another thing about Rocca that made him one of the most intriguing men in the business—a detail I'd figure most fans didn't know. He had the biggest cock most of the boys had ever seen. You should have heard them go on and on about it. They'd hold their hands apart and talk about the length. They'd cup their fingers together and describe the thickness. They'd talk about the sight of Rocca lying back on a bench in the locker room, with the head of his dick resting on the middle of his chest.

You can rest assured that Freddie Blassie never took part in these lively exchanges. I talked about wrestling and Cadillacs, women and making money. I was never interested in cocks.

There was a vacant lot next to the house where my mother lived with her husband, Eli, in St. Louis. After noticing that people in the neighborhood were using the space to dump their garbage, they both went out to clean it up. They were joined by another neighbor, a nurse. The three of them were joking around, and my mother made some kind of smart-ass remark to Eli. He smiled at the nurse and said, "You see, she always picks on me."

Suddenly, he keeled over. The nurse bent down and took his pulse and there was none. My mother stood there, helpless, as Eli died in the lot, among the weeds and the broken bottles.

Eli had treated my mother better than anyone in her life, and the entire family was hit hard by the loss. I was worried about how she would cope now that she was on her own, and decided to bring her out to L.A. for a while.

Once I took her to the arena, though, I wondered if she would have been better off by herself in St. Louis.

Anna.

She was shocked by the things I did in the ring, biting and punching guys in the nuts, and the way I called the fans "pencil neck geeks." When she sat in the crowd, and heard people talking about how they'd like to dismember me, she was terrified.

That's when she asked me why I didn't make more of an effort to be nice to the spectators.

I responded with the kind of diatribe I usually reserved for the television cameras. I made fun of the balloonlike shapes of certain people in the audience, the women's hairstyles, the spectacles I'd noticed on some of my more vocal detractors.

"I hate being nice to ugly people," I told her.

"No wonder nobody likes you," she replied. "You don't like nobody else."

Yet, I knew that no matter how disapproving my mother sounded, we'd always been on the same side, and—whether I was a heel or a babyface—we still were. In my own home, we didn't have that understanding. Between my wrestling, traveling, and the numerous other distractions I encountered on the road, it had been years since I'd given Nettie the attention she deserved, and our marriage was hanging by a thread. As for my kids, they could have probably counted the number of times they saw me each year on their fingers. Like with my mother, I made an effort to bring my family to L.A. for long visits, and have them enjoy the benefits of Southern California living. But Freddie Blassie the man had turned into Freddie Blassie the wrestler. And even with my wife and kids, I'd become—as the boys like to say—a mark for my own gimmick.

Ron Blassie: When my father worked in California during the summertime, we took our vacations out there. I remember having a great time. My father's friend, Max, not only owned this stand where he rented out surfboards, umbrellas, and rafts on the beach, but some duplexes and stuff nearby. That's where we stayed—in one of Max's apartments. My father was always the kind of guy who kept a distance from people, but he liked Max so much that we felt comfortable calling him "Uncle."

Early in the morning, I'd go down to the beach, and help Max open up the stand. I was probably in his way. But no one ever told me that. On the weekends, John Hamilton, the actor who played Perry White—Clark Kent's boss on *Superman*—would stop by, and read me the funnies, right out of the newspaper. Even then, I knew it was strange to have a father who screamed "pencil neck geek" on television, and spend my spare time with the guy who'd yell "Great Caesar's Ghost" at Superman.

My mother didn't go to the beach a lot, so when I was there with my father, I saw the way he acted without the family around. If he sunned himself on his blanket, there would be women all over him. Maybe he was on his best behavior around me, but I don't remember him seeking out their company. They just saw Freddie Blassie and made themselves at home.

They knew I was Freddie Blassie's kid, and would act nice to me, just to get to my father. Sometimes, they'd even give me presents—shovels and pails and shit like that. My father never had to worry about me going home and squealing to my mother. I didn't want to see any arguments and, I have to admit, I liked having a father who everyone looked up to as a ladies' man.

There was a place on the beach called Hank's, where they sold sandwiches, hamburgers, hot dogs, whatever you wanted. Well, Max brought my younger son, Gary, there one day, and

Gary decided, since his mother wasn't around, he was going to have a beer. So Max bought a beer and gave it to him. And the guy behind the counter said, "Hey, what the hell do you think you're doing? You can't give a child a beer!"

Now, Max must have been in his seventies at the time. But he got all fired up, and belligerent: "Fuck you. You're not his father. A mouthful of beer never hurt anybody."

The guy took the beer off the counter. "I'm not letting any kid drink a beer."

Max's face got red. His body shook, and he balled up his fists—kind of like Hulk Hogan making a comeback in his matches. "I guess I'm gonna have to give you a beating then."

The man thought about his situation, and decided that it wasn't worth making an enemy out of Max. After all, everybody in Santa Monica knew the guy, and probably would have boycotted Hank's if they heard that the counterman had belted him. And if Max kicked the guy's ass, then there'd be the stigma of having lost a fight to an old man.

"Suit yourself," the guy said, putting the beer back on the counter. Max slid the drink over to Gary, who happily brought the cup to his lips and started guzzling.

When Nettie and the kids returned to St. Louis, I went back to dazzling the ladies. People thought I was full of shit when I'd boast about my prowess with the fairer sex on interviews. But, in reality, there wasn't enough of Freddie Blassie to keep all my female admirers satisfied. In fact, I remember one woman seducing Max because I wasn't in the mood to service her. The girl must have been fifty years younger than him, and he couldn't believe his good fortune. I even walked into the room when he was in midthrust, pretending that I had to retrieve an item.

"Sorry to bother you," I said. "I just needed to find something."

"A hell of a time to look for it," Max grunted, through gritted teeth. "Goddammit, Freddie, can't a man get any privacy?"

This time, I respected his wishes. For the next week or two, I had a story to tell everybody. One of the most attentive

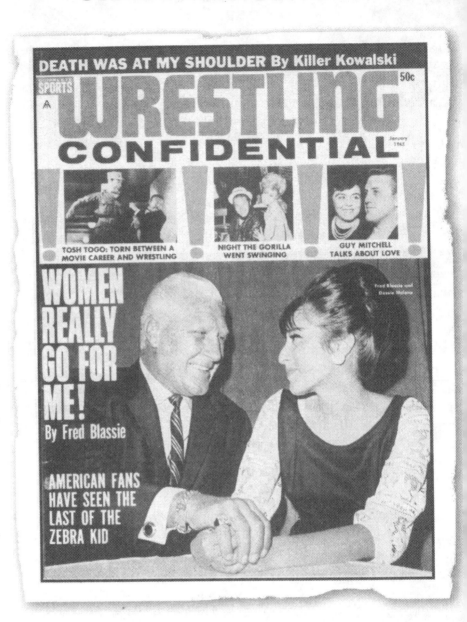

DEATH WAS AT MY SHOULDER By Killer Kowalski

SPORTS **WRESTLING** CONFIDENTIAL

50c

January 1965

TOSH TOGO: TORN BETWEEN A MOVIE CAREER AND WRESTLING

NIGHT THE GORILLA WENT SWINGING

GUY MITCHELL TALKS ABOUT LOVE

WOMEN REALLY GO FOR ME! By Fred Blassie

AMERICAN FANS HAVE SEEN THE LAST OF THE ZEBRA KID

listeners was Honest John Cattore, an Italian-American guy who owned another hot-dog stand on the beach. First, he didn't believe that even the Great Freddie Blassie could get this old Jewish man laid. When we finally convinced him that we weren't bluffing, John wanted to hear every detail, again and again.

I think I understand why he was so interested. When he was in our company, he always stayed celibate. You see, his wife was big-

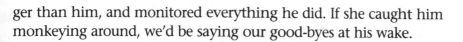
ger than him, and monitored everything he did. If she caught him monkeying around, we'd be saying our good-byes at his wake.

Sometimes, it was hard to remember that I was the same wrestler who'd traveled from one territory to another, grateful for a match above the preliminary level. In Los Angeles, I was rarely booked to lose. Once I achieved the number-one position in the promotion, I wasn't going to relinquish it. Fortunately, I didn't have to work hard to convince Mike LeBell of my marketability. As long as I was making him money, I had my spot.

On July 7, 1961, Lou Thesz—between NWA title reigns at the time—came to California, challenged me for the WWA Championship, and put me over in a two-out-of-three falls match, refereed by former Heavyweight Boxing Champion Jersey Joe Walcott. Not only did a victory over the perennial NWA king-pin add to my credibility, it proved that the WWA belt was a serious title (Thesz would later hold the WWA Championship himself, for two weeks in 1966).

As I stood on the canvas and gloated, several fans slipped into the ring, outraged that such a brutal, arrogant heel had toppled a legend, and managed to retain this important championship. Security managed to pull the intruders to ringside, but I was starting to notice the same fanaticism in California that I'd experienced in Atlanta, and tried to remain alert whenever I walked to the ring.

Still, I didn't have eyes in the back of my head. One night, I was scheduled to defend my title against Lord James Blears. As the challenger, he stepped through the ropes first. Then, I came out, and as I was halfway down the aisle, a couple of teenagers doused me with acid.

I didn't notice anything at first. The ring announcer introduced Blears; as the champion, I would be announced last. But as the introductions lingered, I began to feel hot. The skin around my stomach and legs was burning.

The odor of scorching flesh hit Blears first. He vomited, right there in the middle of the ring. Now, I felt like someone was holding a lit torch to my skin.

"I've got to go," I told the referee, and ran back to the dressing room. The first person I saw there was this elderly black man, who made a few bucks washing the wrestlers' backs and doing other chores.

"God," he said, "you smell awful."

"I'm on fire."

He grabbed a bucket, filled it with cold water, and dumped it on my skin. But the acid had gotten into my pores. Small blisters were rising on my flesh. He filled the bucket again, and splashed me another time, then a few times after that.

Outside, the punks who tossed the acid had run out of the building. We had off-duty L.A. police officers working security at the Olympic, but do you think any of them gave chase? Not a chance. This was a second job, and they didn't want to hustle. So the kids got away—as fans often do when they hit a wrestler with an object. Everyone's looking at the performer, and not the perpetrator. And that gives him the time he needs to get lost in the crowd.

I don't remember if anyone suggested going to the emergency room, but if they had, I would have said no. As much as possible, we treated ourselves in those days. I just kept pouring water on my skin over and over and over again. Still, I was too injured to return to the ring and have my match. I went home, and nursed my wounds the best way I could.

Three days later, I was back at work, defending the WWA Championship.

SIX:
CALLING PRESIDENT KENNEDY!

It was during my WWA title reign, sometime in 1961, that this Irish-American kid from the Bronx attached himself to me. The guy had no interest in being a wrestler. His goal was becoming a television personality. He'd been a gofer at a TV station in California, and now had a little show broadcast out of San Diego at something like one in the morning. When it came to booking guests, all he seemed to want was Freddie Blassie, week after week after week. After a while, we got into a routine. On Saturday nights, I'd wrestle in San Bernardino. Then, I'd run to the airport in my wrestling gear, with my clothes under my arm, and catch a small, chartered plane to San Diego. A limo would pick me up at the airport, and I'd change into my clothes during the ride to the studio.

I want to go on the record by stating that Regis Philbin was nothing until he met "Classy" Freddie Blassie.

Regis let me do whatever I wanted. Or, more specifically, I did whatever I wanted, and Regis stood there, looking like a goof. I destroyed furniture on his set. The desks, the reclining chairs—I threw them all over. I'd insult the other guests, and physically intimidate them. The people who worked for the show couldn't believe that anyone would act like this on live TV. But Regis was a glutton for punishment. Every Saturday night, that plane was waiting for me without fail.

Even people who weren't wrestling fans began watching Regis Philbin just to see Freddie Blassie. And once this new audience was exposed to me, their personalities changed. One Saturday night, when I was chasing Regis around the set, a chair went soaring through the air, whizzing by me.

The Hollywood Fashion Plate shows his jewelry on Regis Philbin's first show—a late-night program in San Diego.

"Who the hell threw that?" I yelled.

"My barber," Regis said.

"Your barber? Some barber."

"He's the most mild-mannered guy in the world, Freddie. You just bring out the worst in people."

"Yeah. You probably go to him because you get free hair-cuts, pencil head."

Regis Philbin: I consider "Classy" Freddie Blassie a pioneer. He was a bridge between what wrestling was, when people would be locked in a single hold for an hour, and the entertainment spectacle it's become. Everyone who ever saw him on television will never forget that bombastic personality. And to my way of thinking, he was even more interesting than the guys you see in WWE today. Not to put them down, but he was my favorite, the best of them all.

When you have your own show in a local market, you start worrying about guests because, you know, you don't have big celebrities anyplace but New York or Hollywood. In San Diego, people would sometimes come down for the weekend, and I'd be lucky

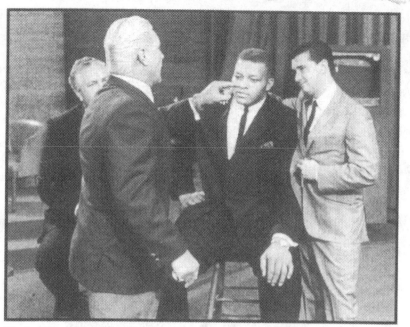

Blassie rages, with Ernie Ladd looking on.

enough to get them on the show. But I always liked wrestling. The first match I ever saw was Hardy Kruskamp versus Gino Garibaldi at the Winter Garden in New York. Kruskamp was the villain and Garibaldi the favorite. The arena was heavily Italian, and when Kruskamp won on a fluke, there was bedlam. People went nuts, throwing chairs around. I said, "Wow. This is really something."

Now, I was in San Diego, and guess who worked for the promotion there? Hardy Kruskamp. So I called him up and said, "I'd like to book some of your more colorful wrestlers on my show." He sent a couple of them, but Freddie Blassie was, by far, the most colorful of all.

I had a wildman on my hands. He never revealed to you that when he screamed and threw furniture, he was kidding. It was his persona and you had to get used to it. But the more tumult he created, the more people watched, and the more I liked it.

One night, we had this challenge. He said, "I'll do anything you want. I can do anything." Well, Blassie called himself the "King of Men." So I got a big pot, and filled it with water and lobsters, snapping ones, and gave him a throne, put a crown on his head, the whole thing. I said, "Okay, King, put your feet in that." He hemmed and hawed, and dipped a toe in. Then, he screamed a little bit more. But he wouldn't do it.

Well, at this point, we're running out of time, and we kept Martha Raye, the next guest on the show, waiting. She came out and started yelling at him. And Blassie, of course, is always ready for a fight, and he started yelling back. It turned into a nasty feud right there, on live TV, in this little San Diego market. Martha finally gave him the finger on the air. Maybe people are used to this gesture now, but in 1961, no one could ever imagine somebody doing that on television. But that's what Freddie Blassie drove people to do.

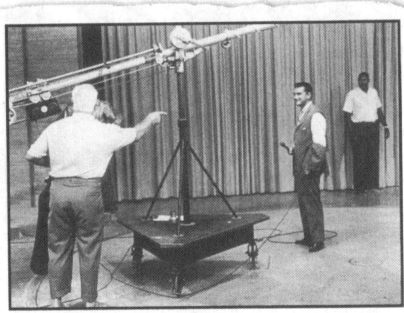

Blassie shouts at Regis after tearing his coat.

A few years later, in the summer of 1964, I was asked to fill in for Mike Douglas for a week in Cleveland, Ohio. Who would I like as my guest? Freddie Blassie was the first name I picked.

They fly Blassie in, and these guys on *The Mike Douglas Show* are used to rehearsing and writing cue cards. I said, "No, not with Blassie. Just bring this guy out. I don't know what's going to happen, but something will happen."

Well, out he came. We were talking about clothes, and I ran my hand through his blond hair, and messed it up. So he began chasing me through this studio, which was quite a large studio. Now, there were all women in the audience, and they were aghast because this animal was yelling and screaming, "I'm going to break your arm." He finally grabs my jacket, and he tried to tear it in half, right off my back.

I say, "This is a pretty good jacket, you know, and I don't know if anyone can replace it." But he doesn't stop. We're grabbing and pushing back and forth, and I broke my middle finger. Boy, did it hurt! I've always told people that everything about me is beautiful except for the finger that Freddie Blassie destroyed.

My career continued to move forward. When Steve Allen quit his show, I got the job. There's an old saying, "You can't punch your way out of a paper bag." So we got a giant paper bag and put Freddie Blassie inside. He smacked his way out—banged right through it—and growled at the audience, and it was great, great stuff.

We had wonderful times on TV. I used him on my morning show, *AM Los Angeles,* in the '70s. Once my national show began in New York, Blassie was there, too. When Blassie talks about making my career, he's not exactly lying. I took him everywhere I went because I knew he'd pay off.

Before Rikidozan came to the Olympic Auditorium to wrestle me, few Americans had ever heard his name. But in Japan, he was considered a deity—the "father of puroresu," or Japanese pro wrestling. The irony is that Rikidozan wasn't really Japanese. His real name was Kim Sin-Nak, and he was born in what is now North Korea. But in Japan, where racism against Koreans was probably worse than prejudice against blacks in the United States, Rikidozan changed his name to Mitsuhiro Momota, and claimed that he came from Nagasaki. It wasn't until after his death that fans learned that Rikidozan's Japanese identity—like so much else in our noble profession—was a work.

He became a sumo wrestler, using the name Rikidozan because it meant "rugged mountain road." He was talented, but had a short temper, which didn't go over in the sumo world, where obedience to tradition came before everything. After losing a close match by a technical decision, he screamed at an official—something a sumo never did—and quit.

I have to credit the guy for having good timing. When American troops occupied Japan after World World II, they pushed pro wrestling on the Japanese like a bunch of evangelists. In 1951, after former boxing champion Joe Louis led a tour of boxers and wrestlers to the country, a number of athletes from sumo and judo decided to train for the new sport. The same year, Rikidozan had his first pro wrestling match, a ten-minute draw against American Bobby Bruns. In February 1954, Rikidozan and his partner Masahiko Kimura took part in a tag team tournament televised on two separate networks. Many Japanese could not afford televisions yet, so the matches were broadcast in Tokyo store windows. Thousands of people jammed the streets on the first and third days of the tournament, when Rikidozan and Kimura appeared.

After Panasonic became the first Japanese company to manufacture televisions, and working-class people had the money to purchase them, Rikidozan became a national celebrity—just like Gorgeous George in the United States.

On December 22, 1954, Rikidozan and Kimura met in a match to determine the first Japanese heavyweight wrestling champion. According to Kimura, the match was supposed to be a work and end in a draw. But Rikidozan suddenly started shooting on his opponent, and helped himself to the belt.

Like Jack Pfefer, Rikidozan was an outsider in his society, watching from the sidelines and figuring out what the people wanted to see. He started his own promotion, the Japanese Wrestling Association (JWA), and dojo, or training school. Rikidozan understood how much the Japanese hated America for defeating them in World War II and stationing soldiers in their country. He made it a point to import American heels to Asia, and cut promos about their poor training habits and inferior character traits. Every time he defeated these guys, the whole country celebrated.

On March 28, 1962, Rikidozan was in L.A., challenging me for the WWA title. This was a great thing for the promotion because it meant that we weren't just a California territory, but an organization that attracted interest on other continents. No other

Japanese wrestler had ever traveled to the United States for a championship match, and the battle was carried on television over there. Japanese fans living in the Los Angeles area packed into the Olympic, cheering for their national hero and—like almost everyone else in the arena—booing Blassie.

The match was supposed to be two-out-of-three falls. Rikidozan knocked me out of the ring in the first fall, and I didn't

Blassie's war with Rikidozan was front-page news in Japan.

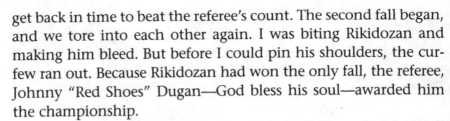

get back in time to beat the referee's count. The second fall began, and we tore into each other again. I was biting Rikidozan and making him bleed. But before I could pin his shoulders, the curfew ran out. Because Rikidozan had won the only fall, the referee, Johnny "Red Shoes" Dugan—God bless his soul—awarded him the championship.

I went out of my mind, tearing off Dugan's shirt. The California State Athletic Commission oversaw both boxing and wrestling at the time, and applied the same standards to both. Obviously, a boxer wasn't allowed to manhandle a referee, and neither could I. So I ended up having to pay a fine. How was I supposed to defend myself—tell the commission that wrestling was a work? That wouldn't have been protecting the business.

When Dick Lane rushed up to me with a microphone, I was breathing heavily. "I was robbed!" I screamed. "Title matches are supposed to be two-out-of-three falls! This is a conspiracy! I'm going to take this all the way to the Supreme Court if I have to! I'm going to call my good friend President Kennedy. You saw what happened! It was out-and-out robbery!"

The next day, Rikidozan returned to Japan with the belt. His entire country was in a frenzy. It seemed like the Japanese had finally gotten revenge for Hiroshima and Nagasaki. Of course, the story line didn't end there. I also flew to Japan, chasing after Rikidozan, and promising to reclaim my championship in his backyard.

Kosuke Takeuchi (President, *Weekly Gong Magazine*): In 1962, we were still feeling the loss of World War II, and when Rikidozan beat Blassie for the WWA Championship, he defeated the Americans.

Everybody I knew watched Blassie's match with Rikidozan on TV. The televisions were only black-and-white then, so Blassie's hair looked white. His eyes were popping out and he had blood all over himself. He was really frightening.

I'd seen lots of foreign wrestlers—Americans had been coming into Japan for several years as heels—but never a heel like this. We were used to wrestlers picking up chairs and hitting opponents with them. That was as bad as it got. Blassie was the first one we ever saw bite somebody and draw blood. Blood would not only pour down the front of the face, but the chest, and even the back of the head. It was shocking.

In the past, the foreign heel would come in and lose. Then, he would accept his loss, like a Japanese athlete would. Blassie was the only wrestler who, when he lost, still wanted to bite someone. In Japan, which is an orderly society, we didn't understand this maniacal kind of man.

Blassie always bragged that when Japanese people saw him on TV, they had heart attacks and died. This is true. TV was still very new in Japan, and only 50 percent of the population had TVs. So big groups of people sat together.to watch wrestling. There still wasn't an understanding of the distance between yourself and the television. It was like Freddie Blassie was coming into your house. And there was a certain type of hysteria that upset some of the older Japanese people to the point where they had heart attacks and died.

Blassie knew about what happened. The reporters in Japan told him about the deaths. I don't know how he felt privately. But in public, he didn't seem to care. He said, "If you're too old and too ill, don't watch me on TV. If you do, you get what you deserve."

When I got off the plane in Tokyo, there were hundreds of people waiting in the airport, along with about fifty reporters. They'd only seen me on TV, and didn't believe I was real. Now, they had the chance to look at me with their own eyes. I got through customs, and the crowd started shrieking. Finally, Freddie Blassie was there, breathing the same air as them.

The reporters circled around me, snapping flashbulbs and shouting questions. Some were yelling in Japanese. The others had accents so thick, I couldn't understand a fuckin' thing they uttered. But I kept hearing one word over and over again: *kyuketsuki*.

When a translator materialized out of the crowd, I yelled, "What the hell does that mean?"

He smiled timidly, "Vampire." Just as I suspected, the reporters were fascinated by my biting. So I gestured them forward, and went right into my gimmick.

"Come here," I barked. "Look at this."

I had a nail file in my pocket, and held it up. Then, I began filing my teeth—not too much, but enough so no one could accuse me of being a faker. The reporters let out a low, guttural *ooooooh* all at once. Cameras were thrust at my mouth so photographers could get a close-up.

I knew I'd get a reaction, but not one this powerful. For the rest of my career, I'd continue filing my teeth during interviews, usually with the microphone held next to my face, so the audio of the metal gnawing against my enamel could be heard in everyone's living room.

The translator was now standing next to me, holding up his finger to indicate one question at a time. Somebody hollered something, and the translator turned to me. "What do you think of Rikidozan as a wrestler?" he asked.

"He's a bum," I spat.

The reporters gasped in unison. Rikidozan was more than a wrestler in Japan, and I knew it. He was this force who gave his people life, convincing them that—as they repaired the cities shattered by American bombs—Japan would rebound and one day overtake the United States. To call Rikidozan a bum in Japan was like stepping up to the altar in a Catholic church and cursing God.

I was booked on a four-week tour, and there was the threat of a riot every time I walked out to the ring. The Japanese—like American fans—wanted to kill me. But never did I worry about some nut firing a bullet into my car or knifing me outside the arena. There's an inbred respect in their society that Americans will never have. When I was out on the street, the people thought I was the greatest thing since water. They called me the "blond-haired, handsome vampire," and followed me everywhere like I was their imported pet.

In the train station, the people would walk backwards, looking at me as I went about my business. When I moved toward them, they continued backing away, afraid of a face-to-face encounter.

In the store, dozens of people loaded in behind me. Japanese shops are usually small, and the place would suddenly fill up. I'd be pressed up against the counter, unable to turn around, with people craning their necks and twisting their heads, gaping at this freak who could commit murder from the other side of a television screen. When I wanted to browse, I'd pick up my leg and smash my heel on the insteps of the people behind me. They'd clear a little aisle, and I'd be on my way.

As the rivalry heated up, the media couldn't get enough of Blassie and Rikidozan.

I had my rematch with Rikidozan on April 23, 1962. He'd never lost a battle in a Japanese ring, and this night was no exception. He was the booker, after all, and I would have been insane to think that he'd want to drop the strap in his home country. But he still made me look like a killer. When the match ended, he was soaked in gore, and the fans were as scared of me as they were before I left Los Angeles.

* * *

Masashi Ozawa, a.k.a. Killer Khan: I was still a fan when I saw Freddie's matches with Rikidozan, but what I remember most was that Blassie wouldn't "sell"—or react strongly—to Rikidozan's big moves. Rikidozan had this powerful karate chop and when other wrestlers would get hit with it—*boom!*—they'd take a bump. But here's Blassie, taking one chop, then another—*boom! boom!* His bleached blond hair is wet, and it snaps in all directions, like straight points on his head. And the crowd is all heated up. "What a guy! He won't go down!" And there's that image of the blood in his bleached blond hair. There was such a hatred towards Blassie.

Later on, when I became a wrestler and thought back on those matches, I realized that Blassie could read the crowd. With every single move, he gave the fans exactly what they wanted. From one second to another, there was no slack.

There's a story that Freddie went out one night and tried some *saki*. He hardly ever drank, so the alcohol hit him right away. He got into the elevator at his hotel, and leaned against the wall, with his hand over his face. The elevator stopped on another floor and a woman got in. Blassie didn't even know she was there. The door closed, and he let out a growl, *"Aaaaaah,"* and turned, staring right at her. She stood there, looking at Freddie Blassie—The Vampire— and passed out. Blassie wanted to help this woman out, but he didn't want to be in a messy situation. So he just picked her up, took her to the lobby, and left her on the front desk.

Rikidozan and I actually had a lot in common. He was a rebel, who set the rules instead of following them, and he loved the night life. When the wrestling matches were over, he was always in the nightclubs, with women all around him.

When you went to the kind of places that Rikidozan liked, you had to deal with the yakuza, or Japanese mob. They were vicious guys. If one of them fucked up an assignment, the first joint of a finger would get chopped off. If he fucked up again, he'd lose another joint. From what I understood, a gangster would voluntarily place his hand on a block, while someone else—probably a friend—would wield the cleaver. They didn't weep about it or anything. They had their way of life, just like the members of the wrestling fraternity had ours.

The yakuza had a lot of power, but these racketeers seemed to like me. They knew I was a roughneck just like them—only I didn't have to use knives or clubs to get my point across. When I shook hands with someone missing a joint, I'd rib him, yanking on the damaged finger and pointing at him. Another guy pulling a stunt like that would have ended up mutilated in a rice paddy. But the yakuza went out of their way to do me favors, sending cars to my hotel to take me places, and giving me presents. By the time I left the country, I had two suitcases filled with custom-made shirts and jewelry.

As you know, I never had a problem finding female companionship. But these gangsters still insisted on helping me out. They'd take me to a nightclub, and ask if I saw anybody who struck my fancy. If I didn't, they'd drive me somewhere else. When I saw a woman I'd like, they'd translate, asking her to join me back at my hotel. I don't recall anyone hesitating or saying no—but, then again, that rarely happened even when I didn't have a couple of hoodlums as recruiters.

The only trouble I had with the yakuza occurred when I was in a taxi with two referees, going back to my hotel after a match. We were about a block from the arena, when we suddenly got stuck in traffic. I asked the cabdriver what the problem was, and he pointed at two drunks, standing in the middle of the street, blocking the cars.

We were idle long enough for some of the fans to notice me in the taxi, and begin circling the car and pointing. "Who the fuck are these fucking assholes?" I yelled at one of the refs, motioning at the drunks. "Get them away from the cab so we can get the fuck out of here."

The referee walked over to the guys, and told them to move. That's when he realized that they were gangsters, and had no intention of going anywhere.

Now, I got out of the cab. The fans watched in wonder, as I shouted, "You motherfuckers! You sons of bitches!" The mobsters stopped staggering and stared, taken aback by my angry tone and complete disregard for their status. Because they couldn't understand English, I decided to express myself by slapping one guy. Then, knowing that I had an audience, I jumped up and zapped the other one with a real flying dropkick.

A day or so later, I got a message from one of the yakuza leaders. "He likes you, Mr. Blassie," I was told, "but he requests that you no longer hit his men." I understood what was happening. The boss had to save face, and speak up on behalf of the two idiots. Not wanting to aggravate a bad situation, I sent a reply: "If your men don't stand in the middle of the street and block traffic, I agree to never humiliate them again."

That was all the boss needed to feel satisfied that his honor had been restored. I received a message back, informing me that the yakuza chief wished to take me out, buy me presents, and introduce me to more women. I responded that I appreciated his goodwill, and would happily accept, in the spirit of friendship.

The next time I met Rikidozan was back in the United States. On July 25, 1962, he returned to the Olympic Auditorium to defend the WWA title against me. For most of the match, he

The Blassie-Rikidozan feud took place on both sides of the Pacific.

held the upper hand. Then, he slung me into the turnbuckles. He attempted to charge into me, but I slumped down, and he went headfirst into the ring post, falling to the arena floor. When he got to his feet, he was wobbly and drenched in blood.

As the referee attempted to count Rikidozan out of the match, I reached through the ropes, grabbed my opponent's head, and pulled him back into the ring. Then, I quickly delivered a Southern neckbreaker that pulsed through the arena, stood and lowered my knee onto him, not once, but close to a dozen times. Rikidozan was a battered man when I pinned him. The referee handed me the belt, and I taunted the crowd, parading around Rikidozan's beaten body and pounding my chest.

The Japanese were pissed off, but excited about a rematch. Unfortunately, it never took place. Rikidozan had become a wealthy man, purchasing his own wrestling arena, along with nightclubs, apartment buildings, a golf course, and hotels. As his business ventures increased, so did his involvement with the yakuza. But that didn't mean that he ever buckled to what they said. When they told him how the game was played, Rikidozan often told them to fuck off.

On December 8, 1963, he got into an argument with a gangster at a nightclub in Tokyo. The guy followed him into the bathroom and stabbed him. There's a great story about Rikidozan tottering back into the ballroom, grabbing a microphone as he held in his guts, and cursing his attacker, like the whole thing was a giant wrestling angle. But this scenario is pure fiction. Instead, an ambulance rushed Rikidozan to the hospital, where he was told that his injury was not that serious.

He was also warned to take it easy. The doctors instructed him not to eat certain foods, but he ate whatever the hell he wanted. While the other patients were lying quietly in their beds, Rikidozan carried on like a lunatic, supposedly slapping some of the doctors around. About a week after the assault, he started bleeding profusely and died of peritonitis.

Kosuke Takeuchi: Rikidozan was just thirty-nine when he died. Even though his death came about because he'd been fighting, there was nothing romantic about it. To the Japanese people, he was a hero, and heroes don't die at the hand of a yakuza gangster.

SEVEN:
AGE OF THE DOUBLE CROSS

One Christmas season—I'm ashamed to admit this, but I can't even remember the year—I came back to St. Louis to spend time with my family. The promoter in Knoxville had contacted me and asked if I wanted to work the main event on Christmas night. I didn't think my wife would mind. I was never home as it was, and she didn't even grow up celebrating Christmas. But Nettie wanted the family to spend the entire day together. I didn't take her request too seriously. We all exchanged presents during the day; then I snapped shut my suitcase and got ready to leave.

"Freddie, I don't want you to go," Nettie said.

"Come on, you know how it is. If I don't leave now, I won't catch my plane."

"Freddie, you have three kids."

"Hell, I know that. But I'm booked in the main event."

There was no way that I was going to get a reputation as a no-show. I could imagine an arena full of crazy fans demanding their money back because Freddie Blassie decided to have Christmas dinner. Just like I always did, I said my good-byes, and went to the airport.

We'd had big fights in the past, but, somehow, this was different. When I called Nettie on the phone later on, she was hurt, and nothing I said could snap her out of it.

I had kept my apartment in Atlanta—I was still wrestling in the south against guys like Ray Gunkel and Eddie Graham—and when I returned there, Nettie flew down to meet me.

"I've done everything to make this marriage work," she said. "And I still want to. But there's something I need you to do."

"What's that, Nettie?"

"I want you to quit the wrestling business."

My heart dropped. She was giving me an ultimatum, but I believe that, deep down inside, she knew what the answer was going to be.

"Nettie, you know I can't do that."

And so we divorced. It was a sad time for me, but what else could I have expected? Nettie was a good woman, and had known me since I was a goofy kid. Unfortunately, I'd gotten swept up in a way of life, and shut her out. She had been both a mother and father to the kids, so they felt no special obligation to me. The two younger ones—my son Gary, and daughter, Cheryl—barely spoke to me again. As the years passed, the resentments piled up. Gary was a hell of a Little League baseball player, and caught a no-hitter at Sportman's Park—the stadium where both the St. Louis Browns and Cardinals played their games. But while all the other fathers were coming up to him and slapping him on the back, I was nowhere to be found. I heard that he never forgot that, or the other shit I did. Of the three, only my oldest boy, Ron, stood by me.

As much as he loved his mother, he worshipped the ground I walked on—so much so that I worried about it. Eventually, I felt that I had no choice but to tell him, "Christ, if you want to follow someone's footsteps, Ronnie, you could do a hell of a lot better than me."

Ron Blassie: My father brought everything on himself. My mother never did a bad thing in her life. He'll tell you that. But my father really didn't do anything on purpose. It was just part of the business, the traveling, the women, and all of that. You know, it happened.

My mother was upset. But, to her credit, she never bad-rapped him to us. She had a lot of other things to worry about. It's not like I was a stable older brother. So it was up to her to hold the family together.

Even after the divorce, I remained connected to the wrestling business. My father arranged for me to get a job working for Sam Muchnick, the promoter in St. Louis, carrying the wrestlers' robes back to the dressing room at the Chase Park Plaza and Keel Auditorium. It was only like five hours a week, but a lot of fun. I met

Lou Thesz, and (former NWA champion) Pat O'Connor. When (future NWA titlists) Dory and Terry Funk were starting out in the business, I hung out with them and their crazy father, Dory Funk, Sr.

Because I was the oldest kid, I remembered the good times with my father the best. I never had it in me to condemn him. Maybe it's because I understand that you can't be good all the time.

After I won back the WWA Championship from Rikidozan, my reign lasted exactly two days. On July 27, 1962, the masked Destroyer defeated me in San Diego. Dick Beyer, the wrestler underneath the Destroyer gimmick, was one of the sharpest guys in the business. He'd earned a master's degree in education long before every bum too lazy to work took off and went to college for four years. When he spoke, he sounded like a professor, and knew how to make money off his book smarts. During interviews, he'd rile up the blue-collar crowd, demanding that the announcer refer to him only as "The Sensational, Intelligent Destroyer."

Beyer was also a hell of an athlete, and could tell a story physically in the ring, working over a body part, backing off, then pouncing on it again—convincing the fans that if he kept at it, his opponent would walk out a cripple. He'd do this routine where he'd put people in the figure-four leglock, and offer a thousand dollars—a small fortune in 1962—to anyone who could break the hold. He excited the spectators with his dropkick and airplane spin. What he would do was drape you over his shoulders and spin you around. The only problem was that you didn't know where he planned to drop you, or how you were going to land. Still, it was a risk worth taking. I knew that if the promotion matched me up with Beyer, there'd be money to burn.

Dick "The Destroyer" Beyer: I knew Freddie from when we worked together in Tennessee in 1958, and had run into him in early 1962 in Hawaii, where he'd gone to defend the WWA title. I was just Dick Beyer then, and presented as a collegiate babyface. They announced me as "from Syracuse University." Blassie, of course, was the nasty heel, and we had a great match, the biggest crowd they'd had in Honolulu in a while.

Freddie used psychology to draw money. His interviews were

great, and he had the biting. He could build the people up during a match, set them back down, then build them up again.

In the dressing room, we used to laugh all the time. He loved to talk about broads, and this stuff, Lubricane, that he'd rub on his dick so he wouldn't come so quick. He'd put it on before he had a date, and the stuff would be dripping on the floor while you were talking to him. You'd say, "Jesus Christ, Freddie," and he'd wrap a piece of toilet paper around his cock. Then, he'd want to play cards. But, fuck, who wants that Lubricane getting all over the cards after it's been on Freddie's dick?

Anyway, after we had our match in Hawaii, Blassie went back to Los Angeles and told Jules Strongbow, "You gotta bring that Dick Beyer to L.A. He's the greatest babyface in the business." A few weeks later, after they turned me heel in Hawaii, he said, "Jules, you gotta bring in Dick Beyer. He's great as a heel, too." Either way, he was the catalyst for me coming to California.

So I went to L.A. and Strongbow tells me, "Tomorrow night, you're working down in San Diego, and you're working as the masked Destroyer."

I said, "What? You gotta be kidding. I don't even have a mask."

"Don't worry about it. Vic Christie (another wrestler) will have one for you."

Now, other than Blassie, Vic Christie was the biggest jokester in the business. When I got to San Diego, he threw me this thing, and told me to go in the back room and change. It was a full body mask. It slipped over your head and over your body, and my arms went through a couple of holes and then it buttoned in the crotch. It was dark blue and moth-bitten and made out of wool. And it only had two little eyeholes, nothing for your nose or mouth.

I had no peripheral vision, and I couldn't breathe. I had my match, and went back to the dressing room, and said to Hardy Kruskamp, the local promoter in San Diego, "You've just seen the first and last of the Destroyer." I took off the outfit and threw it at Vic Christie. Of course, everyone's laughing, because the whole thing was a rib.

Now another wrestler, Ox Anderson, is sitting there, and he throws me a different mask. He says, "Try this one on instead." I tried it on. I could see. I could breathe. I had peripheral vision. And it

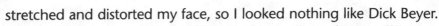

stretched and distorted my face, so I looked nothing like Dick Beyer.

"This is great," I said. "What's this mask made out of?"

"A woman's girdle. You use this for your gimmick, and you'll be the only person in town who can go around telling people that you put your head in a woman's girdle every night."

A lot of guys when they start wearing a mask are in their forties or fifties—they're trying to hide an old face from the fans, and

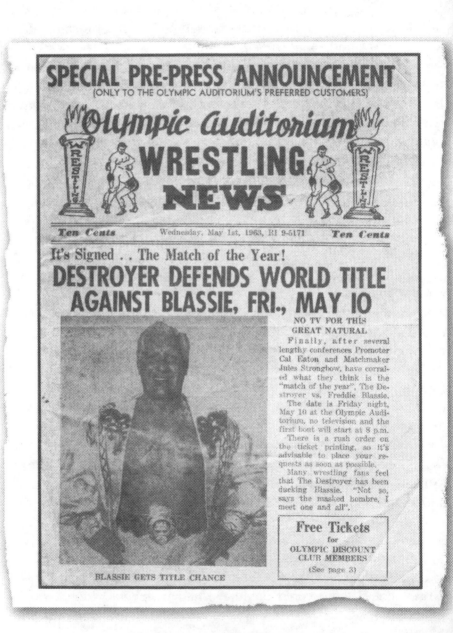

SPECIAL PRE-PRESS ANNOUNCEMENT
(ONLY TO THE OLYMPIC AUDITORIUM'S PREFERRED CUSTOMERS)

Olympic Auditorium WRESTLING NEWS

Ten Cents   Wednesday, May 1st, 1963, RI 9-5171   Ten Cents

It's Signed .. The Match of the Year!

DESTROYER DEFENDS WORLD TITLE AGAINST BLASSIE, FRI., MAY 10

NO TV FOR THIS GREAT NATURAL

Finally, after several lengthy conferences Promoter Cal Eaton and Matchmaker Jules Strongbow, have corraled what they think is the "match of the year", The Destroyer vs. Freddie Blassie.

The date is Friday night, May 10 at the Olympic Auditorium, no television and the first bout will start at 8 p.m.

There is a rush order on the ticket printing, so it's advisable to place your requests as soon as possible.

Many wrestling fans feel that The Destroyer has been ducking Blassie. "Not so, says the masked hombre, I meet one and all".

Free Tickets for OLYMPIC DISCOUNT CLUB MEMBERS (See page 3)

BLASSIE GETS TITLE CHANCE

extend their careers for a few more years. I was young, and my body was good. Then, Freddie Blassie put me over for the WWA title, and I was on my way.

I kept the championship for nearly a year, getting my picture in all the wrestling magazines. But Blassie was always right behind me, on the verge of winning back the title every time we met. On May 10, 1963, we had a match where Blassie promised not only to win the belt, but unmask me in the middle of the ring. It was time for me to do the honors for Freddie, and put an end to the Destroyer mystery. But I didn't want my face exposed. I was leaving the territory for Oregon, and decided to double-cross the promotion and keep my gimmick.

In the dressing room, I told a couple of my friends, "As soon as Blassie rips the mask off, I'm getting out of the ring. I want you to throw a towel over my head, and we're going right up the aisle, out the door, and into my car."

We had the wrestling match we planned—two-out-of-three falls. In the third fall, Blassie beat me with the Southern neckbreaker, and got ready to take the mask off. I saw my friends coming out of the dressing room, and resisted when Blassie tried to grab my head. We began wrestling back and forth—this time for real—until Blassie managed to hook his fingers underneath my mask, and tug it off.

I put my hands over my face and rolled out of the ring. My friends surrounded me, and I put the towel over my head. Blassie and the ref were standing in the ring, watching me, as I took off down the aisle.

Now, the fans were confused. What the hell just happened? Jules Strongbow came into the ring, grabbed the microphone, and said, "We still don't know who he is."

You'd think that I'd never work in L.A. again, after double-crossing the promotion like that. But after I left, the Destroyer gimmick continued to pick up steam. I was becoming a star because of that fuckin' mask. So nine months later, Strongbow calls me up. "You did a good thing, leaving the way you did," he tells me. "We want to bring you back as The Destroyer."

Five days before Martin Luther King, Jr., delivered his "I have a dream" speech to 250,000 people gathered for the March on Washington, I put over Bearcat Wright for the WWA

Championship. Wright, who'd show off his strength by ripping phone books in half in interviews, and used his large hands to apply his dreaded "claw" to people's heads and stomachs, had held a world title for a much smaller promotion in Massachusetts in 1961. But his victory over me, on August 23, 1963, was revolutionary in pro wrestling. While blacks were still restricted to wrestling each other in certain territories, the WWA had given an African-American a title recognized as far away as Hawaii and Japan.

Bearcat was a big drawing card, but he was no Jackie Robinson. Very quickly, he let the win get to his head, and became delusional. To hear him speak, he was America's number-one role model for the black race, and now that he had the title, he wasn't going to give it up.

This posed a pretty big problem for the LeBell family. By the end of 1963, they were planning to put the belt on someone else, but Wright refused to cooperate. I remember breaking some ribs and convalescing in the hospital when Aileen Eaton came to see me, with her husband, Cal, and son, Mike LeBell.

"Bearcat was supposed to do the job for Edouard Carpentier," Mike told me. "But he double-crossed him in the ring, and kept the strap."

"What's his problem?"

"He doesn't want to lose."

"Hell, match him with me. He and I are good friends. He'll do whatever I tell him."

Our match was scheduled for December 13, 1963. Bearcat and I talked everything out beforehand. "You know you're putting me over?" I asked him.

"Yeah."

"And that's all right with you?"

"Sure, Freddie."

"There are no other problems? The money's fine and everything?"

"Yeah, everything's okay."

So I got in the ring with my guard down, thinking that even if Wright didn't respect Mike LeBell, he'd never do anything to screw with me. After all, I was the guy who'd agreed to drop the championship to him in the first place. As the match went on, though, he was tightening up on me, clamping on a hammer-lock and really shoving it up behind my head. I was a little tired from just coming out of the hospital, and felt like he was taking advantage of me, using his strength to muscle me around. Towards the end of the match, he tossed me out of the ring, just like we planned. I was supposed to come back in and rally. But when I was climbing onto the ring apron, he hit me with his Sunday punch smack in the chin. It knocked me goofy, and I fell back down to ringside, where the referee had no choice but to count me out.

Now, I was pissed. I'd always treated Bearcat as a friend. But he didn't see it that way. In his mind, I was the enemy, just because I was white.

I still hadn't recovered 100 percent. But Wright was a loose cannon, and the promotion needed to get the championship away from him. Because of his lack of cooperation, all his conspiracy theories had come true. Everyone really *was* against Bearcat Wright, and, for once, Mike LeBell and I were on the same side.

I agreed to a rematch, but when Wright came out of the dressing room, he got a big surprise. There was going to be a last-minute substitution. Gene LeBell—judo champion and legitimate shooter—was standing next to me in wrestling trunks. Gene, the family enforcer, wasn't only going to grapple the belt away from Bearcat, he was going to torture him. Bearcat stepped through the curtain and considered the situation in the ring, before a jolt of common sense struck him. He turned around, and left the building.

The WWA announced that Wright had forfeited the championship, after no-showing a defense against Carpentier in Indio, California. Then, on January 30, 1964, I defeated the "Flying Frenchman," and the title was finally back where it belonged.

Martin Margulies, a.k.a. Johnny Legend: My friends and I were always trying to peek into the dressing room at Valley Gardens, the little arena we had in San Fernando. Once, we even managed to sneak in and pry a door open. Blassie and Mr. Moto were inside play-

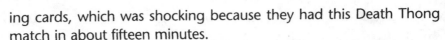

ing cards, which was shocking because they had this Death Thong match in about fifteen minutes.

When we couldn't look into the dressing room, we always had our ears open for rumors and gossip. One night, we hear about some kind of disturbance in the parking lot. I have this weird memory—I'm not even sure if it's true or not—of Bearcat Wright outside, acting crazed. We heard that he'd been caught trying to break into Freddie Blassie's trunk and steal back the belt. It was one of the few times I remember where a wrestler actually snapped.

About a month after I regained the title, I was working a show in Albuquerque, standing behind the dressing room curtain, and holding it open a crack to watch the match in the ring. I heard a whisper behind me, "Blassie, Blassie." I looked around, but it was dark, and I couldn't adjust my eyes.

"It's me, Bearcat."

I turned away from the curtain and, sure enough, it *was* Bearcat Wright. He wasn't scheduled to wrestle on the show or anything. I was so surprised that I didn't know what to say.

"Listen, Freddie, I'm sorry. I can't get booked nowhere in the United States. I'm not making no money. No one wants to touch me because of what happened in L.A."

"Well, you should have thought about that before you pulled that bullshit."

"Freddie, do you think you could speak up on my behalf?"

"Not on your fuckin' life."

I never saw Bearcat Wright again after that, but he didn't vanish into thin air. He worked in San Francisco, Georgia, Calgary, and a bunch of other places—and did pretty well for himself—before dropping dead of a heart attack in 1983, when he was fifty years old.

Johnny Legend: At a certain point, Jay North, the kid on *Dennis the Menace,* began showing up at the Olympic Auditorium. I remember ring announcer Jimmy Lennon saying, "Ladies and gentlemen, we have here at ringside, TV's *Dennis the Menace,* Jay North." He would stand up and greet the crowd, and spend a lot of time hanging out in this back area, near the dressing room, where some of the wrestlers stood to watch the other matches.

I tried talking to Jay North a couple of times, but it was hard to engage him. He'd say things like, "Freddie Blassie—wow," and run off.

These other kids had started a Freddie Blassie Fan Club. So my friend, Glenn Bray, and I began our own group, the International Freddie Blassie Fan Club. We wanted to have an advantage over the other guys, so one night, when Jay North went shooting by, I said, "We're starting an International Freddie Blassie Fan Club. Would you like to be honorary president?" And he said, "Oh, I love Freddie Blassie," and went zooming off. I said, "That's enough of a commitment to me."

Back then, the wrestling magazines would have fan club listings. And we included the International Freddie Blassie Fan Club, with my home address, and the line, "Honorary President: Jay North."

The only letters we got were from these barely pubescent girls, sending scented stationery and these Polaroids they considered racy. We sent letters back, and addressed them from Jay North. Only we made believe he was retarded. We had a lot of misspellings, and wrote things like, "I are big Blassie fan. I have photo of me I sell. One is dollar. Five is dollar and dollar and dollar and dollar and dollar." And that pretty much shook them out. No one ever wrote back.

No matter how many sellouts I drew in L.A., I always felt like I was being cheated. I noticed that my pay would sometimes decrease, even though there were just as many fans in the building as the week before. I was sure that the office was skimming more than its cut, but when I asked Mike LeBell about this, I sensed that he wasn't taking me seriously. I was the number-one boy in Southern California—and taking home more money than a lot of the other guys—so he probably thought that I wouldn't go anywhere else. But just because I was on top didn't give anyone the right to fuck with my money. I began feeling like I wanted to go somewhere else for a while, just to take a vacation from Mike LeBell.

In the spring of 1964, there was a new number-one contender in the WWA: Dick "the Bruiser" Afflis. Bruiser was a thick-bodied, crew-cutted bastard who chomped on cigars and called himself the "world's most dangerous man." He'd played football for the Green Bay Packers, and was a crazy son of a bitch. In 1963,

Blassie uses the ropes to steady his chokehold on Dick the Bruiser.

he got into an argument with Alex Karras, the all-pro defensive tackle for the Detroit Lions, in his Detroit bar. Karras was dabbling in wrestling, and was scheduled to work against the Bruiser, but Dick got it in his head that he wanted to have their match right there and then. Karras was a tough fuck who didn't back down from challenges, so the two of them busted up the place, and pummeled a couple of observers unfortunate enough to get too close to the action.

In 1957, Bruiser and Dr. Jerry Graham lost a match to

Edouard Carpentier and Antonino Rocca in Madison Square Garden. As Rocca celebrated his victory, Graham slugged him, drawing blood. Rocca then banged his rival's head against the ring post, bloodying him.

The fans went berserk, and charged the ring. Bruiser stood there, and hurled spectator after spectator back into the stands.

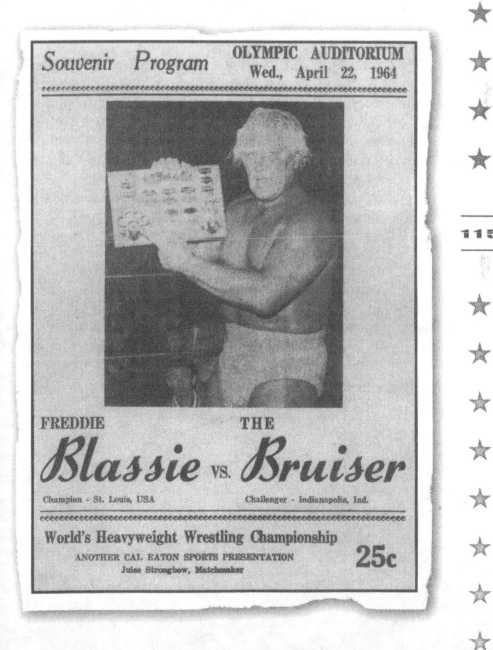

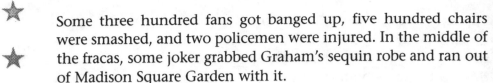

Some three hundred fans got banged up, five hundred chairs were smashed, and two policemen were injured. In the middle of the fracas, some joker grabbed Graham's sequin robe and ran out of Madison Square Garden with it.

The New York State Athletic Commission cancelled the next card at the Garden while they tried to figure out which measures to impose. Eventually, they came to a decision: The Bruiser was banned from wrestling in New York State for life.

"I was suspended longer than the Brooklyn Bridge," he later said.

Fortunately for me, there were no laws in New York restricting Freddie Blassie from making a living. I'd wanted to become a regular there since I was a green boy, and the promoter, Jess McMahon, advised me to come back when I had more experience. Now, I'd gotten that experience, and Jess's son, Vincent James McMahon—also known as Vince, Sr.—had taken his father's place.

"What's going on, Freddie?" he asked when I called him on the phone.

"I want to come east."

"When do you want to come—next week?"

"Well, I have commitments out here."

"Finish them up, call me again, and you're booked."

On April 22, 1964, I dropped the championship to Dick the Bruiser. There were several rematches scheduled, and I told the fans that if I couldn't win back my belt, I'd leave California. On June 12, I challenged the Bruiser for the last time in San Diego, came up short, packed my things, and began my career in the World Wide Wrestling Federation.

EIGHT:
SFACCINO

Like the LeBell family in California, Vince, Sr. and his partner Toots Mondt—an old shooter who'd been associated with Ed "Strangler" Lewis when I was growing up—operated independently of the NWA. This was a recent development. When Buddy "Nature Boy" Rogers won the NWA Championship in 1961, McMahon and Mondt controlled his bookings. With his bleached blond pompadour, graceful moves, and arrogant strut, Rogers was a tremendous draw in the rough, northeastern cities where McMahon and Mondt promoted (and the inspiration for another "Nature Boy," Ric Flair, who came along in the 1970s). The other NWA promoters accused the pair of hogging Rogers all for themselves, and making him unavailable for weekend bookings in the rest of North America. Eventually, the NWA board voted to get the belt away from him.

On January 24, 1963, Lou Thesz defeated Rogers for the title in Toronto. But Thesz never drew that well in New York, and McMahon and Mondt felt screwed. Instead of accepting the decision, they announced that Rogers had defeated Antonino Rocca in the final round of a tournament in Rio de Janiero to become the first World Wide Wrestling Federation Champion.

Rogers was a fuckin' prick, and a lot of the wrestlers hated him. In 1962, Karl Gotch and Bill Miller beat the shit out of him in a dressing room in Columbus, Ohio. I heard that Rogers had to flee in a jock strap, nursing a broken hand. If you ever had any dealings with the son of a bitch, you'd understand why Gotch and Miller were driven to violence. There was nobody worse.

He could have cared less about your body. Instead of protecting you like a good opponent, he'd go out of his way to hurt you. If you were working out a high spot with him—whispering to each other in the middle of your match about which move to execute next—you could never trust his word. For example, he might tell you, "I'll whip you into the ropes, then leapfrog you when you come off." Instead, when you'd be bouncing back towards Rogers, he'd hit you in the head with a potato.

Lou Thesz once warned me, "Don't let him get a hammerlock on you because he'll try to go home with it." In other words, if you allowed him to get in a position where he could manipulate your body, he'd punish you—and maybe even stretch you until you submitted, regardless of what you'd worked out beforehand.

Because of my look—the bleached hair and flashy ring jackets—I was often compared to Rogers, as well as another rotten scumbag who worked in the WWWF, Johnny Valentine. We all enjoyed a good practical joke, but Valentine took it to the extreme. There was a spot in one dressing room, where the wrestlers could peek through a hole and look into the bleachers. The rumor was that when Valentine found out about it, he took a shit, grabbed a fan, and blew his bowel movement through the hole, all over the spectators. That's a fuckin' asshole for you!

"The Alaskan" Jay York was asthmatic, and kept an inhaler in the dressing room. When he was in the ring one time, Valentine got a hold of the inhaler and filled it with lighter fluid. York came back into the dressing room, wheezing, and reached for his inhaler. But instead of getting relief, he received a jolt of lighter fluid in his lungs, and threw up all over the place. York was a hotheaded guy to begin with, and liked playing with weapons. After the incident, he supposedly began packing a gun with his ring gear and, when he saw Valentine again, stuck it in his face and chased him out of the arena.

If you looked at our pictures in the old wrestling magazines, I understand why you would think that Freddie Blassie shared a natural kinship with "Nature Boy" Buddy Rogers and Johnny Valentine. But I didn't want anything to do with those motherfuckers. In fact, I went out of my way to disassociate myself from them.

By the time I got to the WWWF, Rogers was gone anyway. On May 17, 1963, he met Bruno Sammartino for the championship at Madison Square Garden. Bruno had recently held the U.S. title for the Toronto promotion, and had almost a cultlike following—not only among Italians, but all immigrants, who believed that he was one of them, and got an emotional boost from his victories. He was powerful as hell, and despised Rogers as much as I did. In the past, he'd had problems with McMahon, and apparently wasn't willing to come to the WWWF unless he got the belt. I don't know what kind of deal was made behind the scenes, but in the match, Sammartino grabbed Rogers, lifted him up in a backbreaker, and took the title in forty-seven seconds. Rogers would later claim that he was sick that day. Bruno still insists that the match was a shoot.

Some promoters thought that Sammartino was a pain in the ass. He had conflicts with both Vince McMahon, Sr. and his son—the current owner—Vincent Kennedy McMahon, or Vince, Jr., as we called him. No one admires the McMahon family more than I do. But, to this day, I have enormous respect for Bruno, not only as a wrestler, but as a human being. Despite the fact that he was the top guy in the WWWF, he'd complain on behalf of the boys. It wasn't enough that he was making money. He wanted the boys to get their fair share as well.

I wanted to wrestle Bruno in the worst way. In the WWA, I was recognized as the world champion in California, Hawaii, Asia, and a few places in the Midwest where the promoters had a working arrangement with Mike LeBell. Sammartino defended his WWWF title in arenas from Washington, D.C., to Maine. Our confrontation was considered something of a dream match. But because we'd be battling in the WWWF, the buildings—and the payoffs—would be larger than in the WWA.

Without a doubt, Bruno had come a long way since his days wrestling an orangutan in the carnival. For one thing, he was richer. Vince, Sr. was more generous than other promoters I'd known. And when he promised you something, he kept his word—which almost made him an aberration in the wrestling business.

Vince McMahon: My Dad treated the talent with great reverence and respect. The other promoters around the country didn't. Many of the promoters were former wrestlers, and they had hardly any respect for these people who'd once been their co-workers. They took every opportunity to take advantage of the boys, skimming cash money off the grosses, lying about what the actual gross was. It was every man for himself out there, and these promoters had kind of a clique, united by one philosophy: "How can we screw the talent?"

Freddie and I immediately hit it off. I just gravitated to him. Even when the television cameras weren't on, he'd cut a promo on someone in the dressing room, and make the other boys laugh. Of course, every other word would be an expletive. When he was riled up, Freddie had the foulest mouth of anyone I'd ever known. He'd talk about someone's mother, and the look on the face of the person on the receiving end was not to be believed. He was almost eloquent in his use of expletives.

He and Toots Mondt used to compare what they called their "kits." And in those kits were vibrators of different shapes and sizes. I think they were advertised as "marital aids," and they could only be purchased at certain types of retail establishments. One time, Toots was showing off some item, and Freddie decided to top him. He pulled out a vibrating dildo that he had just acquired and said, "Look at this. It's so sophisticated, you have to wear an aviator's cap to operate it."

Willie Gilzenberg had managed Two Ton Tony Galento—a number-one contender for the Heavyweight Boxing Championship who later drifted into wrestling—and promoted WWWF shows in New Jersey. He was listed as the "president" of the WWWF in all its advertising. It always made sense to have a figurehead president in the wrestling business. If a match ended with a questionable finish, you could entice the fans into buying tickets for a rematch by saying, "Because of the controversial results, President Willie Gilzenberg has demanded that the next time they meet, this will be a no-disqualification contest." I guess Gilzenberg was so happy to have a title that he never told his family the real story. When he died, his wife contacted the company looking for her cut; she wanted to know when all the money would be coming.

As soon as I entered the WWWF, Gilzenberg smelled cash, and tried to get me in a main event with Bruno right away. This wasn't how it normally went in the WWWF. A heel would come

120

in, and squash jobbers on TV for a couple of weeks. Then, he'd beat a second-tier wrestler like Don McClarty or Tony Marino, and finally get a title match with Sammartino at Madison Square Garden. After two television appearances, though, Gilzenberg noticed how I agitated the crowd, and asked McMahon if he could match me up with Sammartino at Roosevelt Stadium, the old baseball park in Jersey City.

McMahon was still building me up for the big clash at the Garden. But since fans in New York were oblivious to anything that went on across the Hudson River, he didn't think that there'd be any harm in granting Gilzenberg's request.

Even though I'd dropped the WWA title to Dick the Bruiser, news traveled slow in those days. The WWWF claimed that I was still the champion on the west coast, and advertised the match as a title unification battle. Some fourteen thousand fans—most of them Italian—packed Roosevelt Stadium on June 26, 1964, to see their idol put me in my place.

I had to exit the dressing room through the dugout—the ring was located on the pitcher's mound—and when I walked up the steps and turned to taunt the audience, their profanity even took *me* by surprise. Not only were the fans cursing me in English, they were spitting out some Italian phrases I'd never heard before.

"Va fanculo, sfaccino!"

Bruno and I had a real brawl. I grabbed his cauliflower ears and twisted them, then paused and looked at the crowd to piss them off. On the canvas, I snatched his arm and tied the bottom rope around it, like a tourniquet. About forty-five minutes into the match, the referee got knocked out of the ring. When Bruno bent over to help him back in, I booted him in the balls from behind, kicking him to ringside. That's where he stayed, as the referee counted him out and I raised my arms in triumph.

The WWWF had a rule that the title couldn't change hands on a disqualification or countout, but the fans were still furious. I sensed that they were going to riot, so I told the usher standing at ringside, "Come on, let's go."

He shook his head from side to side.

"What's the fuckin' holdup?" I shouted.

"The people are too mad. We have to wait awhile."

The guy was a half-wit. I knew that the longer you waited,

the angrier the people would get. And that's what was happening. The sight of me pacing around the ring while Bruno was still down on the ground with his hands on his balls inflamed the crowd. When some ringside attendants raced to Sammartino with a stretcher in their hands, the fans even got hotter.

"We're gonna kill you, Blassie!"

The people in the back of the stadium had now joined the fans at ringside, pushing their way towards the ring. I looked at the usher again.

"What the fuck are you waiting for?"

The guy shrugged, as if the whole situation was out of his hands. From the dressing room, Gilzenberg called out the heels—Dr. Jerry and Crazy Luke Graham, Killer Kowalski, and some other guys—to storm the ring and rescue me. As soon as they got out of the dugout, the fans jumped them, and they were fighting for their lives. I used the distraction to step through the ropes and hop off the ring apron. Then, I advanced towards the dressing room, glaring at anyone entertaining thoughts of making a move on me. When I got to the dugout, Kowalski and the Graham Brothers were still fighting the crowd, and I didn't have a scratch on me.

Roosevelt Stadium was laid out in a way where each dugout led to a separate locker room. There was no corridor connecting the two. After I stepped through the dugout, I realized that I was walking towards the babyface dressing room. I can't imagine what would have happened if I'd gone back out to walk across the field to my changing area. So I went into Bruno's dressing room—he was still out at ringside—and wondered what to do next.

Herbie Freeman, the guy who ran the dressing rooms for McMahon, joined me. "Have any ideas?" I asked him.

"Yeah. I'll send someone into the heel dressing room to bring your clothes over. Why don't you take a shower, and wait for the fans to leave?"

As I was talking to Herbie, Bruno came in on a stretcher, still selling my blow to his nuts. He had a whole entourage around him, which was pretty typical. In every town, the most powerful Italians latched themselves onto Sammartino, and decided that they were his protectors—whether Bruno wanted them there or not. Some of these guys were businessmen, others were political types, and a few—I'm sure—were mobsters. I'm not implying for a second that Bruno would ever have any dealings with the mafia on his own. But he'd gotten so famous that he couldn't always pick the boneheads who chose to band around him.

The dressing room was the size of a basketball court. I looked across at Sammartino and his cohorts, recognizing Jilly Rizzo, Frank Sinatra's number-one sidekick and the owner of Jilly's saloon on West Fifty-second Street in Manhattan. Bruno had met Sinatra once. Afterwards, Sammartino brought his parents to see the Chairman of the Board in concert. This was a big thrill for Sammartino, and he planned to take his parents backstage. When he got there, though, Sinatra was very busy. There were fifteen guys surrounding him—Sinatra would fart, and they'd pass the gas. Bruno made it clear that he wanted to introduce his mother and father to Frank Sinatra. He was told that he'd have to wait. That was the wrong thing to say to a stubborn guy like Bruno Sammartino.

"I don't have to put up with this bullshit," Sammartino raged. "Fuck Sinatra." And he and his parents left.

Nonetheless, Jilly Rizzo was a big Bruno Sammartino supporter, and a true-believer wrestling fanatic. From across the dressing room, he eyed me suspiciously. Bruno and I were still in character, so I yelled, "Look at that! Typical Italian stunt! You hit him in the neck and he grabs his balls!"

Rizzo reached for his gun. "Motherfucker," he said. "I'll kill the son of a bitch."

Bruno looked over at me and made eye contact. "No, let him go," he told Jilly. "I want him for myself the next time we step into the ring."

My guess is that Rizzo was bluffing, acting like a tough guy when he had Bruno Sammartino around to back him up. But, if he wasn't, Bruno had just saved my life. Now, I had to figure out a way to get out of Roosevelt Stadium. Herbie asked for my car keys, and sent someone to get my vehicle. It was driven right up to the employees' entrance, and I got in. There were two motorcycle policemen waiting for me, and Herbie told them, "Take Blassie to the Jersey Turnpike."

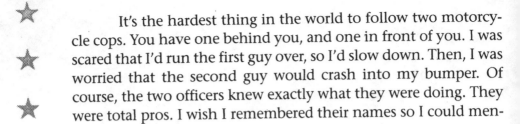

It's the hardest thing in the world to follow two motorcycle cops. You have one behind you, and one in front of you. I was scared that I'd run the first guy over, so I'd slow down. Then, I was worried that the second guy would crash into my bumper. Of course, the two officers knew exactly what they were doing. They were total pros. I wish I remembered their names so I could mention them in the book.

We got on the Turnpike and pulled over to the side. I got out of my car, shook their hands, and complimented them. Then, I said good-bye and drove to my hotel. It had been a hell of an ordeal. And my time in the WWWF was only starting.

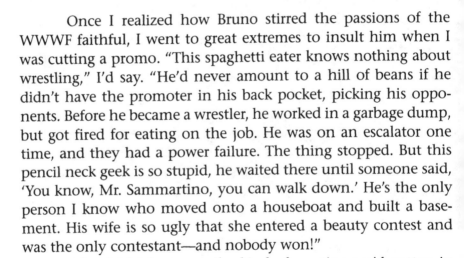

Once I realized how Bruno stirred the passions of the WWWF faithful, I went to great extremes to insult him when I was cutting a promo. "This spaghetti eater knows nothing about wrestling," I'd say. "He'd never amount to a hill of beans if he didn't have the promoter in his back pocket, picking his opponents. Before he became a wrestler, he worked in a garbage dump, but got fired for eating on the job. He was on an escalator one time, and they had a power failure. The thing stopped. But this pencil neck geek is so stupid, he waited there until someone said, 'You know, Mr. Sammartino, you can walk down.' He's the only person I know who moved onto a houseboat and built a basement. His wife is so ugly that she entered a beauty contest and was the only contestant—and nobody won!"

After McMahon saw the kind of reaction we'd gotten in Jersey City, he fell right in line with everything Gilzenberg had told him. Sammartino and I had our first match in Madison Square Garden on July 11, 1964. There were close to nineteen thousand fans there, and every one of them was a Bruno fan. Today, even if Rob Van Dam is supposed to be the hero in a match, a large portion of the audience is still rooting for his opponent. In 1964, I doubt that anyone ever came to an arena hoping that Bruno would lose. Emotions were so high that I thought, "Jesus, maybe I should get on the Sammartino bandwagon, too."

The weeks of insulting Bruno on TV had paid off. Everyone believed that he was legitimately pissed and wanted to annihilate me. The match ended when he put me in his bearhug. My body flopped around, like I was losing consciousness. The referee told Bruno to break the hold and he refused, clamping on more pressure. Finally, the official disqualified Sammartino, and as I fell to the canvas, I raised my limp arm, to the great distress of the audience.

We had our "blow-off"—an old carny term for final confrontation—at the Garden on August 1. As with every challenger, Sammartino finally cut me down, and got a decisive victory (we'd later re-do our two clashes in other WWWF cities). What I remember most about the match was Bruno's incredible strength. At one point, he picked me up with one arm and slung me over his shoulder like I was a sack of flour.

I shouldn't have been surprised. Bruno had actually gained his reputation in New York with a feat of remarkable might, wrapping an arm around the leg of massive Haystacks Calhoun, hoisting him into the air, and dumping him onto the mat. Calhoun was said to weigh more than six hundred pounds. He had a hillbilly gimmick, sporting a long beard, overalls, and a "lucky horseshoe" around his neck. When Haystacks got pissed during a match, he'd sometimes grab the horseshoe and belt his opponent with it.

125

Calhoun was a freak, and the only reason he had a job was because he was so fuckin' big. He had no wrestling ability whatsoever, and never took the time to try to learn how to work a match. In that way, he was different than the French Angel, Swedish Angel, and other so-called anomalies of the mat world. A lot of these other guys wanted to fit in, and earn the respect of their peers. The Swedish Angel, in particular, was appreciated because he had a name that drew fans to the arena, but understood that he was only as good as the opponents who put him over.

Calhoun, on the other hand, was an obnoxious bastard convinced that he was the number-one attraction in wrestling. Whenever you saw him in the dressing room, he was sitting on his fat ass and bitching: "I made a lot of money for Vince McMahon. Look who he puts in the main event? Does he think *they* drew that house tonight?" I never heard anyone complain so much. He'd even complain about his complaints.

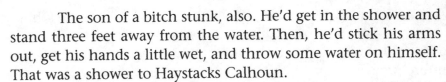
The son of a bitch stunk, also. He'd get in the shower and stand three feet away from the water. Then, he'd stick his arms out, get his hands a little wet, and throw some water on himself. That was a shower to Haystacks Calhoun.

When you wrestled him, you were limited because he couldn't do anything athletic. Essentially, you'd do all the work— hit him with tackles and bounce off him, bend to try to lift him up until he smashed you on the back of the head, sell like hell when he bumped you with his stomach. All of this led up to Calhoun's finish, the "big splash," which consisted of him falling on top of you.

The only good thing about Calhoun was that he was an easy target when you were cutting a promo. "There would not be a food shortage if he cut down on his diet," I said during one interview. "This man here, I know for a fact, just recently ordered sixteen hams—*sixteen* hams—eight bushels of potatoes, two pecks of grits, and then he had half a hog jaw as a snack, as he was waiting for his breakfast to come. . . . Three weeks ago, he was locked up at the beach because he didn't have a license, and was renting himself out as an umbrella. When they arrested him, they pulled that flab up and eight pigeons flew out."

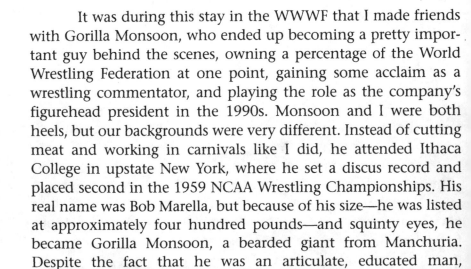

It was during this stay in the WWWF that I made friends with Gorilla Monsoon, who ended up becoming a pretty impor- tant guy behind the scenes, owning a percentage of the World Wrestling Federation at one point, gaining some acclaim as a wrestling commentator, and playing the role as the company's figurehead president in the 1990s. Monsoon and I were both heels, but our backgrounds were very different. Instead of cutting meat and working in carnivals like I did, he attended Ithaca College in upstate New York, where he set a discus record and placed second in the 1959 NCAA Wrestling Championships. His real name was Bob Marella, but because of his size—he was listed at approximately four hundred pounds—and squinty eyes, he became Gorilla Monsoon, a bearded giant from Manchuria. Despite the fact that he was an articulate, educated man, Monsoon growled out his early interviews, and his manager,

Bobby Davis, claimed that he'd discovered his protégé bathing nude in a stream during an overseas talent-scouting tour.

Monsoon was well established when I arrived in the territory. He and Killer Kowalski had held the company's Tag Team Championship in 1963, and he had credibility among the boys. Once, he cracked two ribs while wrestling Sammartino, but kept going, finishing a ninety-five-minute match. With so many stars in the WWWF dressing room, I wasn't sure how I'd be received. But Monsoon went out of his way to make me feel welcome. I remember once, before a trip to Baltimore, he heard me mention that I was planning to rent a car. "You don't have to do that," he said. "Just ride with me."

I was glad to be accepted by this big guy who everyone liked. But when he started driving, I saw another side of Gorilla Monsoon. Without glasses, he could barely see two feet ahead of him. It made me wonder whether Monsoon was being considerate, or he'd invited me along because nobody else wanted to get into his car.

127

Bobo Brazil was another popular character. He was the first African-American wrestler I knew who was a real superstar. Even white bigots couldn't help cheering for Bobo. As for black fans, I'm fairly certain they would have skinned me if he'd asked.

I remember meeting Bobo's kids at one of the banquets Vince, Sr. would occasionally have for the wrestlers and their families. I was standing with a bunch of the boys, and Brazil walked over and said, "Freddie, I'd like to introduce you to my family."

"Yeah," I joked. "If they're anything like you, they're a bunch of shit heels."

Bobo shook his head and laughed, then brought me to the table. One of his daughters looked up at me and said, "Daddy, what are you doing with him? This is the one who bites and hits foul when the ref isn't looking."

Clearly, Brazil's family had been kept in the dark about the business. So I said, "Man, I can tell there's no sense talking to you. You talk like your father. You talk like an idiot." And I just walked away.

One night, Bobo and I wrestled in Washington, D.C., and I swear I didn't see a white face in the audience. I was walking to the ring and there must have been—I'm not lying—sixteen or seventeen ushers surrounding me, all taking small steps.

"Jesus Christ," I hollered. "We're never gonna get to the ring at this rate."

"Well, Mr. McMahon told us to stay with you," one of the ushers blurted.

"Congratulations. You're doing your job. You're *with* me. Now goddammit, let's move."

As soon as I set my foot on the ring steps, the first thing happened. *Bam!* An empty quart bottle hit the ring post and shattered. I got into the ring, and Willie Gilzenberg's old crony, Two Ton Tony Galento, was the special referee. "Blassie," he muttered, "don't pull none of your shit tonight." He was scared to death.

"What the hell are you so afraid of?" I sneered.

I started giving the people the arm, and the elbow. *"Up your ass!"* I shouted.

Now, Bobo ran down the aisle to a cascade of cheers. In Washington, Brazil always came to the ring with James Dudley. Dudley had started off doing odd jobs for Jess McMahon, then became an indispensable part of Vince, Sr.'s operation. Vince broadcast his shows out of the two-thousand-seat Turner Arena in D.C., and, in 1956, appointed Dudley its manager, making him the first black man to run a major arena in the United States. In 2002, Vince, Jr. included him in a vignette on *SmackDown!*; he played an old man being wheeled into the arena by scheming Stephanie McMahon—the fourth generation of the family to work with ninety-two-year-old James Dudley.

The moment Brazil stepped through the ropes, he put his hand on the back of my head, wound up, and began slugging me. I backed away from him, shaking my body and throwing my head back. The crowd went wild. But their euphoria didn't last. Soon, I unloaded on Bobo, rocking him with punches, then snatching him around the throat and taking him down to the mat, choking him.

Bobo was a master at selling a chokehold. Spittle was forming at the edge of his lips. *"Ah, ah, ah, ah!"* he groaned, loud enough to be heard in Arlington.

"Break it, Blassie," Galento demanded. "Break it."

I ignored Galento and continued to choke. And Bobo continued to sell: *"Ah, ah, ah, ah!"*

"I'm not joking," Galento reiterated. "Break the hold, you crazy bastard. They're coming to the fuckin' ring."

I looked up, and, sure enough, the fans had broken past security and were streaming down the aisle to get me.

"For Christ's sake, Blassie, do something," Galento begged.

Thinking quickly, I released the choke, grabbed Bobo's hand, and pressed his fingers around my neck. Now, it was my turn to sell: *"Ah, ah, ah, ah! Fuck you, Bobo. The way you sell, you're gonna get me killed."*

Galento looked on in amazement. But I hadn't been in professional wrestling this long without learning anything. With Brazil in command, the people were happy, and forgot that they'd planned to tear the building down.

The match ended in a double disqualification. Then, I had to leave the arena and walk to my car. I showered, changed my clothes, and waited a long, long time to exit. Most of the fans had gone home by the time I left the building. But a couple of hundred diehards were still hanging around.

"Holy shit, it's Freddie Blassie!"

Some oranges, apples, and wadded-up wrestling programs were tossed my way. But I could read the mood of the crowd, and realized that it would be suicidal to go into my gimmick. I just looked straight ahead, not reacting to anything, and walked. The crowd followed behind me. But because I was out of character, they weren't sure what to do. There was an eerie quiet, as I found my car, put my key in the lock, and gradually opened and closed the door. Once in a while, some asshole shouted an insult—to scattered laughter. As a rule, though, the group was tense, but cautious.

I turned on the ignition and backed up—very slowly because I didn't want to bump anybody. If I'd run someone over, it would have been the end of Freddie Blassie. There were some

people in my way, but I didn't honk the horn. I just kept going at an easy pace, until the people moved out of the way. Then, I shifted into drive, and got out of there.

A block or two away, I remembered my Catholic upbringing. Looking heavenward, I said, "Thanks for everything."

NINE:
WANNA BUY A FORD?

After my first trip to Japan in 1962, I always looked forward to returning there. Even when the people booed me, I was treated with awe. The Japanese moved at a faster pace than Americans. After having their country destroyed during the war, they were in a rush to make up for lost time. Everywhere you went, you could see advances—in technology, business, and the wrestling profession.

While I was touring Asia in 1965, I noticed that, since Rikidozan died, two of his old students had filled his spot. One was Kanji "Antonio" Inoki, a high school track star who'd been raised by Japanese parents in Brazil. Not only was Inoki a natural athlete, but—with his full head of jet-black hair and pelican jaw—he was extremely charismatic. Inoki's goal in life was promoting himself. I never liked the guy personally, but I have to give him credit for doing the most with his talents. Over time, Inoki ended up running a huge wrestling company, and even getting elected to the Japanese *Diet*, or Senate.

I had much warmer feelings for Rikidozan's other trainee, Shohei Baba. He stood at least six-foot-nine—monstrous for a Japanese guy—and had been a pitcher in the Japanese major leagues. After training with Rikidozan, he was renamed "Giant" Baba and billed at seven-foot-three. Some fans may have considered Baba a freak, but once they saw him wrestle, they changed their minds. He was a real athlete and, because of this, didn't have to act like a typical, salt-throwing Japanese heel when he toured the United States. Instead, Baba was treated as a serious contender, and had long, strenuous matches against the champions in every territory—Bruno in the WWWF, Thesz in the NWA, and me when I held the WWA title.

Souvenir Program

OLYMPIC AUDITORIUM
Friday, February 28, 1964

Freddie Blassie
CHAMPION

VS.

Shoehi (Big) Baba
CHALLENGER

World's Heavyweight Wrestling Championship

ANOTHER CAL EATON SPORTS PRESENTATION
Jules Strongbow, Matchmaker

25c

132

What shocked me about Baba was the way that he was treated during these visits. He traveled with Mr. Togo—an older wrestler who I'd once chewed up on Japanese television—and was completely submissive to him. After matches, Togo would scream at Baba in the dressing room, and hit him alongside the head with these Japanese clogs called *getas*. This really bothered me. Baba was a great kid and, from time to time, I'd try to defend him.

"What the hell are you doing?" I'd yell at Togo.

"This is how I teach him," Togo would answer. "Otherwise, he'll be an idiot his whole life."

If Togo wanted Baba to learn, I didn't understand why they didn't go to the gym and work out on the mats. But the rules about teachers and pupils were different in Asia, and Baba never

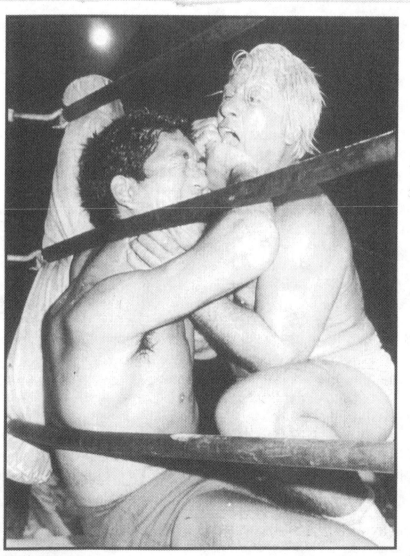

Shohei "Giant" Baba.

said a word on his own behalf. What's ironic is that Baba was already a bigger star than Togo. In his lifetime, Baba would become one of the most significant figures in the wrestling business, starting All-Japan Pro Wrestling—Inoki's promotional rival—and setting a record that will never be broken: 3,764 straight matches—from 1960 to 1984—without time off for illness or injury. If his bouts in North America are added in, the number is probably closer to 4,100.

Baba became so well liked that Bruno Sammartino, who never got along with authority figures, said that, if money was ever short, he'd work for All-Japan for free. In the years ahead, when I'd observe the way that other wrestlers honored Shohei Baba, it behooved me to think that this was the same guy who was still a clumsy kid when I toured Japan in the spring of 1965.

Peter Takahashi: I refereed so many of Freddie's matches in Japan that I can't even guess the number. I also spent a lot of time with him alone. We would exercise together, but Freddie always wanted to suntan. One time, we were staying in Kumamoto City for five days, and Freddie wanted to tan on the roof of the hotel. But it was raining for all five days. Every morning, Freddie would come to my room, yelling, "Peter, it's raining again. Do something about it." I'd say, "Freddie, just because I'm Japanese, I can't control the weather. Tomorrow will be a better day."

On the last day, he told me, "You said tomorrow would be a better day. This is a nice day—for a frog. Get two umbrellas. We're going up to the roof."

Freddie was hoping that if we stayed on the roof long enough, he'd get some sun coming through the clouds. But we sat there, holding our umbrellas, getting rained on. It was cold. "What's the matter with this country?" he complained.

"I don't know, Freddie," I told him. "It doesn't rain in America?"

Freddie kept grumbling. I was feeling upset. This was a very difficult guy to satisfy. Then, I looked over at his face. He was staring at me and smiling. He was only having fun with me.

He was always bored, looking for something new to do. In Sapporo once, he decided to go to a strip club. I said, "Freddie, maybe you shouldn't. You're very famous. There could be trouble." Blassie didn't listen. He went into this club, and instead of sitting in the dark and watching, he walked right up to the stage. Everybody there was saying, "Look, look, it's Freddie Blassie."

A girl started dancing in front of him, completely nude. No one was watching her. Everybody wanted to see Freddie's reaction. On the stage, she got down in front of him, and opened her legs. Freddie held up his hand and said, "Hold on a minute." Then, he pulled out his glasses, slowly unfolded them, adjusted them on his face, and stared right at her vagina.

"Oh," he shouted, "that's much better."

Everybody was laughing. And when Freddie got up to leave, the girls all stopped dancing, followed him to the door, and asked for autographs.

The other American wrestlers who'd been to Japan were very different than Freddie Blassie. Some of them would get drunk, act like idiots, and get into fights. Freddie was nothing like that. He liked cake, chocolate, and ice cream—not alcohol. If I hadn't met him, I think I would have hated all Americans.

Often, the Japanese would arrange for foreigners to tour the country all at the same time, participating in tournaments with local wrestlers. In 1965, I went all the way to the finals of the Seventh World League Tournament, losing the last match to Toyonobori, a former sumo wrestler who never quite became the superstar some expected. But as much as I enjoyed working a big event in front of an energized Japanese crowd, the highlight of my trip took place not in a wrestling arena, but a train station, where I met a beautiful girl in a kimono.

Miyako Morozumi: My family was strict in every way. My father was a physics professor at Chuo University. One brother became a Navy captain, the other a major-general in the Japanese Air Force. I was not allowed to watch boxing or wrestling as a child. My mother wanted me to be graceful, patient, and tolerant. Boxing and wrestling would not teach me anything about those qualities.

In 1965, my brother, Yoshihiko, was getting married in Sasebo. I was nineteen, a few days short of twenty, and attending school in Nara. In order to get to the wedding, I had to pass through the train station in Kokura. That's where I met Freddie.

I was walking up the steps while Freddie was coming down.

I didn't see him because I was looking at the ground. But I heard a voice say in English, "Oh, you have a beautiful kimono on." I'd studied English in school, and I could understand that much at the time.

I looked up and saw this handsome man, with blond hair, blue eyes, and a big smile. He was American, but that wasn't strange to me because there were many American sailors stationed in our country. He had a radiant face. I wasn't used to that because Japanese men don't show their emotions on their face in the same way.

"Thank you," I said. Then, I went upstairs and didn't think about it.

I wanted to get something to eat. But I couldn't get into the restaurant. There was a big crowd surrounding a very tall man there. I looked closely and recognized him as "Giant" Baba. Even though I wasn't a wrestling fan, everybody in Japan knew "Giant" Baba because he was a celebrity. There was also a department store in the station, so I decided to go there instead.

I walked around the department store for about a half hour, then went back out into the main part of the station. Once again, I heard somebody speaking to me in English.

"Miss, miss, can I talk to you for a moment?" It was the blond man, but now he had a Japanese friend with him. I later found out it was Seiji Sakaguchi—a wrestler Freddie had brought as an interpreter.

"I was following you all over the station," he told me. "Where do you live?"

My mother had told me to never tell the truth to a stranger. So I said, "I'm living in Tokyo," even though I was living in Nara.

"That's good," he said, writing on a piece of paper. "That's where I'm staying. Do you know who I am?"

I wasn't sure.

"I'm Freddie Blassie," he said. "I'm an American professional wrestler."

Because wrestling was so popular, I'd probably seen his picture in magazines and newspapers. But I didn't realize that this was the same man because, in all the pictures, he was wrestling and sweating. He told me that he was staying at the Daiichi Hotel, and they were having a farewell party for all the American wrestlers at the end of the tour on May 16—my birthday.

I took the piece of paper, and then I had to go to my brother's wedding. Afterwards, I told my friends, "I met this American man in the train station. Look, he gave me this piece of paper."

My friends jumped up. "Do you know who that is? That's Freddie Blassie! He bites people!"

"He seems very nice," I told them.

"No, he is not. He's very mean. He bites people and makes them bleed."

But my friends wanted me to go to the party. The boys I knew were especially excited. "You have to go," they said. "This is a once-in-a-lifetime opportunity. You can tell us everything afterwards. Go for us."

So I went to the party. All the wrestlers were there. Freddie seemed very happy to see me. But then, something terrible happened. He had a kidney stone attack—right at the party. He was holding the wall with his eyes closed, screaming, "Ooooh! It hurts! It hurts!"

I was starting to get worried. What if there was a story about this in the newspaper, and my mother saw a picture of me at a hotel in Tokyo, with all these wrestlers? "Oh God," I said. "I'm getting out of this one."

People were rushing to get a doctor. I gave someone from the wrestling office my address and phone number, and left. There was nothing I could do, anyway, to help him.

The next day, Freddie called me. But I didn't know what to talk about. I couldn't speak English. I could understand, but I couldn't speak. I just said, "Yes, yes, yes, yes."

Then, all of the sudden so many packages started coming to me. He sent a music box, fans, Japanese umbrellas—*three* umbrellas—porcelain *hakata* dolls, the kind of things American tourists buy in Japan to give to other Americans. I didn't need any of these souvenirs because I was already Japanese.

After he left Japan, he sent me a letter from Hawaii, and more letters when he got back home. Then, one day, the letters stopped. I later found out that he didn't want to write anymore because he believed that his wrestling career was over, and he would never visit Japan again. So I wiped Freddie Blassie out of my life. I wasn't in love with him or anything.

On the plane home from Japan, I was in tremendous pain. When I got to Hawaii, I decided that I couldn't wait, and checked myself in for kidney stone surgery. The doctor was a fuckin' quack, and punctured my urine pipe. I didn't realize it, returned to the mainland, and continued wrestling. But I was now becoming exhausted easily. I was forty-seven years old, and wondered whether I was too old to be lacing up the boots. Then, I realized that I also had no appetite; and that had nothing to do with wrestling. When I visited a doctor in Atlanta, I was diagnosed with hepatitis. Thanks to the medical care I'd received in the Aloha State, my kidney had dried out, and I had to have it removed.

On November 9, 1965, I underwent surgery at Emory Hospital in Atlanta. The procedure took everything out of me. I dropped a lot of weight, and felt weak as a kitten. The promoters were afraid to book me; they thought I'd die in the ring. Whenever I ran into any of the boys, they shook their heads sadly. They all concluded that I was finished with the business.

Among the fans, a rumor started that I'd passed away. People would talk while standing outside the arena, waiting for autographs. Maybe someone had heard from one of the wrestlers that I looked like shit. By the next day, the story would change: Freddie Blassie was dead. With no Internet—and everything kay fabe to begin with—there weren't any web sites to quell the gossip, and inform the fans that I was recuperating. To tell you the truth, it wouldn't surprise me at all if some of the reports about my demise had to do with wishful thinking.

It was a terrible time, being at the top of the heap one week, and at the bottom the next. I'd always thought I was invincible, and never bothered holding on to money. Hell, I figured that there was always another payday down the road. Now, on top of everything else, I had to find a fuckin' job. For most of 1966, I was in Decatur, Georgia, working at Al Means' Ford City. The dealership ran my face in newspaper ads, over the words: "Get the Blassie deal on a new '66 Ford car or truck or good used car. No other dealer can beat my deal. *They wouldn't dare.*"

Ron Blassie: I spoke to my father, and he was trying to line me up with a convertible. He was working hard to get me a good deal. As I remember, he was a decent salesman. He was trustworthy, and I'm sure a lot of people were excited to buy a car from Freddie

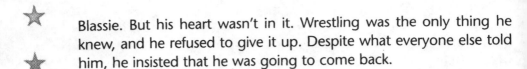

Blassie. But his heart wasn't in it. Wrestling was the only thing he knew, and he refused to give it up. Despite what everyone else told him, he insisted that he was going to come back.

I'd worked too hard, and come too far in the wrestling business, to admit defeat. I began working out, and putting on weight. I spoke to Paul Jones, my old partner in Atlanta, and told him that I wanted to get back into the ring. He was cautious, but agreed. In my first match, I was pitted against some jobber, but as soon as the bell rang, I felt like I wasn't ready. The last time I'd experienced this type of trepidation, I was a mark hoping to catch a break in the wrestling game. With my credentials, I knew that I shouldn't have been so unsure of myself. But I hadn't really recovered. I guess I could have worked out for ten years, and still felt the same way. In wrestling, you can never completely come back until you work off the ring rust. And the only way to do that is by getting in the ring.

I won my first match, then came back to the dressing room and collapsed into a chair. The fatigue—just like my fears—was my little secret, though, and I told Paul Jones that I felt great. I asked for another match, then another and then another, until I finally felt like I was putting the surgery behind me. Eventually, I was booked into a feud with Don McIntyre, the guy I'd originally beaten for the Southern Heavyweight Championship in 1954.

Don and I knew how to work together, but I was still readjusting, and the rivalry lacked the kind of intensity I would have liked. The fans really didn't care about a renewal of the old Blassie-McIntyre conflict. It was a different age, and there were new stars in town: Buddy Fuller, Tim "Mr. Wrestling" Woods, Butcher and Mad Dog Vachon. But I was getting in shape, and felt like I had my life back.

In the middle of all this misery and bullshit, I got married a second time. This time, I picked a southern corn pone. It seemed like no matter how much I bashed the south during TV interviews, the women there always threw themselves at me. In the northeast, I always had to work a little bit before I got laid. In the south, the females were readily available. I don't know how this one managed to marry me, but she did.

The day of our wedding, I knew that I fucked up. My wife was so useless that I can't even think of her name. About the only good thing I can say about her was that she had these poodles that she'd taught to do tricks. Other than that, she had no redeeming qualities.

While we were together, a guy who cleaned the dressing room at one of the arenas told me that he'd become acquainted with Elvis Presley. Elvis was a big wrestling fan, and apparently wanted to meet me. I figured that it wouldn't hurt my career to take a picture together, and brought my wife to a concert. When I pulled up in my car, I saw a squadron of police standing outside the arena and holding back hundreds of women.

"Who are those girls?" my wife asked, sounding a little bit suspicious.

"I don't know those girls. They're looking for Elvis. They sure as hell ain't looking for me."

Backstage, we were led to an area where Elvis's father, Vernon, was talking business with Presley's manager, Colonel Tom Parker. No one was in any rush to bring us to Elvis, until my wife opened her mouth. I don't remember what Colonel Parker said, but she replied, "Sure enough, honey child."

Both Parker and Vernon perked up: " 'Sure enough, honey child'? Hey, you're one of us!"

"I guess you gotta be a fuckin' southerner to get any service with these guys," I mumbled loud enough for my wife to hear, but not so loud that we'd get booted out of the building.

Someone went back and fetched Elvis. He still looked great at that time, and—like so many others who crossed paths with him—I was impressed by the fact that he was so humble and friendly. While my wife was busy with the other two, we talked about wrestling for a little while. A photographer came over and took some publicity shots; then I kind of whispered, "Hey, Elvis, what about your pussy situation?"

Elvis let out a big chuckle. "Man," he said, "you wouldn't believe it."

"I believe it. I believe it. I mean, I'm doing excellent

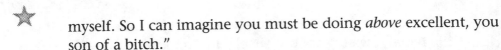

myself. So I can imagine you must be doing *above* excellent, you son of a bitch."

My wife and I only lived together for a few weeks. When I'd go on the road, she'd catch a plane with one of her poodles and wait for me after the matches. I paid for the airfare, of course. And whenever we were together, she always seemed to squeeze money out of me for some reckless shopping spree. After a while, I started giving her money just to stay away from me. Looking back, I imagine that she thought that I was loaded. When she realized that I was pretty close to broke, she disappeared.

I didn't bother looking for her. Ten minutes in her company was enough to make a man shy away from ever talking to a woman again.

Ron Blassie: My father was always charming with the ladies. So when I was going out with the girl who became my first wife, I introduced her to him, hoping to make a good impression. My brother was there, and we all decided to go to the movies together. We're outside one of those big theaters in downtown St. Louis, waiting in line, and he's dressed up in white leather, with that blond hair, and everybody's gawking at him. As the line's moving down, he's peeking into clothing stores, and giving my brother money to run in and buy stuff. So he's buying clothes while we're in line for a movie.

Inside the theater, this black kid, a teenager, accidentally kicks my father's chair. He turns around and tells the kid to stop. A few minutes later, the kid kicks the chair again. My father jumps up, and hollers in that gravelly voice of his: "Listen, you son of a bitch. If you hit that chair one more fuckin' time, I'm gonna squeeze your head like a pimple!" Honest to God, everyone in the theater was on their feet, watching. Up until that point, my girlfriend thought my father was a really nice guy. Now, she looked a little frightened of him.

We continue watching the movie, and five minutes later, my father doesn't even remember what happened. I look behind me, and the whole theater's buzzing, and the poor kid has left.

Occasionally, (St. Louis promoter) Sam Muchnick would call my father to come in, work a card, and fly back out. One time, my friends and I picked him up at the airport and brought him to the Chase Park Plaza Hotel for a TV taping. The Chase was an interesting place. There would be wrestling in this ballroom called the Khorassan

Room. The ring was surrounded by tables. And people would get dressed up and eat dinner during the show.

After the matches were over, we met my father in the lobby so we could take him back to the airport. He looks at me and says, "You know, I wish I could have stayed longer." I'm thinking that he's going to say, "I really wanted to spend more time with you," you know. Instead, he points across the room and goes, "You see that redhead over there? I hear she gives a good hooter-tooter." Oh, he was terrible.

TEN:
"JAPANESE-LOVING PERSON"

    During my Japanese tours, I'd sometimes think that—while I was being chauffeured around by the yakuza, and getting followed by ravenous fans all over Tokyo—on the same continent, American soldiers were dying in Vietnam. As a World War II veteran, I was becoming worried about our role in Vietnam. By 1968, I was fairly certain that this was a war that we couldn't win. The Vietnamese were fighting us on their terms, luring us into ambushes in the hills and the jungle. And our servicemen, raised eating in restaurants and sleeping in feather beds, seemed lost.

    Fortunately, neither of my sons had to serve in Vietnam. But my family was still affected by the war. My cousin, Air Force First Lieutenant Michael Blassie, was twenty-four and on his one hundred thirty-eighth combat mission when the wing was blasted off his plane near An Loc, South Vietnam. For years, he was listed as Missing In Action. Then, in 1998, DNA testing revealed that he was the one buried in the Tomb of Unknowns at Arlington National Cemetery.

    I have to admit that, once I returned to wrestling after my operation, family issues were a long way from my mind. All I cared about was the wrestling business, and in 1968, I had one of my biggest matches ever in Japan, teaming with Tarzan Tyler against "Giant" Baba *and* Antonio Inoki.

    In the weeks leading up to my trip, I kept remembering that pretty girl I'd met in the Kokura train station in 1965. There was a certain sweetness about her that seemed to balance out my rough edges. I wanted to see her again. But between the kidney surgery and all the other disruptions in my life, I'd misplaced her address and phone number. As I traveled around Japan in the spring of 1968, I kept my eyes open, hoping that—even in a country of more than 126 million people—I'd somehow run into her again.

Miyako Morozumi: My friends who were wrestling fans read in the newspaper that Freddie Blassie was back in Japan. They said, "Go see him." I told them, "He won't remember me. He's famous. He meets a lot of people." But my friends pushed me. So I called Kourakuen Hall, the arena in Tokyo, and left a message for Freddie Blassie.

A half hour later, Joe Higuchi, the referee, called me back. "Miyako, I'm so glad you called," he said. "Freddie has been bothering me since he arrived in the country. He kept asking me to find you. He only remembered your first name, Miyako. He forgot your last name."

"How am I going to find someone if I only know her first name?" Higuchi told him.

"Japan is a small country. You'll find her."

Every time Freddie saw Higuchi, he wanted to know, "Did you find her? Are you trying?" Now, Higuchi was very relieved.

Freddie called me up the same day. "Hi, Miyako," he said. He still couldn't speak Japanese and I couldn't speak English. I didn't know what to say. "Hi, Freddie," I answered, and then kind of laughed.

He had his schedule sent over to me, and I arranged to visit him in Himeji, near Osaka. I was studying classical literature in college now, and working in an office. I took a two-hour lunch break to meet him, but it took almost an hour to get there from Nara; you had to pass through Osaka and change trains there. I called the hotel to leave a message before I arrived, and when I was walking into the building, Freddie was coming to the door, looking so happy.

He grabbed me in the lobby and kissed me all over. Everybody was standing there, just watching. This isn't the custom in Japan, to start kissing people in public like that. And it was even stranger because the person doing the kissing was "The Vampire" Freddie Blassie.

I was feeling embarrassed, with everybody looking at me. Then, Freddie brought me over to a couch in the lobby. Joe Higuchi was sitting there to translate. And right away, Freddie proposed to me.

Now he was talking faster. He was still married to his second wife, but they were separated. He was living in L.A. again, and she was in Atlanta. The divorce would be legal soon, and he wanted me to give everything up and move to California.

"That's ridiculous," I said. "I don't even know you."

"Okay," he said. "Take your time. But I want to marry you."

I was very young, and no one had ever asked me to marry him before. Even though Freddie and I had never had a real conversation, I liked the attention. It felt good. And I didn't want to just say good-bye and not see him anymore.

We stayed in touch throughout his trip; then I came with him to Haneda Airport before he flew home. I walked with him all the way, as far as I could, before he had to pass through customs. There was a balcony where I could stand and see his plane on the runway. He turned around and waved to me, went on board, then came off the plane. A truck was parked right under the balcony, and Freddie climbed up on it—with everyone looking—and got on his toes and tried to touch my hand. It was too far to reach, but it was very romantic. I thought, "Wow, this guy really loves me."

Every day for three and a half months, he wrote me two letters—sent by special delivery. Even though I couldn't have a conversation in English, I could read and understand his letters. There wasn't too much to write about because we didn't have any memories. We never even had a date. So every letter was the same thing, where he was traveling, who he was wrestling, and always, "I want you to come to America to marry me."

His handwriting was beautiful. Most people, by the time they finish a letter, their hand has gotten tired, and their writing changes. This didn't happen with Freddie. Every letter of every word was perfect.

I started to show my friends his letters. They were saying, "Look at the way he writes. His handwriting is so nice, even we can read it. He must be a very good person."

I had one friend who knew English well enough to help me write back to him. I didn't write every day—more like every two weeks. I never said, "Yes, I want to marry you." But I did say, "I want to meet you. I want to see you." So he took that as, "I'm coming to get married."

At that time, the American Embassy was very careful about

Miyako and Freddie in Japan, before their marriage.

single women from Asia coming to the United States. They were afraid of mail order brides. So I had to create a story that I was coming to California to stay with Mr. Moto and his wife, Violet.

I arrived on September 8, 1968. Freddie met me at the airport. Before we got in the car, he asked me, "Want to get married?"

He had an apartment in Santa Monica, and I stayed with him

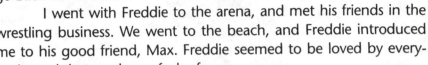

there. For a long time, my mother thought I was still in Japan. I was afraid of what my family would do to me if they knew that I'd gone to California to spend time with a man, and thought, "I really can't go back home now."

I went with Freddie to the arena, and met his friends in the wrestling business. We went to the beach, and Freddie introduced me to his good friend, Max. Freddie seemed to be loved by everybody, and that made me feel safe.

But it was still very stressful. In Japan, I'd been more mature than my friends. In America, I was a helpless child. I could not express myself. There were cultural differences. I felt depressed. When we got married on September 30—three weeks after I arrived in America—I looked like a ghost.

Charlie and Violet Moto were the best man and maid of honor. They were very good to me. But I felt that I was getting married because I didn't have other choices. Fortunately, Freddie was a wonderful person because I really would have been in trouble otherwise.

Eventually, I had to call my mother and tell her that I was living in California and I was married. She just said, "okay," not "congratulations" or anything. Then, while I was in America, my father died. So I felt responsible for that, too.

Eight months after I got married, I went with Freddie for another wrestling tour of Japan. We got off the plane, and Freddie had to leave me to go to a press conference. When I turned around, my two brothers were standing there, in the middle of all the reporters and fans. One of them said in a very stern voice, "Miyako, come with us."

We went to my mother's house, and the whole family was waiting for me: two aunts, two uncles, my brothers' wives, my sister and her husband. My mother said, "If you are happy, we are happy for you. But what you did—leaving school and disappearing without telling anyone—is unforgivable. Who is this man you married? Do you even know him? You must be a bad girl to leave Japan and live with a man like this."

"My husband is very nice," I told her.

"Who is he?"

"He's an athlete."

"What kind of athlete?"

"A wrestler."

"A wrestler. What's his name?"

I looked down and mumbled, "Freddie Blassie."

My mother started to cry. *"Freddie Blassie?* What's the matter with you? He's very, very bad."

"No, he's only bad in the ring. At home, he's a very good person."

My mother was disgusted. "If he's so bad on television and so good in person," she said, "he must have seven faces." That was a terrible insult. It meant that you were an insincere person, who created a different personality to manipulate every situation.

I wanted her to meet Freddie, and see for herself. But she was very angry. Finally, my brothers spoke to her. "This is her husband now," they said. "He's in our family. We must meet him."

My brothers took my mother to the hotel where Freddie and I were staying. Freddie understood that she was in a bad mood. But he was kind and gentle and friendly. When she walked down the stairs, he took her arm and helped her. He pulled out a seat for her in the hotel restaurant. He lit her cigarettes. No Japanese man had ever treated my mother like that, and she kind of felt good.

A group of wrestlers were at another table. She asked, "Those men are very big. Are they wrestlers, too?"

Freddie nodded his head.

"But they're not acting like wrestlers," she said. "They're acting respectful."

"We're different than we are on TV," Freddie told her, and I think she finally understood.

Afterwards, my mother admitted that she liked Freddie. "If anything goes wrong in your marriage," she told me, "it will be your fault."

But she had a problem—she'd already announced to her relatives and friends that he was unacceptable. She said, "I will lose face if I tell everyone that I was wrong. Give me a year. In a year, I can say that Miyako made a good choice. Freddie Blassie is very nice."

I felt like a burden was lifted from me. Freddie and I went back to California and continued our life. I had a new job at home, removing Freddie's stitches. I knew that the men Freddie wrestled were not really his enemies because I'd seen him joking with them. But I never asked him any questions about this—just like I never questioned my brothers about secrets they'd learned in the military. There

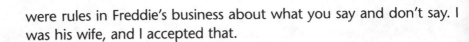
were rules in Freddie's business about what you say and don't say. I was his wife, and I accepted that.

Even if Miyako had asked about what happened when you got in the ring, hell, I wouldn't have been able to explain anything. She understood English, but not *that* well. How would I even begin to describe "shoots" and "works" and "kay fabing"? Where would I start describing the way our business grew into what it did—with characters like Ed "Strangler" Lewis, Jack Pfefer, and Gorgeous George? Luckily, Miyako was young enough to adjust to my lifestyle, and accept that the other members of the wrestling fraternity were my family.

I sometimes wonder what it would have been like to trade places with Miyako, have a stranger take you to another country and basically force you to adapt to that culture. To tell you the truth, I don't think I could have done it. But Miyako is a positive person who can find the best in everything. She eventually became a hairdresser, and joined a church where there were other Asian people she could befriend. No matter how difficult it was for her in the United States, she didn't ask anything of me. All she seemed to care about was that I was comfortable when I came home from the arena, all bruised up.

I was also impressed by Miyako's intelligence. Ask me about wrestling and I can talk for hours. But in other areas, I'm not the quickest guy on the uptake. Miyako would read about different subjects, and educate me about them. She was smart, as well as beautiful.

If anyone had suggested before this marriage that I was going to become a one-woman man, I would have thought they'd gone insane. But I haven't stepped out on Miyako once during our marriage—not because she asked me to remain faithful, but because I was happy just with her.

Because there was a twenty-eight-year age difference between us, I was too damn old to start a family again. I already had three kids, and I fucked up that situation pretty good. Miyako understood the way I felt, and didn't pressure me to become a father when I was already in my fifties. Whatever maternal instinct she had was channeled towards me. I like to say that I'm the little baby she never had.

Peter Takahashi: After Freddie married Miyako, I saw him change. Fans always kept a distance from him because he was so scary in the ring. Now, if he noticed someone holding a pen and paper, he'd nod at them and motion them over. Once in a while, when we were out in public, he'd walk over to a mother and kiss her baby.

One day, we were talking about the Japanese people who died in 1962 because they were shocked by the violent things they'd seen Freddie do on TV. He told me that, no matter what he said in his interviews, he felt guilty about what happened. When I looked at his face, I noticed that he was crying.

Kosuke Takeuchi: It soon became public knowledge that Blassie had a Japanese wife. Although they'd hated him with a passion, the Japanese people began to soften their opinion. In the ring, he was still "The Vampire." But he also had another nickname, *shin-nichika,* or "Japanese-loving person."

I brought Miyako on the road with me as much as possible. One year, I was supposed to take two weeks off and go on vacation with her in Hawaii. Then, the Atlanta office called. Could I help them out down there? I had to tell Miyako, "Forget about Honolulu. We're going to Georgia."

Miyako usually sat in the crowd, and tried to blend in with her surroundings. In San Francisco and L.A., where there are large Asian communities, this was never a big deal. But in Columbus, Georgia, she stood out. First, the fans wanted to know what this well-dressed Japanese woman was doing in their arena. Then, someone blurted out that she'd been seen arriving at the building with Freddie Blassie.

I was getting ready for my match when an usher ran into the dressing room. "Mr. Blassie, you better get out there," he said. "They're ready to jump your wife."

Here was Miyako, sitting there, unaware that these white-trash women standing all around her were threatening to kick her ass. When people cursed her out, she'd smile, apparently thinking that they were paying her a compliment.

I stormed out of the dressing room and shoved people out of my way, stomping up to where Miyako was seated. Everyone turned away from the match in the ring when they saw me, but I didn't give a damn.

"If any one of you assholes just so much as lays a finger on her, I'll come back and kill you," I shouted at the greasy hags surrounding my wife. Then, I looked over their heads at the men they'd brought along. "And that goes for your fuckin' husbands, too. And you know goddamn well I'll do it."

The crowd hushed. Nobody said a word, or made eye contact with me. "Miyako, go back to the car," I said. "Roll up the windows and lock the door. Don't open it for anyone except me."

I watched as she left the arena. People stepped out of her way, cutting her a wide aisle.

I went back to the dressing room, worked my match, and quickly changed out of my wrestling gear. It was snowing slightly when I got back to the car. Miyako was sitting there in the dark, unsure of why I asked her to leave the building. Very slowly, I explained what those idiots meant when they called her a "fuckin' bitch." She seemed genuinely surprised; not for a moment had she imagined that she'd been in danger.

It was sad looking at her face, and seeing the innocence fade away. But, for Miyako's own survival, she needed to learn a very important lesson—about the mentality of American wrestling fans, and the things that could happen when you hung around with Blassie.

Here's Freddie at thirteen, seen with his mother and a friend's daughter.

A shirtless Freddie taking a turn at mess duty.

Already a popular wrestler in the States, Freddie captured the imagination of Japanese fans with his style.

On one of his trips to the east, here's Freddie getting the better of a lion in Tacloban.

Miyako and Freddie were invited to ride in a Christmas parade.

In his fifties, Blassie was *the* headliner.

Freddie was the natural choice to manage Ali and the Japanese press during a wrestler vs. boxer match.

Blassie leads Cowboy Stan Hansen to the ring.

The master of getting heat, Freddie was the best manager at transferring heat.
He's seen here with the Iron Sheik, one of his many protégés.

ELEVEN:
"BITE HIM, BLASSIE! BITE HIM!"

While the WWWF was booming on the east coast, on the other side of the country, Mike LeBell was growing tired of competing with the NWA. The organization was just too powerful, and by keeping himself isolated from them, he was cutting himself off from all the NWA stars who could be flown in for special shows. In 1968, the WWA Champion, Bobo Brazil, wrestled the NWA kingpin, Gene Kiniski, in a unification match. Kiniski won, and the WWA title was abandoned. I'm sure that LeBell thought that, now that he'd joined the NWA, he could accumulate enough leverage to be voted president of the organization—and the most powerful man in wrestling. But the other promoters in the group realized that LeBell was a treacherous S.O.B. After all, it takes one to know one.

Under the new arrangement, the NWA Champion regularly visited Southern California, defending his title. And the America's championship became the most important belt in the territory. The America's title changed hands frequently. But for the next three years, I held the belt more than anyone else, defending it, losing it, and winning it again against guys like Bobo, Mil Mascaras, The Sheik, Rocky Johnson, and John Tolos.

Not long before the WWA was dissolved, I held the group's Tag Team Title with Killer Buddy Austin, a bleached blond brawler much like myself. Austin was a talented guy; he helped train one of the greatest workers of all time, eight-time NWA Champion Harley Race. But he was full of bad luck, like lightning

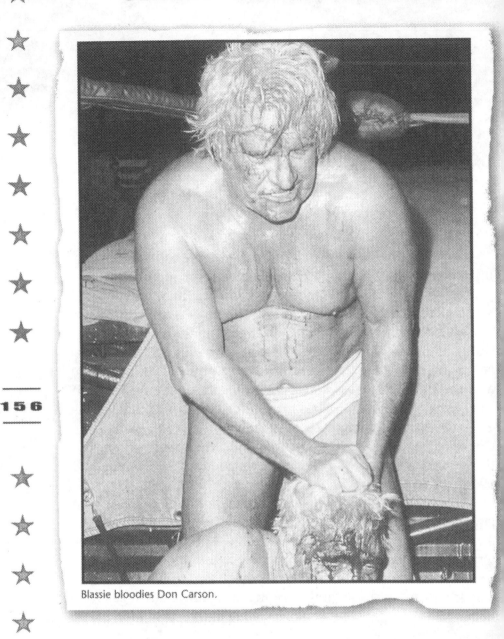

Blassie bloodies Don Carson.

156

struck him twice. In the dressing room, he'd act kind of goofy, and make the boys laugh. When I looked at him, though, I didn't see anything that funny. The guy was a drunk. I'd been stuck with one for a father. Now, I was stuck with one for a tag team partner.

Occasionally, Austin would show up at the arena with too much under his belt. He was professional enough that, once the bell rang, he could shake himself out of his haze and work a good match. But I didn't fuckin' care. What happened if one day he overdid it, and dropped his opponent on the head, paralyzing him?

"Jesus Christ, you gotta come here drunk?" I'd yell at him. "Goddamn, you know I don't like that bullshit."

With some guys, a stern lecture from a veteran is enough to snap them into shape. But Austin had enough experience himself that he didn't need any words of wisdom from me. I guess he'd been wrestling inebriated for so long that he felt entitled to do whatever he damn pleased.

Eventually, I went to Mike LeBell. "I'm carrying this team," I said. "I don't want a drunk for a tag team partner. I can't rely on somebody who doesn't have all their faculties."

LeBell agreed to separate us, explaining our breakup to the fans by booking us in a feud. Austin played the babyface; I was the heel. Despite my lack of enthusiasm about sharing a ring with Austin, we actually did great business. When we had a stretcher match (loser must be so incapacitated that he leaves on a stretcher), four thousand fans were turned away from the Olympic Auditorium.

In 1970, I took part in a similar angle with another bleached blond partner, Don Carson. We held the America's Tag Team Title together, then turned on each other. The strategy was that fans would look at Carson, perceive him as another Freddie Blassie, then lay down their money to see mirror images do battle (World Wrestling Federation pulled this off successfully in 1994, when they had Undertaker clash with an evil impostor at the *SummerSlam* Pay-Per-View). You'd never believe who came up with the idea—Jack Pfefer! Although he was no longer promoting, Pfefer was still scratching out a living where he could in the wrestling business. Apparently, he hadn't lost his gift for delivering a line of bullshit because, behind the scenes, Carson had hired him as a manager.

Unfortunately for Carson, the rivalry didn't draw much money. Plainly put, there was only one Freddie Blassie, and the people didn't buy anyone else—particularly Don Carson— challenging my legacy. I don't know the financial details, but I can only imagine what transpired when Pfeffer negotiated on Carson's behalf with Mike LeBell. Between the two of them, I'd

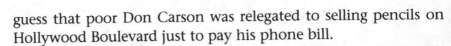
guess that poor Don Carson was relegated to selling pencils on Hollywood Boulevard just to pay his phone bill.

But an unusual thing happened during my feud with Carson. When I cut a promo and called myself "The Great One, King of Men" and "Wrestling God," I wasn't getting typical Freddie Blassie heat. In fact, I noticed that some of the fans were nodding their heads in agreement. After seeing me around for so long, they were finally starting to accept me as one of their own. Sometimes, a promoter decides to turn a guy babyface because he's not getting over as a heel. Other times, the fans make the decision for the promotion. This was clearly one of those cases. But I didn't want to snap my fingers and become a babyface overnight. Instead, we built intrigue over several weeks. Rather than coming out, slapping hands while trotting down the aisle, I made my turn a gradual process.

Fans weren't sure what to expect when I stepped into the ring against Rocky "Soulman" Johnson. Rocky was a handsome, popular athlete raised in Nova Scotia's tiny black community. In the middle of his matches, he'd go into a boxing stance, shuffle his feet, and throw rapidfire punches that looked like they were coming off Muhammad Ali's fists. He collected numerous championships throughout his career, including the America's belt, NWA Florida title, and World Wrestling Federation Tag Team crown with Tony Atlas. But, today, he's best known for being the father of Dwayne Johnson, a.k.a. The Rock.

Dwayne may have been the cutest little kid I'd ever seen in my life. It's too bad he's an only child because his sister would have been stunning. His mother was Samoan—the daughter of my future protégé, High Chief Peter Maivia—and dressed him in Polynesian shirts. He had dark eyes and fuzzy-wuzzy hair, and an inquisitive look on his face all the time. I wasn't surprised at all when he became a movie star because, even as a little boy, his face belonged on a billboard.

Dwayne "The Rock" Johnson: I remember just being in awe of Freddie Blassie's presence. He was flamboyant and creative, and really understood the art of entertaining the people with facial expressions and body language. Whatever role he was playing, he embraced it. He had a lot of different outfits, but I distinctly recall these gold pants he wore with a gold shirt that had a splash of orange on it. When I was a kid, he was my fashion mentor—in a sports entertainment way.

Rocky Johnson and I became pretty good friends, and somewhere along the line, I discovered that he was afraid of rodents. So I went to a novelty shop and bought one of those wind-up mice. We had a card in San Bernardino that night, and I put the toy next to him on the floor while he was tying his boots. When he saw that fuckin' mouse, he jumped out of his skin and literally tried to climb up the wall. A couple of years ago, I tried telling that story to The Rock, backstage at a World Wrestling Federation show. I thought that he'd laugh his balls off, but he wasn't very amused. Hey, it's still his father.

My confrontation with Johnson took place on the promotion's weekly show, now on KCOP-TV. I came out and told announcer Dick Lane that I wanted to have a scientific match with The Soulman. And I kept my word, exchanging headlocks and arm drags, and getting down on the mat and applying old-fashioned wrestling holds. If two other guys delivered the same series of maneuvers, viewers would have been turning on *F-Troop*. But because I'd been such a nasty fuck, no one moved. Everybody expected me to lose my temper and kick Rocky in the nuts or slam his head into the turnbuckle. When I didn't, and gave Johnson a sportsmanlike handshake when the time limit expired, spectators knew that they could make a commitment to me.

Wrestling fans love to forgive. The more vicious you were as a heel, the more they cheer you when you turn babyface. Now that I'd earned their trust, I didn't have to work slow, technical matches anymore. I could pop my thumb into my opponents' eyes, stand behind them and stretch their mouths, and bang their heads onto the timekeeper's table. It was a lot like Stone Cold Steve Austin when he made his babyface turn in World Wrestling Federation in the late 1990s. In the ring, he was the same rotten son of a bitch he'd been before. As long as his victims were heels, though, everyone was happy.

After taunting the crowd for so many years, it was strange to hear applause. But I liked it. At least I knew that when I left the ring, no one was going to stick a knife in me.

* * *

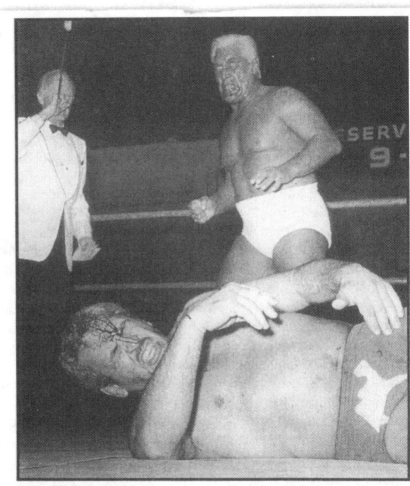

A bloody Ed "The Sheik" Farhat is down, as Blassie hovers; the immortal Jimmy Lennon is ring announcer.

Among heels, perhaps no one was as consistently hated as The Sheik. I'm not talking about my future protégé, the *Iron Sheik*. I'm talking about Ed Farhat, a Lebanese-American guy who—nearly fifty years before Osama bin Laden became Public

Enemy Number One—turned himself into a Middle Eastern terrorist. The Sheik would come to the ring in an Arab headdress, roll his eyes up into his head, stick out his tongue, and pull sharp objects out of his trunks to carve up opponents. He also traveled constantly, making stops in as many territories as he could, so—despite the regional divisions between promotions—it seemed like every fan in North America had seen The Sheik bloody up their favorite wrestler.

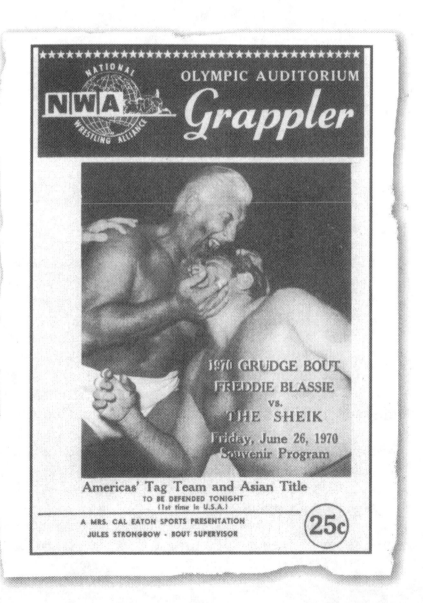

* * *

Mike LeBell: What made The Sheik such an interesting attraction was that he would throw fire. And God Almighty, the people would just go crazy. He once showed me how you did it. He had this little thing, like a flint, that you'd strike, and then throw your hand forward so the flame would shoot out. It was like a match; if you lit it once, you couldn't light it a second time. So he'd throw fire at his opponent, and the guy would cover his face, falling on the mat, kicking. Then, The Sheik would leave the ring, get near the fans, and throw his hand out like he was going to do it again. He couldn't, of course. But the people would be terrified.

LeBell and The Sheik were intimate friends, and I think I know why. In addition to wrestling, The Sheik was the promoter in Detroit. That meant that he could vote for NWA president. One day, LeBell fantasized, The Sheik would help get him elected.

There wasn't anything LeBell wouldn't do for his pal. As soon as The Sheik arrived at the airport, LeBell would have a car waiting to take him wherever he wanted. For a while, LeBell had me shuttling to Detroit on a regular basis just to round out The Sheik's cards. I wasn't even in the main events; the wrestlers there were too scared I'd take away their spots. So The Sheik booked me in preliminary matches, like I was twenty years old again. I guess he was disappointed that I didn't draw a dime. But if you bury a guy in opening bouts, what the hell do you expect?

When The Sheik came to L.A., he'd bring along his manager, Abdullah Farouk. Despite his name, Farouk was a skinny Jewish guy from Canton, Ohio, named Ernie Roth. He was great at getting heat, insulting The Sheik's opponents and the local fans in the same breath. Like most managers, he inserted himself into the action. So before I wrestled The Sheik, I announced that I wanted him alone in a fifteen-foot cage. That way, Farouk—or "The Weasel," as I called him—couldn't interfere.

I took credit for designing the cage—it was made out of steel tubing—and emphasized that I couldn't wait to corner The Sheik in my new contraption. Cage matches were a rarity then, so the concept sparked a lot of interest. Dick Lane described the coop as "The Freddie Blassie Cage." The Mexican fans—who were

The Sheik trapped in the famous "Freddie Blassie Cage."

163

turning out at the Olympic in greater and greater numbers—
called it "*La Jaula de* Freddie Blassie."

To nobody's surprise, The Sheik and I had a great brawl.
He climbed up on the cage, trying to escape, and I chased after
him, beating him back down to the canvas. But before I could
claim victory, Farouk threw a liquid in my face. I collapsed on the
mat, while The Sheik retreated over the top of the cage, to the

safety of the dressing room. Fans were later shown a bottle bearing a skull and crossbones, and told that the substance was iodine.

The next time I appeared on television, I howled that I didn't want any time off to recuperate from my accident. What I wanted was a rematch—also in a cage. And this time, I was building a second, smaller cage, to suspend Farouk from the ceiling. That way, he couldn't get anywhere near me.

"I won't do it," he shouted in an interview. "I am nauseated by height."

Of course, the promotion demanded that he adhere to the provision. Bud Furillo of the *Los Angeles Herald-Examiner* wrote a tongue-in-cheek story about the unique stipulation. Playing off Farouk's Arab gimmick, Furillo told readers, "He agreed to go twenty feet [in the air], while keeping a watchful eye for Israeli planes."

This match was basically a slaughter. From the moment the bell rang, I kicked, punched, and bit The Sheik. "Bite him, Blassie!" I heard the fans scream. "Bite him!" To the delight of the crowd, I ended the match by chucking pepper in The Sheik's face, and scrambling over the top of the cage to win.

The fans were on their feet, rejoicing the way the Dutch did when they were liberated from the Germans. But as I rested in a front-row seat after the harrowing battle, "The Golden Greek" John Tolos attacked me.

At fifty-two, I was about to begin the most famous rivalry of my career. Despite my age, I never gave a thought to retiring. I thought that I was as good as I'd been when I was younger—in fact, better, because I had more experience.

Of course, every time I woke up in the morning, I could feel my bones rattle. Over the course of my career, I broke every rib on the right side of my body, and five on the left. My vertebrae were fused together, and my head literally creaked. I could balance myself on top of a cage and brawl with somebody, but I could only turn my head so far. If I pushed it beyond that, the pain was unbearable. But I'd been living with pain ever since I'd been in the business. It was no different at fifty-two than it had been at thirty-two.

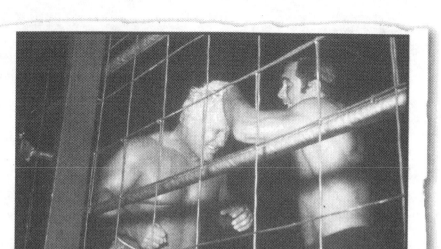

Blassie and "The Golden Greek" John Tolos brawl in a cage match.

Still, I pushed myself. I'd patch up whatever injuries I had, and get out there and work. I knew that some people thought that I looked like an old man when they saw my publicity photo. My goal was proving to them that I was tougher than the ordinary human. And I was! Unfortunately, that's the reason I'm suffering so much today.

In John Tolos, a handsome but roguish, dark-haired man, I had my best opponent. We'd known each other since 1953, and were neighbors in Santa Monica. I thought of him as a brother because our ethic was exactly the same. He was as driven as I was to stay on top. He could cut a great promo—screaming and laughing like a hyena—and wrestle an even better match. It didn't matter if we hurt ourselves in our skirmishes, as long as we did our best for the people who paid to see us. Regardless of what we called the fans in our interviews, that was how we both felt inside—and that's why the public was never disappointed when we tore into each other. I thank God I met him because, together, we made a hell of a lot of money.

* * *

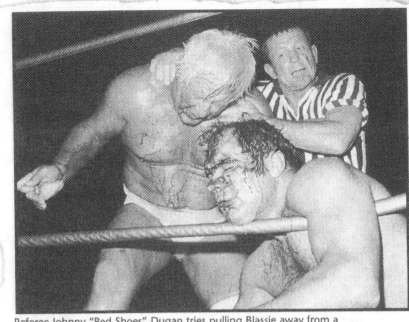

Referee Johnny "Red Shoes" Dugan tries pulling Blassie away from a
bloody John Tolos.

Mike LeBell: Blassie and Tolos were the two hottest wrestlers
back then. I knew them well. At one time or another, they'd both
been my bookers. Blassie, in particular, was very good at it. On
Fridays, we'd have a booking meeting at 3:00 in the afternoon.
Freddie was always there at 2:30, with a notebook filled with what
we'd done in the past, what we should do in the future, what different wrestlers were capable of doing in the ring.

This was going to be his biggest moment. Even though he
was in his fifties, he was in real, real good shape—thin, looked good.
In May 1971, we started the ball rolling. Freddie was defending the
America's title against Tolos. In the middle of the match, Freddie fell
against the ropes. They broke, he knocked himself out, and Tolos
became the new champion.

The next day, we all met at the KCOP studio, where we taped
our television program. We had a ringside physician, Dr. Bernhart
Schwartz, and I went through his bag to see what he had in there.
There were bandages, needles to sew people up, those types of
things. I asked, "Do you have anything that could blind a man?"
Blassie came up with the idea of "monsel's powder," made from the
same clotting material you'd find in a styptic pencil.

We went through a rehearsal of what we were going to do that night. Blassie would be wrestling, and Tolos would sneak around the ring and go into the doctor's bag, then throw the monsel's powder into Freddie's eyes after the match. Dick Lane announced it all, as if we were live. Everyone there—the cameramen, the other KCOP employees—began applauding. I said, "That's it. We got it."

After my match that night, Dick Lane interviewed me on KCOP. He announced that I'd been voted Wrestler of the Year by the fans, and handed me a trophy. Of course, the crowd had seen Tolos steal something from the doctor's bag, but they didn't exactly know what was coming. As I was making my acceptance speech, Tolos came up on one side of me, and threw this cloud of white powder in my face. I fell on the ground, screaming, *"My God! My eyes!"* while Dick Lane was frantically reporting, "We need medical assistance. Freddie Blassie has been blinded."

Tolos stood over me and laughed hysterically. Then, he destroyed the trophy. The fans were falling over the seats, trying to get to us. If anyone had been carrying a gun, Tolos would have spent the night in the morgue.

Mike LeBell: We had to have the police take Tolos out of the building. We called an ambulance for Blassie. And the ambulance went to South Hoover Hospital. The only way to make it look proper and legitimate was to go to the hospital. We had two television programs back then—one in English, one in Spanish—and we explained, "For those of you who want to write Mr. Blassie in the hospital, here's the address."

We also announced special visiting hours. People came by the hundreds and hundreds. Freddie was sitting in a hospital bed, with gauze wrapped around his eye, and Vaseline and some kind of reddish solution underneath. It really looked like his left eye was burned completely.

People were crying. "Don't worry, Freddie," they were saying. "You'll beat this." And Freddie was going, "You don't know what it's like to lose your sight."

Now, this was all done for a purpose. I booked Freddie into Japan for, I think, six weeks, then Korea for three weeks. We told the people that he was going to a hospital in another part of the world for special treatment. And before our Friday-night show, we stood and had one minute of silence for Freddie Blassie, the man who loved wrestling, but lost his sight.

All the fans said they were going to jump Tolos. But they were also afraid of him, after what he did to Blassie. The fans would make a move towards Tolos, and he would raise an arm and roar, "Yaaaahh!" They'd go running because they really believed he was a monster.

In late July, Tolos was in the ring, battling Don Carson, when I charged out of the dressing room. The fans were stunned; they thought I'd been resurrected. Tolos looked at me and started shaking. I jumped in the ring, and Tolos ran out. I followed and chased him around in circles.

Mike LeBell then showed up. "Can you sign this match?" the announcer asked him. "Mr. LeBell, please, *please,* can you sign this match?"

I grabbed the microphone. "Give me a contract, I'll sign right away," I hollered. "I don't want no money. All I want is Tolos."

The match did not take place for a while. We wanted to stretch out the anticipation for weeks. It was announced that I was still regaining my vision, and training against doctor's orders. In the arena, whenever I saw Tolos, I'd rush after him, while people jumped between us, restraining me. Just before our big confrontation, the promotion chained me to a ring post on television, to prevent me from battering my enemy. As I was sitting there, helpless, Tolos dove on top of me, rubbing the chain against my face. As the show went off the air, Dick Lane was shouting for the police.

Because of the buildup, when we finally had our match on August 27, 1971, it was held not at the Olympic Auditorium, but the Los Angeles Coliseum. On the undercard, The Sheik came in from Detroit to wrestle Bobo Brazil, The Rock's grandfather, Peter Maivia, flew down from San Francisco to wrestle Dutch Savage, El Solitario—the NWA lightweight champion based in Mexico—battled Raul Mata, and the Fabulous Moolah defended her women's title against Betty Niccoli. There were 25,847 fans in attendance, and the reported gate was more than $142,000—California records at the time. Outside, scalpers were selling tickets for as much as $100, unheard-of money in 1971.

Not only that, but the show was broadcast on closed circuit at about a half dozen other locations, the first time this had ever been done in professional wrestling. There were even monitors in the dressing room for the boys. Nonetheless, a lot of them stood in the entrance ramp to watch my match; this was the biggest wrestling event ever, and they wanted to see it live.

When you go to a WWE Pay-Per-View today, you see a lot of people joking around before the card starts, as if they're at some kind of comedy performance. That's okay, since WWE calls itself "sports entertainment." But when Tolos and I met at the Coliseum, no one was laughing beforehand. I'd done such a good job of convincing the people that I'd lost my vision that even I believed it. And when a man robs you of your sight, your goal is not to wrestle him, but to murder him.

We split the first two falls, then I basically massacred Tolos. Blood was spilling everywhere, and the fans were shrieking for more. I pulled back Tolos's head, tucked it into my shoulder,

169

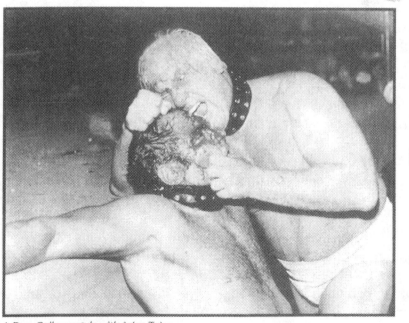

A Dog Collar match with John Tolos.

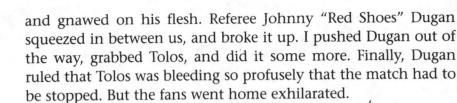
and gnawed on his flesh. Referee Johnny "Red Shoes" Dugan squeezed in between us, and broke it up. I pushed Dugan out of the way, grabbed Tolos, and did it some more. Finally, Dugan ruled that Tolos was bleeding so profusely that the match had to be stopped. But the fans went home exhilarated.

I would have been exhilarated too—if it wasn't for one little episode that took place outside the ring. Before the show, I saw a group of ushers leaving the Coliseum with bags of money. I was sure that this was some kind of attempt to swindle us on the gate. I'll never be able to confirm the theory, but at the time I was convinced that it was true.

After the Coliseum show, Tolos and I kept headlining. Any gimmick you could think of, we did it in the ring: Roman gladiator death matches, Sicilian strap matches, "I Quit" matches. Because he was the heel, Tolos always acted like a coward. For a period of time, he wore a spiked collar to protect himself from my chokehold and kneedrops. On one occasion, he brought out a boa constrictor to keep me away from him. I'd be knocking Tolos around and he'd run to the corner, grab the snake, and wave it at me. I have to say that Tolos's pet was a pretty good worker, wiggling around and performing better than a lot of the wrestlers I knew.

By then, the fans were calling me "Fearless" Freddie Blassie, because I always found a way to undermine Tolos's schemes, and butcher him a little bit more. When the two of us were guests on *The Steve Allen Show*, I snatched him in a front facelock and started biting his forehead. Tolos was screaming for his life, *"Stop! Stop!"* as the blood flowed like ouzo at a Greek wedding. The two of us thought it was a great spectacle—although I'm not sure that people outside the wrestling community particularly appreciated an unscheduled bloodbath on a wholesome, family program.

John Tolos: A feud like this only comes along once in a blue moon. Blassie and I were the right combination at the right time. We started to wrestle each other and, bingo, it just hit. Oh, both of us were high, man. Every time I wrestled Blassie, I knew that house was gonna come down.

The fans hated me so much that I couldn't get out of the ring.

The people were in the aisles, practically rioting. Blassie knew how it was because the fans used to hate his guts, too. So he'd stand there in the ring, laughing at the whole thing. "How do you like it, you son of a bitch? You're gonna get it now."

I had trouble at the beaches, trouble at the store, anyplace people recognized me. All I'd hear is, "Blassie's gonna kill you! Blassie's gonna kill you!" And I'd scream right back at them, "Maybe you wanna try something instead!" A few times, when they got too close, I had to kick a couple of guys in the ass.

I'd be at home and the phone would ring. I'd hear, "Tolos, you rotten motherfucker," and then the caller would hang up. People would knock on my door and run away. When I'd answer, there'd be a hunk of shit on the welcome mat.

Today, some of those same people are much nicer when they meet me. "Boy, I remember you and Blassie," they say. "What great matches." I tell them that I loved it. Those were the best years of my life.

The more violent I acted, the more the Mexican fans seemed to love me. By the time I clashed with Tolos, they'd given me a nickname: *El Rubio de Oro,* or "Golden Blond."

There were wrestlers who bitched that, when they worked the Olympic, they didn't even feel like they were wrestling in America. But I didn't give a shit. In fact, I encouraged the promotion to use Mexican talent. Maybe I called them "pepper bellies" when I was a heel, but I didn't mean it. Race never made a difference to me. If *you* drew money, I made money.

Mil Mascaras was the biggest Mexican name to work Los Angeles. They called him the "man of a thousand masks and a thousand holds to go with it." He was good, but a little too impressed with his own importance. And he became a big star by accident.

In Mexico, masked wrestlers starred in their own films, playing superheroes. In the early 1960s, producer Luis Enrique Vergara was making movies with El Santo and Blue Demon, both superstars in the ring. But in 1966, Vergara was stuck without a leading man. Santo had jumped to a rival movie studio, and the Blue Demon was injured. So the Mil Mascaras character was invented to fill the void. Aaron Rodriguez was picked to play the character because he was athletic, and had an impressive physique. Had Blue Demon recovered a few weeks early, Mil Mascaras would have never existed. And—who knows?—Rodriguez might have been a bore with a different gimmick.

Mascaras was colorful. But he had a lousy attitude. In the ring, he refused to sell his rivals' moves. Doing a job to elevate an opponent was the furthest thing from his mind. If it didn't benefit Mascaras, you could go fuck yourself.

172

I preferred the company of Ray Mendoza. He was a good-hearted guy with a lot of charisma. As an athlete, I think he was better than Mascaras. I have no doubt that if Mendoza spoke English, he would have been a star in the United States (his sons, the five Villano brothers, and daughter, La Infernal, later became famous on the Mexican wrestling scene). With his talents, the American people would have taken him into their hearts, the way the Mexicans did.

We did an angle where Mendoza gave me a sombrero. I wore it everywhere—in fact, I still have it at home, hanging on the wall leading to my basement—until the Spanish-speaking fans started thinking I was Montezuma's third cousin. Then, the heel tag team of Black Gordman and the Great Goliath attacked me, leaving me a bloody mess and—even worse in the eyes of the Latino set—ripping my cherished sombrero.

As a result, Mendoza and I had a series of Tag Team matches against Gordman and Goliath. The rivalry did great business. Gordman and Goliath were not as good as North American tag teams like Pat Patterson and Ray Stevens, or Jack and Gerry Brisco. But they had a lot of heat because of their ring introductions. When the ring announcer listed Mexico as the pair's home country, they'd explode. "We're not low class like the dirty Mexicans,"

Blassie was a fan favorite with L.A.'s Latino community.

they'd yell. "We're from *New* Mexico." All the Mexicans wanted to see was Mendoza and me destroy these two jokers. Unfortunately, whenever we went down to Tijuana for a match, you never knew if they'd show up.

I wasn't a big fan of Tijuana. I couldn't speak Spanish, and the Mexican wrestlers work from the opposite side of the body. For example, Americans apply a headlock while standing on your left. Mexicans do it while standing on your right. Because I had the reputation I did, the Mexicans tried working American-style when they were wrestling me. But being in a tag match with three Mexicans could be damn confusing.

When I went into a restaurant in Tijuana, I never wanted to eat because I was convinced that the cook didn't wash his hands after he went to the bathroom. In the TV studio there, you'd have goats and chickens roaming around the building. I'm not making this up. I'd be doing an interview, building up an important match, and, out of nowhere, a cow would go, *"Moooo!"* It was altogether different than American TV.

Every time we went there, the promoter had to put someone in charge of getting Gordman and Goliath to the arena. The guy would search every brothel in the city, until he found those clowns dancing with the whores, forty-five minutes before their match was supposed to begin.

As far as I was concerned, it didn't matter if I was wrestling Gordman and Goliath, or Milton Berle and Jack Benny. The fans cheered everything because, in Los Angeles, Freddie Blassie could do no wrong. One night, I looked into the stands, and was amazed to see almost the entire crowd wearing cardboard Freddie Blassie masks. As rough as this business can be, few outside of it will ever know the thrill of gazing at ten thousand people sitting together, dressed like you.

In 1971, there wasn't a more popular man in America, in or out of wrestling. Then one day, I answered the phone and Vince McMahon, Sr. was on the other end. Pedro Morales was the WWWF Champion, and they needed a number-one contender. I was fifty-three years old, and knew that I couldn't stay on top forever. If I didn't say yes, I might never get this chance again. So I went back to a place where the people still hated Freddie Blassie, and gave them a little bit more to hiss about.

TWELVE:
"GROUCHIEST MAN IN THE WORLD"

Like Bruno Sammartino, Pedro Morales was an ethnic hero. When he wrestled in Madison Square Garden, the Bronx emptied out, and every Puerto Rican in the borough filled the arena. If you were roughing him up, all he had to do was give the high sign, and he'd have twenty-thousand tag team partners charging the ring.

Gorilla Monsoon was a babyface now, and a very powerful guy in the WWWF office. He loved Morales, and took some credit for

Blassie in the early '70s.

guiding him to the WWWF title. There was no selfish motive involved. Gorilla thought that Pedro was a good kid, and wanted to help him. Every time Pedro sold out a building, Monsoon was thrilled. Morales was his pride and joy.

New heels coming into the WWWF often wrestled Monsoon on the way up, scoring a win and then getting a shot against Pedro. Once your series of matches with Morales ended, you were likely to wrestle Chief Jay Strongbow a few times before moving on to another territory.

As I've mentioned, Strongbow was an Italian-American who did an Indian gimmick. He'd be getting his ass kicked, then go into a war dance and make his big comeback, bending to smack the mat with both hands, and coming up to deliver a string of "tomahawk chops" to his opponent. He was a decent guy, but very, very thrifty. If he made a dime, he saved eleven cents of it. When the boys wanted to rib him, they'd ask him how much he paid for his hotel room. After he answered, they'd claim to have found a cheaper place down the road. The thought of another guy squirreling away more sheckels killed Strongbow, and he'd hit the ceiling, cursing his brains out: "Shit, why the fuck didn't anyone tell me about this before? Motherfuckin' son of a bitch."

I remember when he bought a farm outside Atlanta. There was a lake on the property, and he stocked it with fish. Then, he charged fishermen to use the water. Which I guess is all right. It's just not my cup of tea.

Strongbow was always hanging out with Monsoon. After

Chief Jay Strongbow.

all, the sky was the limit to Gorilla; he threw money around like it was paper. I, on the other hand, spent my spare time with Captain Lou Albano. He'd been made into a manager a few years earlier and, despite the fact that I'd been in the business since the 1930s, I became his protégé.

You might not know it from looking at him—Lou was a

chubby, bearded guy who'd slipped rubber bands through the hoops piercing his face—but Lou was a very intelligent fella. His father, Dr. Carmen Albano, delivered something like five thousand babies in Mount Vernon, New York. Three of his brothers became educators—two of them principals—and Lou was a premed student at one time. But he wasn't dealing with a full deck. There's no question that he knew wrestling from A to Z. Switch the subject to anything else, though, and you could see that his mind wasn't functioning right.

Back when he was wrestling, he and Tony Altimore called themselves The Sicilians. They held the WWWF Tag Team Championship in 1967, but, honestly, they were nothing to get excited about. What made them unique was their gimmick. They each wore a white fedora and black glove, and would clench a fist at each other, muttering, "Mafia." That was until a few guys representing Chicago mob boss Tony Accaro decided to drop in on them.

"You're degrading the Italians," they were told. "There's no such thing as the mafia. We're legitimate businessmen."

Apparently, Albano and Altimore struck a deal with their visitors. The two could continue to call themselves The Sicilians, but they had to get rid of the glove.

Albano never claimed to be Lou Thesz. He was an average wrestler, but an exceptional talker. That's why Vince, Sr. made him a manager. You could bring him out with a protégé who was a complete zero and, in two or three minutes, he'd have you believing that the guy was one of the all-time greats. And because Lou was an experienced wrestler, he knew how to take a good bump after he interfered in the action, and the babyface slugged him.

Unfortunately, Lou was a total fruitcake, and could foul up a match before he even woke up in the morning. We'd have it arranged for him to get involved in one of my confrontations, and he'd be nowhere in sight. The babyface and I would be standing there like dummies, until we spotted Albano in the audience, fighting with a spectator instead of doing his job.

Once, I was beating the shit out of Pedro Morales. After the slaughter was completed, Albano and I were supposed to retreat to the dressing room. Only Albano didn't want to leave.

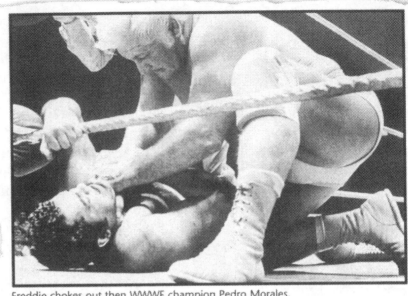

Freddie chokes out then WWWF champion Pedro Morales.

"Come on, Lou, the fans are pissed off," I whispered. "Let's get the hell out of here."

Albano wasn't listening to a word I said. He was just talking gibberish and staggering around.

"What the hell are you doing, Lou?"

He shook his head from side to side, and farted through his lips. As we were leaving the ring, a wooden folding chair came sailing through the air. Lou didn't even see it, until it landed on his head, and spun around his neck like a horseshoe.

When the matches were over, he'd drag me to one bar after another. If you bought Lou a drink, you'd have a friend for life—because he'd keep coming back to you for a second and a third one. If you opened a saloon, you became his cousin.

There was one morning when Lou's son got up and looked out the window. "Hey, Mom," the kid said, "Dad parked his car outside, and left the window open."

Albano's wife went out to investigate. He'd driven home the night before, with the window rolled down, parked, then went to sleep in front of his house. During the night, it started to snow, but Lou didn't know the fuckin' difference. When his wife found him, he was snoring with his arm hanging out the window, covered with snow. If it wasn't for his son, Albano would have become wrestling's first one-armed manager.

"Captain" Lou Albano: You know, I did occasionally have a few drinks. I was hell when well, and never sick, mean when I was drinking, drinking a little bit all the time. I'm a legend in my own mind.

My job as manager was getting out there with the hype: "This man's got the brain of a dehydrated beebee. Put his brain in a parakeet, and it'll fly backwards." I was the one who did it all, putting it together.

Freddie and I usually got along. Of course, we also had a couple of disagreements. He would like to tease, you know, so I teased him back. And if you teased Freddie back, forget about it. You became his enemy. He could tease you, but you couldn't tease him. Freddie could get a little abrupt, so he and I wouldn't talk for a few days. But we always made up, like a husband and wife.

Vince McMahon: I can't remember ever exchanging a harsh word with Freddie. I just so appreciated him and all of his accomplishments. His passion for the business and passion for life was contagious. We were very much alike in that way.

179

My father was a different sort of person. I wouldn't say that he was puritanical, but he had his own set of values, my Dad did, and they were high moral standards and things of that nature. Freddie and I would be joking about personnel or talking about women, and my Dad would see us, and he could almost read our minds.

"What are the two of you doing?" he'd ask, but he really didn't want to know. He understood that we were kind of up to no good all the time.

Vince, Sr. would be in his office, talking with Gorilla Monsoon and some of the other guys in his inner circle. Then, he'd walk out, jingling change in his pocket—the old man was always jingling change—and look at us, and a worried look would come over his face. He knew that his son and I liked the same things—money, big automobiles, dressing well—and always had his eye on us. Vince, Sr. wanted his kid to be conservative like him, not a wild bastard. The last thing he desired was having his

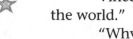

son leading a Freddie Blassie lifestyle. And who could blame him? I wouldn't want a son like me, either. Before Miyako, the only one who really put up with me was my mother.

Still, the old man treated me great, and never tried to separate me from his kid. Sometimes, when Vince, Jr. and I talked, he'd discuss ways of expanding his company's business. While other promoters were worrying about selling glossies of their talent at the gimmick table in back of some high school gym, Vince had his mind on action figures and network television. And his plans went way beyond wrestling. In 1974, he promoted Evel Knievel's jump in a rocket car over Snake River Canyon in Idaho. Whether he was successful or not, Vince was willing to try anything if there was the possibility that he could make a buck out of it. And that was fine with me since we're all on this earth to make a good living.

When Vince, Jr. and his wife, Linda, were living in Cape Cod, he'd ask me to stay at his house if there was a wrestling show nearby. This may not seem like a big deal, but after years of being fucked over by promoters, it was nice to have one who really was my friend. Later on, when Vince's son, Shane, got married, I was invited to the wedding, just like I was a relative. So when people start trash-talking Vince McMahon, I get a little defensive. The guy's always been wonderful to me.

Although we might have had different types of personalities, I also felt at home with Vince McMahon, Sr. Once, Miyako and I went to Florida on vacation. The old man had a home nearby, and insisted on bringing us to dinner.

"And tomorrow," he promised, "I'll take you out on my boat."

Well, it rained the next day, and then it was time for Miyako and I to return home. The next time I saw Vince, Jr., he asked me about my trip.

"I had a good time," I answered. "Your father treated us, Jesus Christ, terrific. We were supposed to go out on his boat, but we had bad weather and had to cancel it."

Vince's lips curled into a smirk. "You're the luckiest guy in the world."

"Why's that?"

"He doesn't know how to stop that damn boat. He just fig-

180

ures he'll hit the brakes, like on a car, and it'll stop. But in the water, you just keep going. He's run into the retaining wall so many times, I've lost count. Who knows? He could have drowned you or something."

Jim Myers, a.k.a. George "The Animal" Steele: The McMahons understood Freddie, and he understood them. And that's not always an easy job. Vince (Jr.) has about seven personalities, and five of them are pretty good. Don ("The Magnificent") Muraco and I used to call him "Sybil."

Even though Freddie was getting older, I loved watching him work. In those days, you wouldn't really know the details of your match until you got in the ring. The heels and babyfaces were in different dressing rooms, and someone would come in to where you were and tell you the finish and, possibly, how the match would start. So the heel usually ended up leading the babyface through the match, beating him up, then selling like hell when the babyface made the comeback. Freddie was a master at setting the pace, so the babyface just had to follow along.

181

If Blassie didn't like you, though, you were in trouble. Haystacks Calhoun had heat with Freddie for years. Blassie thought he was a lazy worker, and a pain in the ass. We were at a TV taping one time in Hamburg, Pennsylvania, and Calhoun left his truck—he was too big to drive a car—by the dressing room. Stacks had this little Chihuahua with him all the time, and kept him in the truck, with the window slightly open. Well, Freddie went over to the window and fed the dog Ex-Lax.

About fifteen minutes later, the dog shit on the upholstery. Freddie went over to one of the windows and tapped it. "Come here, Jules, come here." The dog ran through this slimy shit over to Freddie. Then, Blassie went to the other side of the car, and tapped the window again, so the dog would track more shit in the truck.

By the time Haystacks came out at the end of the night, that truck was a total shit wagon. He and his wife must have spent two hours cleaning it out before they could drive away. Calhoun just thought the dog was sick. No one ever told him it was a Blassie rib.

My disdain for Calhoun only went so far. He kept his little dog in his bed, and I was sad to hear that he'd rolled onto it

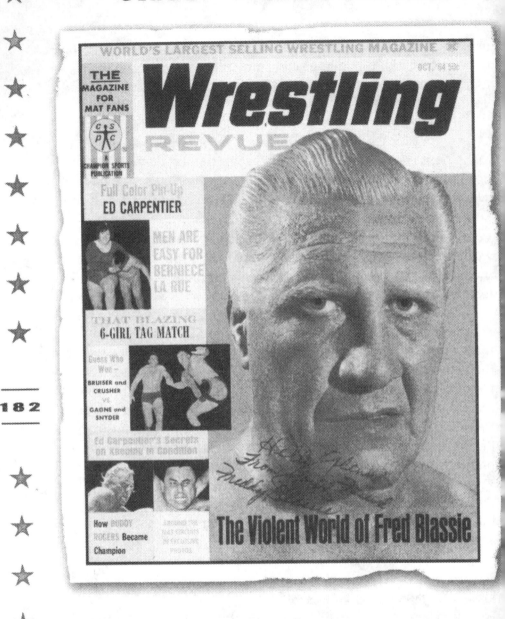

WORLD'S LARGEST SELLING WRESTLING MAGAZINE

OCT./64 50¢

THE MAGAZINE FOR MAT FANS

A CHAMPION SPORTS PUBLICATION

Wrestling REVUE

Full Color Pin-Up
ED CARPENTIER

MEN ARE EASY FOR BERNIECE LA RUE

THAT BLAZING
6-GIRL TAG MATCH

Guess Who Won –
BRUISER and CRUSHER vs GAGNE and SNYDER

Ed Carpentier's Secrets on Keeping In Condition

How BUDDY ROGERS Became Champion

The Violent World of Fred Blassie

one time, crushing the poor animal to death. In 1989, Haystacks died after a long bout with diabetes. Earlier, he'd had his leg amputated, and I'm told that he didn't come out of his house. When he received a letter from a wrestling fan, it made his week. Calhoun was only fifty-five when he passed away, and that's too young. He might have been an aggravating prick, but I took no pleasure in his misery.

* * *

Fans who didn't know any better sometimes put Andre the Giant in the same category as Haystacks Calhoun, a curiosity placed in the ring only because of his size. This is not entirely true. Andre, who was listed as seven-foot-four and more than five hundred pounds, was as athletic as a young man. He could deliver a flying dropkick, and once tried out for the Washington Redskins. Even as he aged and his body began falling apart on him, Andre remained one of the strongest men in wrestling. Once, when he was in the ring, wrestling Hulk Hogan, Andre got it in his head that Hogan wasn't hustling enough. Trapping Hogan in a full nelson and clamping on the pressure, Andre growled in that deep, distorted voice of his, "Work, Hulk, work." Hogan never realized that anybody on earth could be that powerful; he thought that Andre was going to snap his spine in half.

Andre's real name was Andre Rene Roussimoff, and he grew up in France, hoping to become a schoolteacher. But he had acromegaly, a disease sometimes called "giantism." Because of some glandular problem, everything grew on Andre—his head, face, chest, feet, and hands. Although he was marketed as a kind of colossus, he could be sensitive about his condition; at one point, the writers from World Wrestling Federation's magazine were instructed not to call Andre's hands "paws" because it hurt his feelings. When he was growing up, the other kids teased him, and—even though he could annihilate them by sneezing in their direction—he wanted to escape from his hometown.

183

Not surprisingly, Andre ended up on the wrestling circuit, first in Europe, then in New Zealand, Japan, and North America, billed as "The Eighth Wonder of the World" and using a variety of names, including Andre "The Butcher" Roussimoff, Monster Roussimoff, Monster Eiffel Tower, and Jean Ferre. It was Vince McMahon, Sr. who christened him Andre the Giant, and became his official booking agent, leasing him out to promoters all over the world.

Although I liked Andre, I found him revolting. We were once on a train in Japan, and he pointed out a Canadian woman, who was sloppier-looking than Haystacks Calhoun. She had on a white dress that was almost black with filth. "I eat that," he told me in his French accent.

"What?"

"I eat that. *Ah,* delicious."

"You're kidding?"

Andre smiled. Because of his condition, he had a gummy grin, and it seemed like his teeth stretched all over his mouth. "No, very good. Very good."

"Oh well, Andre. I'll let you have your choice. I have mine."

Actually, Andre got laid more than you'd think. He was a mark for greedy women who knew that he'd buy them presents and clothes. But he wanted to be seen with them, so people would think that he was a ladies' man, and not just some carnival attraction. From the moment he arrived in America, he was one of the highest paid guys in the business, and never minded spending that money.

He had legitimate friends—like "Golden Boy" Arnold Skaaland and referee Tim White. A few of the other boys, though, socialized with Andre only because he picked up all the tabs. Sometimes, I felt that he was trying to buy friendship. But it wasn't my business to get involved.

After the matches, Andre never wanted to call it a night. He'd keep people in the bar with him, demanding, "One more, boss," if they said that they were tired. I believe that he had some kind of ill feeling that he was going to pass away in his sleep. So every night had to be a party.

On my birthday one year, he insisted on throwing me a celebration. We went to this narrow diner, where there wasn't a lot of room to move around, with a bunch of the boys. The waiter brought the food out, then Andre went up to the door, held it shut, and let out a big fart.

Everybody was choking. And Andre was laughing his ass off. "Eat, eat," he was saying. "Do you think it smells nice?"

Needless to say, I lost my appetite. When we left the diner, Andre was still gloating over his rib, and handed me a piece of cake. "You forget to finish it," he chuckled. *"Ho, ho, ho."*

"Ho, ho, ho, your balls," I said, and threw the cake in his face.

* * *

Although I was a headliner in the WWWF, I hadn't completely divorced myself from L.A., flying back there frequently to work Mike LeBell's shows. This was a strange situation because I was a heel in the east, and the fans still loved me on the west coast. One of the wrestling magazines created a worked story about my split personality, even inventing a psychoanalyst they could quote about my condition.

Some of my friends wondered why, with the kind of money Vince, Sr. was paying me, I continued to work for LeBell. But LeBell had nothing to do with it. The people in L.A. had been very good to me, and I felt loyal to them. I wouldn't think of writing a book about my life without mentioning Jeff Walton and Art Williams, two kids who'd grown up as Freddie Blassie fanatics and ended up working in LeBell's office—Walton as a writer and photographer for the programs, Williams as a referee. Still, between the travel and the bumps I was taking, I was running myself into the ground, like an old car being held together with spare parts.

I desperately needed knee surgery. So on February 11, 1972, I wrestled Killer Kowalski at the Olympic, and he jumped on my leg, "crippling" me. Now, the promotion could not only explain my upcoming sabbatical, but show pictures of me with my leg in a cast, as I prepared for yet another return.

186

After we shot the angle, I went in for the long-overdue operation in Allentown, Pennsylvania. Miyako and I had moved into a place just north of New York City, in Westchester County, and Vince McMahon, Jr. offered to drive me home.

Vince was bodybuilding at the time, and the car was full of barbells. He pushed them out of the way, helped me into the backseat, rolled up the window, and took off. When he turned the corner, the barbells fell against me, and I had to push them out of the way. Vince rolled the window down. Now, the wind was blowing my hair all over the place.

"Goddammit, Vince," I hollered, "roll that fuckin' window up."

"Okay, Freddie." He turned another corner, and more barbells banged against me.

"Jesus Christ, Vince. I would have been better off taking a fuckin' cab."

That's the way it went for the whole ride, with the window coming down and my hair getting messed up, and barbells tumbling on me. By the time I got home, I felt worse than I did in the hospital.

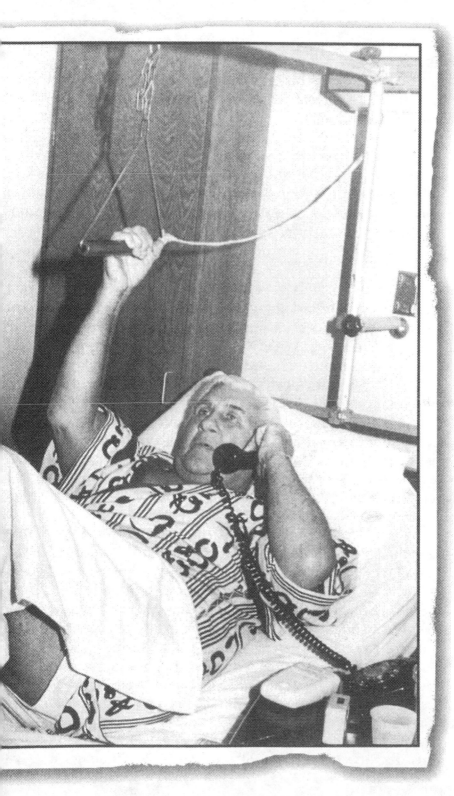

"How's everything?" Miyako asked when we pulled into the driveway.

Vince shook his head from side to side. "I don't know how you stand living with him," he answered. "He's the grouchiest man in the world."

On June 16, 1972, I had yet another homecoming at the Olympic Auditorium, throttling Kowalski in the main event. The fans were told that my leg had never been better, and when I was in the ring—hearing the roar of the crowd again—I felt like I could do this forever. In the back of my mind, though, I knew that my career as an active wrestler was nearing its conclusion. With all the punishment I'd taken, I was part dead.

I was afraid to leave the business. It was the only thing I really knew or cared about. Without it, I was nil. When you spend every day with a certain type of people, you become a breed of your own. What was I supposed to do now, play golf and regale a bunch of retired insurance salesmen with stories about Mr. Moto and Bearcat Wright? They wouldn't have understood half the shit that came out of my mouth.

I also wasn't sure that I could support myself—certainly not in the style to which I'd grown accustomed. I loved to spend money, and never saved a fuckin' penny.

For a couple of months, I thought about my different options. Then, at the end of 1973, I approached Vince McMahon, Sr. at a show in Philadelphia.

"I think I'd make a good manager," I told him. "I'm a good talker, and have real knowledge about this business. There are a lot of guys out there with talent, but no color. I could go on TV with them, and *give* them the color they need."

This wasn't a line of bullshit. I knew that I could manage because I'd briefly done it in Los Angeles. My protégé was a giant masked guy called The Convict. In L.A., he came and went. But in the 1980s, he was given a hillbilly gimmick and received a little more notice as Uncle Elmer in World Wrestling Federation, getting married in the ring on the *Saturday Night's Main Event* show on NBC.

Vince nodded his big head of swept-back hair. "Well, Freddie," he began, "we already have two managers." That was true. Along with Albano, the WWWF had the Grand Wizard—actually Ernie Roth, who also jetted to different territories to play The Sheik's manager, Abdullah Farouk. As the Wizard, Ernie wore a sequin turban, wraparound sunglasses, and deliberately mismatched clothes, mocking the babyfaces with fifty-dollar words and sarcasm. "I don't know if we need another one."

What could I say? Albano and the Wizard *were* the best when it came to getting "on the stick"—or microphone—and putting over an angle. I thought that I might be able to add something, too, but if I wasn't there, the WWWF wouldn't go out of business.

The Unholy Trinity: Blassie, "Captain" Lou Albano, and The Grand Wizard of Wrestling (kneeling).

I had to wrestle that night, so I went back to the dressing room and got ready. I worked my match, showered, and was preparing to leave when the old man tracked me down and told me that he wanted to continue our discussion.

"Fred, I think I'll make a manager out of you," he said.

I hadn't been so happy since Jim Crockett, Sr. told me that I was going over in the main event, all those years ago in Charlotte. To this day, I don't know why Vince came around to my way of thinking; I never got to ask him before he died, and if he ever shared the information, his son doesn't remember. But his decision to change his mind—

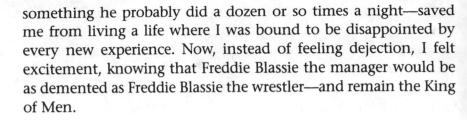
something he probably did a dozen or so times a night—saved me from living a life where I was bound to be disappointed by every new experience. Now, instead of feeling dejection, I felt excitement, knowing that Freddie Blassie the manager would be as demented as Freddie Blassie the wrestler—and remain the King of Men.

THIRTEEN:
LEATHER LUNG

As soon as word of my retirement got out, I started getting calls from wrestlers I hadn't heard from in years. Since I didn't need my ring jackets anymore, they wondered if I was interested in selling them at a discount price. I told them that I wasn't going into the retail business. A few of my jackets went to friends—as gifts, not merchandise. The "give-me boys" got nothing.

As a manager, I had to come up with a whole new wardrobe to wear to the ring. I ended up with a bunch of sequin outfits in a number of colors. Obviously, given my size and the unusual style favored by men in my line of work, they had to be custom made. Fortunately, Miyako was a seamstress with finesse in her fingertips—something I didn't realize when we married. She made every outfit I ever wore as a manager, along with the slacks and Hawaiian shirts I preferred outside the ring.

I took pride in managing, and made my protégé a priority, using the same techniques to draw attention to him as I did to attract publicity to myself when I was wrestling. Because of my reputation, fans often stopped and listened when they saw me on the stick. That was my job, giving my guys "the rub" from my fame. My goal was never adding to Freddie Blassie's notoriety—I had plenty of that already—it was making someone else into a superstar. When the bell rang, I usually backed away from the action, letting the wrestlers work their match. I'd already played my part, building up the confrontation. Now, it was up to the guys in the ring to keep the fans interested.

Of course, there were times when I also raised heat by inserting myself into the proceedings. I'd pace back and forth at ringside, then suddenly stick my cane through the ropes, and jab

Freddie jabs his cane at one of his protégé's adversaries.

my protégé's opponent in the ribs. The fans would boo me for being a dirty bastard, and my protégé for letting someone else fight his battles.

People have asked me if I used a cane because my knees were so bad. But if you look at old tapes of me managing, I'm not hobbling to the ring, leaning on my cane. I'm holding it in my hand, gesturing across the ring or at the fans with it. I was "Classy" Freddie Blassie, The Hollywood Fashion Plate. And a cultured man of my distinction required a walking stick.

Thank God, I was born with a leather lung voice. I'd always been a loudmouth, even as a kid. Back then, of course, that really wasn't considered an asset. After a few years of wrestling on television, I figured out, "Hey, I have this voice. I might as well use it." As a manager, I could yell at my protégés from ringside, and it sounded like I had a microphone in my hand.

With Albano and the Grand Wizard as my peers, I knew that I had a huge challenge ahead of me. Because of his numer-

2

ous mental defects, Albano was probably the most entertaining man on television in the early '70s—a cut above even Archie Bunker and Lou Grant. And the Wizard, a former radio announcer, could have had his own drive-time morning show. Like me, he didn't memorize lines before his interviews. Whatever was in his mind just flowed out. Once, when he was managing "Superstar" Billy Graham, the Wizard predicted that his protégé's upcoming victory against Bruno Sammartino would devastate the morale of Italians everywhere.

"Flags will be flying at half-staff from Mamma Leone's," the Wizard said, referring to the popular Italian restaurant in Manhattan.

Now that I was a manager, I found myself in Albano's and the Wizard's company all the time. Albano and I were already in a routine of driving together, and sometimes I thought of him as a little brother—the kind who follows you around and talks in your ear until you want to throw him off a bridge. I remember driving for miles and miles, listening to him snore because he was sleeping off a drunk. In the dressing room, he'd hide my clothes. I'd come out of the shower and search around, screaming, "There's no clothes. Where the fuck did they go?" Just when I'd think I was going senile, I'd look over and see Albano laughing like a dope.

Lou was very compulsive with his money. In the car, he'd take it out, count it, fold it and unfold it, and put it in order: fives together, tens together, twenties together. This went on everywhere we went, not just once, but five, six, seven times a ride. We were driving with Ed Cohen, the guy who books the arenas for WWE, one time, when I just exploded on Lou.

"Does the fuckin' amount change every time you count it?" I yelled. "What do you think—I'm stealing your money when you're not looking? What the fuck's the matter with you?"

Christ, we were fighting constantly.

In all fairness to Albano, I'm sure I also had a lot of quirks that got under his skin. When you're in this business, you see your co-workers more than you see anyone else. And all those little things become big things until you feel like you can't take it anymore.

I never liked Ivan Putski. He was one of the top babyfaces in the WWWF, doing a Polish gimmick, chewing on kielbasa and singing Bobby Vinton songs after his victories. He was a muscular guy, and the fans loved him. But he acted as if he didn't know that the office was giving him the push. To listen to Putski, you'd think that he did it all on his own.

He was also a fuckin' slob. All day long, he'd eat egg whites. What he would do is peel the outside layer off a hard-boiled egg and let it drop on the dressing room floor. He'd drop the yolk too; he didn't give a damn. After months and months of taking off my shoes at night and looking at egg yolks embedded into the bottom of my soles, I'd had it.

I don't remember what exactly happened. But one day, I was taping an interview in Allentown, while all the boys were standing around, watching. Putski was sitting on a chair, and he piped up with some stupid remark, mocking my promo style. If Albano had come out with it, I probably would have shrugged; Lou and I were at each other's throats all the time, but at least we *liked* each other. I hated Putski. So I stopped my promo and started walking over to where he was seated.

"What the fuck did you say, you gutless motherfucker!" I screamed. *"I'll kick the shit out of you right here!"*

I called him every name I could think of, trying to irritate him enough so he'd get up and take a swing at me. Vince, Jr. and Gorilla Monsoon came running over, getting between us. Putski never got out of his chair. And that was the end of it.

Luckily, for every Ivan Putski I met in the wrestling business, there were a dozen Nikolai Volkoffs.

Josip Peruzovic, a.k.a. Nikolai Volkoff: I was Freddie Blassie's first protégé in the WWWF. They made me into a Soviet bad guy. See, even though I'm from Yugoslavia, my mother's Russian, and I speak the language. My father is Croatian and Italian, and there were too many Italians already in wrestling. Croatians nobody knew about. So I had to be a Russian.

I didn't like the gimmick. I told Blassie, "I don't want to be a bad guy. Yugoslavia's a communist country, and I couldn't wait to escape. I hate communism."

Blassie said, "Well, Nikolai, if you hate those bastards, what's the best way to insult them? Show people how bad they are."

But it was hard. I didn't know what to say on interviews.

Volkoff.

Then, I learned: "You know, in Russia, everybody is rich. We only keep our cars for six months, 'til the style wears out. Then, we call the junk-yard."

You see, a heel can never tell the truth. If you're telling the people things they don't know already, they feel like you're smarter than them, and they don't like that. When you tell a lie—and people know it's a lie—they feel superior to you.

One time, I did an interview and I said, "America did a very cowardly thing by dropping the bomb on Hiroshima and Nagasaki. They killed all the Japanese civilians. And those American soldiers who went in to clean up the mess, they're all today dying from leukemia. And the American government won't do anything to help them."

Guess what? That was no good. The fans watch wrestling to escape. Nobody wants to listen to that shit.

But Blassie understood. He had so much experience, and knew that you couldn't get better without making mistakes. He let me work my gimmick in my own way. He said, "You know how a Russian thinks, how a communist lives. Don't copy anyone else. Be yourself." And that's what I did."

Nikolai couldn't speak English that well when I met him. It was hard to relay information to him, and his accent was so thick that half the time, I didn't understand what he was saying. But I liked the guy. When I found out that he was Croatian, I liked him even more. My stepfather, Eli, was from the same country, and anyone who had something in common with Eli was all right with me.

One thing I respected about Nikolai was his devotion to his family. He had two daughters, and he looked at the wrestling business as a way to pay for their college educations. Instead of eating in the restaurant with the rest of the boys, he'd buy a bag of groceries and cook in a hot plate in his room. If his pants ripped, he pulled out a needle and thread and darned it. Once in a while, I'd buy him a sweatshirt or something because his clothes were falling apart. He'd be so happy, but I knew that he'd never go into a sporting goods store and purchase one for himself. He wouldn't spend a penny to see Jesus Christ jump down Main Street on a pogo stick.

Like a lot of guys from the Old Country, Nikolai was stubborn as hell. You'd say, "White is white," and he'd argue, "No, white is green." He was so bullheaded that, after a while, I'd find myself agreeing with him: "Yeah, Nikolai. You're right. It's green."

What would have been my alternative? Knocking some logic into the guy? He'd be the wrong person to mess with, I'll tell you that. Nikolai was strong as a bull.

We'd do this routine on TV where I'd pull apples out of a bag, and claim that each represented one of his opponents. "You know, it so happens here," I'd say, "that I have two Pedro Morales, and two Bruno Sammartinos." I'd hold up two apples. "*This* is Pedro Morales, and *this* is Bruno Sammartino. Now, the world's strongest man will show you what he's gonna do." I'd raise my voice: "*The most powerful hands in the world!*"

Volkoff would grimace into the lens, squeezing juice from each apple, first with the right hand, then the left.

Vince, Jr. was still working as an announcer then, and he'd grab a fresh apple, and ask, "Do you mind if I hold these apples?" Then, to the audience at home: "*Wow,* these are very strong, very strong."

Nikolai would shove one of the demolished apples in his mouth and chew it, while squeezing another two simultaneously.

"*Oooooow!*" I'd yell, selling the hell out of the performance.

What always amazed me was the way that the juice came out of those apples. I wondered if Nikolai had hidden a rag dipped in water, and kept it in his hand while he was squeezing. When I'd ask him about it, he'd insist that everything you saw was the real thing. I'm not so sure, but Nikolai never let me in on his secret. And with a guy that stubborn, it made no sense probing any further.

While I was managing Volkoff, the WWWF gave me two other protégés, the Canadian Wolfman and Waldo Von Erich—the gimmick brother of Fritz Von Erich, an evil Nazi who became a Bible-quoting Texas hero after he bought the promotion in Dallas. At a certain point, my role became managing the "foreign" wrestlers who passed through the organization—among them, Ivan Koloff, Shozo "Strong" Kobayashi, Masa Saito, Tiger Chung Lee, and the Polish Prince. I also had my share of Americans, like Blackjack Mulligan, Cowboy Stan Hansen, Swede Hansen, and Big John Studd. Victor Rivera and Bad News Allen Coage—later known as Bad News Brown—were in a kind of gray area, since they were from Puerto Rico and Canada, respec-

Black Jack Mulligan.

tively. After a while, the fans stopped keeping track of the birth-places of my charges, convinced that—no matter who I man-aged—I was an "American turncoat" dedicated to obliterating my countrymen.

It didn't take long to be accepted as an equal to Albano and the Wizard—by them, as well as the wrestling public. When teenage boys and barroom bouncers flexed their muscles in the mirror, dreaming of a life between the ropes, the notion of having Freddie Blassie as a mouthpiece often went along with the fantasy.

Vince McMahon: There was this one kid who Freddie called a "goof." There really was no other way to describe him. He claimed to be related to "Nature Boy" Buddy Rogers—never knew if he was or not. He would have done anything to get into this business.

One afternoon, before a TV taping, Freddie had this kid come over for a tryout. He said, "Kid, it's one thing to see your work in the ring"—which was average, at best—"but we want to see what kind of interview skills you have. I'll be your manager."

Freddie tells us that this is his new protégé. Of course, we were all in on it, except this kid. Freddie gets on the microphone: "I'm gonna make this man a champ*peen*. Look at the body on this kid. Take your shirt off." The kid takes his shirt off. "Look at the shape this kid is in. Hell, he can do one-hundred push-ups without taking a breather. Show 'em, kid."

The kid gets down and starts doing push-ups. But after twenty or thirty, he starts to huff and puff a little bit. Freddie says, "Come on, dammit, you can do it! This kid can do one-hundred push-ups! I've seen it with my own eyes!" He starts counting, "Eighty-nine! Ninety!" I mean, this kid is nowhere near eighty-nine push-ups. Freddie's just entertaining us.

Then, he says, "I'll even step over this son of a bitch to add additional weight. Ninety-three! Ninety-four!" Freddie's straddling the kid, but the guy's really tired. He can barely get up off the floor. "You're my protégé, dammit, you can do it! Now come on! Try! *Try!*"

Freddie gets one last push-up out of the guy, and he says, "Now, turn over onto your back." The kid is exhausted. He turns over and when he looks up, Freddie takes his penis out. The kid tries to sit up a little bit, and Freddie's business is dangling right there in front of his face. It was a surreal moment, like, "What the hell am I looking at? I'm having the biggest tryout of my life, and Freddie Blassie is gonna actually manage me, and now I'm looking at his unit? What the fuck just happened?"

Of course, all of us just burst out laughing. I mean, come on, we couldn't contain it. The kid knew he'd been had. And Freddie had a wonderful joke at his expense.

* * *

When it came to ribs, nobody was worse than Mr. Fuji, not even Johnny Valentine. Valentine's ribs were incredibly cruel, but Fuji's were nonstop: in the arena, in hotels, in airports, in restaurants. And Fuji was an instigator. He'd find weak-minded wrestlers and have them do ribs *for* him, just to wreak more havoc. The man was incorrigible.

If you were sitting across from Fuji, drinking a cup of coffee, he was liable to slip in some laxatives when you weren't looking. It would be time to go to the ring, and you'd be on the toilet, shitting your guts out. If he heard you on the phone, making airplane reservations, he'd call up the airline after you hung up, and cancel your trip. You'd miss a booking, lose money, and Fuji would think it was funny.

When I first found out that I was going to be Mr. Fuji's manager, I was less than thrilled. Right away, I told him that he could fuck around with the other boys all he wanted; that was their problem. *I* was off-limits. "I don't want none of your bullshit," I said. "Either you're with me or you're not with me. The first time you cause me a fuckin' problem, we're through. There are plenty of other people I could manage."

At that point of his career, Fuji couldn't afford for me to dump him, and he knew I would if I had reason. So he gave me the respect I wanted. For the rest of my career, I was immune from Fuji's mischief.

To the fans, Fuji was a pretty typical Japanese heel, playing off the prejudice that started when Pearl Harbor was bombed. Like Mr. Moto, he and his tag team partner, Professor Toro Tanaka, would sneak "illegal" martial-arts moves into their matches, and throw salt in their opponents' faces. By the 1970s, though, Japan was different than the country we'd left in ruins at the end of the war. In a lot of ways, Japan was overtaking the United States because we'd become lazy, and the Japanese people showed greater ingenuity. There was a joke about a Japanese mother finding her son jerking off. "Don't do that," she said. "Make a radio."

In greater and greater numbers, Americans were buying Japanese products while, at the same time, resenting the fact that our old enemies were making money off us. It was a sentiment I used to exploit when I'd cut promos with Fuji and Tanaka.

"These two men come from a long line of bankers," I said once. "They have more money than Carter's got pills. You could dump IBM in the ocean, and it wouldn't be missed. But if you pull all the money from the Fuji family off the stock market, the whole thing would collapse."

From Tanaka's point of view, he was passing time with Fuji because it made sense to team up with another Japanese villain. The two certainly had no great admiration for one another. Tanaka was a by-the-book guy, who looked at wrestling as a means to make a living. He wanted to work his match, shake hands with everyone afterwards, and save some money. He was a professional.

If you wanted to talk about an angle beforehand, you always went to Tanaka. He was the ring general, who'd lead everyone else in the match. Fuji was certainly a good performer, but you couldn't control him. So, in addition to worrying about their opponents, Tanaka had the responsibility of making sure that Fuji didn't get out of hand. I guess he did a pretty good job because, years later, when Tanaka was relegated to working these tiny independent shows to earn a few extra bucks, Fuji himself had become a manager.

Some of my protégés became close friends. The Rock's grandfather, High Chief Peter Maivia, and I were already buddies from California. He was older by the time he entered my stable, so his movements were limited. But he still knew how to sell out buildings. In the ring, he acted as if he were impervious to pain, just standing there as his opponent kicked and punched him, then flooring the guy with a big headbutt. Because of his Pacific Island ancestry—he had tribal tattoos up his legs and around his midsection—he was called "Savage" Peter Maivia.

Maivia was not a savage; he was a gentleman. But when provoked, he may have been the meanest man in wrestling. He was a true blue wrestler, who could snap your arm or leg if you

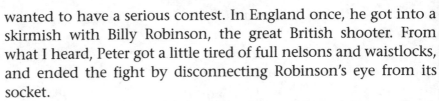

wanted to have a serious contest. In England once, he got into a skirmish with Billy Robinson, the great British shooter. From what I heard, Peter got a little tired of full nelsons and waistlocks, and ended the fight by disconnecting Robinson's eye from its socket.

Another guy I really enjoyed was Spiros Arion, a Greek wrestler who'd resettled in Australia. Whenever Spiros visited the United States, he was catapulted into the number-one contender's spot in the WWWF. But I think that he's best remembered for an angle in which he disgraced Chief Jay Strongbow, tying him up in the ropes, and shoving the feathers of his beloved Indian headdress in his mouth.

Because so many Greeks owned restaurants around the country, I went out of my way to travel with Arion when I managed him. Whichever town we were in, all the restaurant owners knew Spiros. It didn't matter if it was noon or two in the morning, when you hung out with Arion, you were going to get a good meal.

202

Johnny Legend: When Freddie became a manager, a whole new group of fans were exposed to him—people who'd never seen him wrestle, but couldn't tear themselves away when they heard him on an interview. Not all these people were traditional wrestling fans, either. Freddie didn't realize it, but what he did transcended wrestling. He'd become something of a cult figure.

By the late 1960s, I was a musician, and started thinking that it would really be great to do a record with Fred. I wasn't really sure how to pull it off. It was pretty hard to do anything with wrestlers back then. I knew that Freddie had appeared on *The Dick Van Dyke Show* a few years before (doing a new dance called "The Twazzle," which consisted of Freddie putting Dick in an airplane spin), but those kinds of things were rare. Wrestlers and promoters were afraid that if they got involved with too many outside things, it would leave the business open to scrutiny. And they didn't want their secrets getting out.

It took a couple of years to actually consummate the project. In 1975, we went into the studio. My friend, Pete Cicero, and I had written a song called "Pencil Neck Geek," and I wrote one by myself called "Blassie—King of Men."

In the studio, recording "Pencil Neck Geek."

203

* * *

    I didn't know anything about music. I couldn't keep a beat, and never even sang in the shower. These guys had already recorded the music by the time I got into the studio. Then, they handed me the lyrics and just told me to talk through the songs.

"Pencil Neck Geek" was supposed to be a tirade against my opponents. The words were pretty true to my own, and went like this:

> If there's one thing lower than a sideshow freak
> It's a grit-eating, scum-sucking pencil neck geek
> You see, if you take a pencil that won't hold lead
> Looks like a pipe cleaner 'tached to his head
> Add a buggy whip body with a brain that leaks
> You got yourself a grit-eating pencil neck geek.

On the other side of the record, I recorded "King of Men." It was the kind of tribute to me I should have received twenty years earlier:

> You can go through life acting mean and sassy
> But you better play it cool when you come around Blassie
> And that goes for all you women, living or dead
> You'd best watch your step when you're messing with Fred
> I've said it before and I'll say it again
> My name is Blassie—King of Men.

Johnny Legend: Over the years, we released these songs a couple of times—we made about fifteen hundred copies—and on an album called *I Bite the Songs*. There was a weird novelty radio program called *The Dr. Demento Show,* and I knew that Dr. Demento himself was a big Blassie fan. Right after "Pencil Neck Geek" was pressed, my sister actually drove to his house and gave him the record. The show was syndicated in over one hundred markets and, within weeks, it was number one on the program.

Some people think I made a lot of money off "Pencil Neck Geek." But a lot of what Dr. Demento played was unavailable, or audiocassettes of things people recorded at home. People would tape his show, and that's how stuff would circulate. I called every major label and said, "Hey, I have a hit record here." And they'd tell me, "We're looking for long-range plans, bands that are gonna be around for ten years." It was very frustrating. Freddie Blassie didn't fit into that category.

* * *

The only thing I ever got from "Pencil Neck Geek" was a cheap little check, and a lot of publicity. To this day, people bring it up all the time. About a week ago, a fan was telling me, "I was just listening to 'Pencil Neck Geek.' Boy, that was a great song." I thought, "Jesus Christ. This guy is stuck for an answer when you say hello." A great song? Shit.

I still haven't learned the words to it.

FOURTEEN:
ALI VERSUS INOKI

In 1976, Japanese superstar Antonio Inoki announced that he was going to battle Muhammad Ali in a "wrestler versus boxer" match in Tokyo. The clash would be broadcast at closed-circuit locations around the United States, including the Olympic Auditorium, Omni in Atlanta, and Shea Stadium in Queens—home of baseball's New York Mets—where the WWWF was also going to include its own card of live wrestling. To build interest, Vince McMahon, Sr. asked me to become Ali's special adviser, traveling with him, and cutting promos on Inoki.

It was easy for me to cut a promo on Inoki because I considered him a conceited jerk. In 1972, he helped start the New Japan wrestling promotion and pushed himself as the reincarnation of Rikidozan. He was a very good athlete, but the Japanese people thought that he was even better because he forced himself on them. Still, he didn't mean shit to American fans and it killed him. He desperately wanted to headline arenas in the United States, but every time he crossed the Pacific Ocean, he was a flop. That was going to change, he figured, the moment he slaughtered Muhammad Ali at Budokan Hall.

Hisashi Shimma: I was Inoki's promoter in Japan, and I knew how much he wanted to receive worldwide acceptance. There was no athlete more famous than Muhammad Ali, so a victory over Ali would change everything. But we had to convince Ali to agree to this match. We did it by offering him $6 million—more money than any boxer had ever received.

* * *

When I began traveling with Ali and his entourage, he told me that he was a Freddie Blassie fan. He used to watch me wrestle in his hometown of Louisville, Kentucky, and even copied my line of delivery. You had to admire Ali. He had a magnetic personality, and could back up every boast when he laced on the gloves. Yet, deep down inside, I wanted Inoki to win. After spending my entire adult life being called a fake, I couldn't wait to see a fellow wrestler knock The Greatest on his ass.

In the weeks leading up to the match, Ali and I bounced all over the United States, humoring the press with catch phrases, and hitting every talk show. In Japan, Inoki defeated Dutchman Willem Ruska, a two-time Olympic gold medalist in judo, with three back suplexes in a worked match—to prove that he could beat any athlete from the legitimate sports world. I appeared with Ali on ABC's *Wide World of Sports* with Howard Cosell, as he squashed two jobbers at an American Wrestling Association (AWA) event in Chicago, then squared off against Buddy Wolfe, a wrestler who wasn't exactly a superstar, but still won his share of matches.

207

Ali was such a great entertainer that he could have been one of the boys. He sold Wolfe's wrestling maneuvers, then pounded him. After the match was stopped because of blood, manager Bobby "The Brain" Heenan stepped into the ring. Ali hit him with a haymaker, allowing Heenan to take a dramatic bump on the canvas. It was just what ABC wanted. They showed it again and again on instant replay.

The most memorable angle leading up to the Ali-Inoki match took place on a WWWF program in Philadelphia. Gorilla Monsoon was wrestling Baron Mikel Scicluna, as Ali stood outside the ring, heckling. Monsoon threw Scicluna over the ropes, and Ali decided to come in and take his place. The fans were going wild, as Muhammad removed his shoes and went into the Ali shuffle. But while he was showboating, Monsoon bent down, draped Ali over his shoulders, twirled him around in an airplane spin, and dumped him on the mat.

The exchange was probably the highlight of Muhammad Ali's little foray into the wrestling world. It certainly was a hell of a lot better than his match with Inoki.

*   *   *

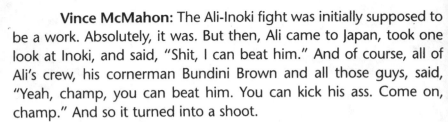

Vince McMahon: The Ali-Inoki fight was initially supposed to be a work. Absolutely, it was. But then, Ali came to Japan, took one look at Inoki, and said, "Shit, I can beat him." And of course, all of Ali's crew, his cornerman Bundini Brown and all those guys, said, "Yeah, champ, you can beat him. You can kick his ass. Come on, champ." And so it turned into a shoot.

I was in Japan, supposedly representing my father, and Freddie and I had a wonderful finish set up which no one to this day knows about. Gene LeBell—Mike LeBell's brother—was the referee. He was a wildman and a good friend of Freddie's. Gene would have done anything in the world that Freddie said. Freddie's idea was that Gene would bring a blade with him into the ring, and maybe wear it on his thumb. As soon as there was any contact at all, Gene was going to put himself in the middle of the combatants, and accidentally trip or whatever and headbutt Ali. And when he did, Gene would have to go up with his hands, you know, to check the forehead of Ali. Then, Gene would start sawing Ali with the blade. Even Ali wouldn't know what the fuck was happening. We had the deal where Ali wouldn't get hurt, but he would bleed profusely because Gene would do a damn good job, and Gene would have to stop the fight because of blood. Thus, the fans would want to see a return match or some damn thing.

I don't know how my Dad found out about this—wind, telegraph, telephone—but he knew I was up to no good over there. He said, "Goddammit, you're dealing with Muhammad Ali, and you're going to get into trouble legally in Japan. Get your ass back here now."

Masashi Ozawa, a.k.a. Killer Khan: I was a "green boy" at the time, training at the New Japan dojo. I remember hearing that, after Ali arrived in Japan, he kept changing his mind. First, he wanted to do the match, then he didn't want to do the match, and so forth. The arguing went on up until the day the fight was scheduled to take place. No one could agree on the rules. Tickets were sold out, and Ali was threatening to go home. So Inoki had to agree to certain conditions in order to get Ali in the ring.

Hisashi Shimma: Inoki wanted to be able to use his elbows and karate chops. But he agreed to no thrusts to the throat, chokes, or bare-knuckled punches to the face. Inoki wanted to be

able to use his knees, but he could not kick Ali with the bottom or side of the foot. Essentially, Inoki could wrestle Ali—if he got a hold of him—and Ali could box. He had gloves on, so that limited other things he could do. But he could punch Inoki if they were down on the floor.

We held a press conference in Tokyo, just before the match took place. Ali was shadowboxing. Inoki was sparring with some of the New Japan green boys. At a certain point, Muhammad looked over at the wrestlers and began taunting them. Like a good heel, I mocked them, too. This really pissed them off. They didn't seem to understand that Vince McMahon, Sr. had put me in this position. They thought that, by siding with Ali, I'd betrayed the wrestling fraternity.

In reality, once I realized that there wouldn't be any funny business in this match, I assumed the role of an honest-to-goodness adviser. I understood wrestling, and now I was going to

pass on some of that knowledge to Ali, teaching him about coun-
termoves, and avoiding certain pitfalls on the mat. Here's how I
looked at things: I wasn't doing anything to hurt wrestling. In
fact, because of all the publicity surrounding this match, we
might even win a few new fans. Rather, I was working to defeat
Antonio Inoki, a guy I never liked to begin with.

The New Japan wrestlers couldn't understand this logic.
To them, Inoki was the messiah, and I was an infidel. When I got
near a few of these guys at the press conference, they grabbed me
and tried to pummel me. Well, I'd been in this kind of situation
before, and began hitting right back. Ali jumped in to try to break
things up, but I shoved him out of the way. This was inside stuff
between members of the wrestling family.

Needless to say, when the match took place on June 25,
1976, people were pretty fired up.

At Shea Stadium, thirty-two thousand fans watched a
WWWF undercard featuring Bruno Sammartino—in his second
title reign—against Cowboy Stan Hansen. This was Bruno's big
comeback, after Hansen legitimately broke his neck in a stiff—or
exceptionally rough—match a few months earlier, and the fans
went berserk when Sammartino retained his championship. And,
in another "wrestler versus boxer" confrontation, Andre the
Giant clashed with "The Bayonne Bleeder" Chuck Wepner, the
hard-luck fighter whose story was the inspiration for *Rocky*. The
match ended when Andre lifted Wepner and threw him over the
ropes. Then, both corners piled into the ring—with Gorilla
Monsoon at the center of the action—and started brawling.

There were fourteen thousand people in the building at
Budokan Hall, but the gate was $2.5 million—an amazing
amount when you consider that no U.S. house at the time had
ever exceeded $150,000.

After the hype was over, and Ali and Inoki actually had to
fight each other, everything got blown to hell. Feeling restricted
by the rules of the match, Inoki spent most of his time on his
back on the mat, wiggling around like a crab and kicking at the
back of Ali's legs. The strategy—forcing Ali to fall onto the canvas,
where Inoki could stretch him into submission—would have
worked with a lesser man. But Ali was a class apart from the rest
of the world. The few times he fell to the mat, he was able to

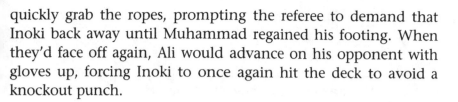

quickly grab the ropes, prompting the referee to demand that Inoki back away until Muhammad regained his footing. When they'd face off again, Ali would advance on his opponent with gloves up, forcing Inoki to once again hit the deck to avoid a knockout punch.

Killer Khan: I was standing at ringside, with a number of other students from the New Japan dojo. Ali wouldn't let Inoki lure him into a brawl. If it had been Mike Tyson, I'm sure the result would have been different. But Ali was a very intelligent fighter, who thought before he acted. He had come all the way to Japan, and wasn't going to lose to this Japanese guy. I guess that's why the match turned out the way it did.

I knew Inoki's strategy before many other people because I'd practiced with him. Along with other students from the dojo, I got in the ring with a rubber pad around my thighs, tied with a rope and wrapped with a towel. After feeling those kicks, I thought that Ali would eventually lose. I was amazed that Ali could take it for so long. It was a shitty match, but I don't think Inoki had any other choice. One punch from Ali and that's it. Game's over!

Between rounds, Ali would come back to the corner, and say to his manager, Angelo Dundee, "I'm sick of this. Just let me get down on the mat with him, and knock him out."

Dundee would look at me to try to talk some sense into Muhammad. "You don't want to do that," I'd say. "This guy really knows how to *wrestle*. All he has to do is get behind you with an armbar or an anklelock, and he'll break your arm or leg."

This happened over and over again. Ali really believed that he could handle Inoki. I knew what was going to happen if Ali followed his own instincts, and Dundee agreed with me.

So Ali kept going out, circling Inoki for fifteen rounds and getting kicked in the back of the knee and thighs. From where I was standing, I could see that his legs were all black and blue.

In the stands, the fans were bored out of their minds. From the fifth or sixth round, they were booing. Hell, I was even losing interest, and I was part of the match. My wife was in the crowd, and heard the spectators yelling in Japanese,

"Get Ali out of the ring, and put in Blassie! We want to see a show!"

When the bout ended in a draw, I shook my head from side to side. I couldn't comprehend why Muhammad took this match in the first place. I know he got a great payday, but there were a lot of things Muhammad Ali could have done for money. From the second he arrived in Japan, everything was stacked against him. There was no way that he was going out a winner.

In the upper deck of Budokan Hall, a couple of fans began throwing chairs. Although the closed-circuit telecasts in WWWF cities did well—Bruno and Andre, after all, put on great performances—people trashed the venues in other parts of the country.

After the fight, I went backstage and tried to work my way over to Inoki's dressing room to pay my respects. The green boys from the New Japan dojo were guarding the door and refused to let me go through. That fuckin' Inoki sure had them brainwashed. They couldn't figure out that with his performance that night, he did more to hurt the business than I ever could.

Hisashi Shimma: Ali had to go to the hospital after the match with a blood clot in the back of his legs. A lot of people believe that the punishment he endured that night shortened his career as a serious boxer. The Japanese fans were disappointed because they really believed that Inoki would win. No one expected him to lie on his back for the entire match. It took us a long time to win a lot of them back. Inoki was satisfied because he'd fought to a draw with the great Muhammad Ali. But he's the only one who thought it was a good match.

FIFTEEN:
"HE LOVES HUMAN FLESH"

Blassie uses his teeth on an opponent's skull.

Old wrestlers never really pack their trunks away. You find yourself sitting at ringside thinking, "Shit, I can do a better job than these guys." Even after I turned sixty, I still believed that I had a couple of good matches left in me. So I made a few brief comebacks, wrestling my old rival, John Tolos, and Andre the Giant for Mike LeBell, and even had a novelty match with Lou Albano—after he turned babyface—at the Nassau Coliseum on Long Island.

I still thought that I was a tough wrestler. And considering my age and injuries, I did a pretty fair job. But I was way past the point where I belonged in the ring. Fortunately, I didn't get hurt. In fact, Andre the Giant ended up doing more damage to me away from the arena.

I should have been prepared for this, but I didn't see it coming. I was on a hotel elevator with a couple of the other boys, when the doors opened and a smiling Andre got on. He nodded at us, then—once the doors closed—turned around and passed gas. That little elevator stunk like a skunk. It was terrible. We wanted to get out, but Andre blocked the doorway. We threw punches at him, and hit him with tackles. But Andre didn't move. It was like water off a duck's back.

It was during one of my comebacks that I first ran into Andy Kaufman, a stand-up comedian who was starring in the hit TV show *Taxi*. Andy was a maniac wrestling mark; he'd seen Bruno Sammartino defeat "Nature Boy" Buddy Rogers for the WWWF Championship live in Madison Square Garden, and repeated the story about twenty times a day. He wore a title belt in his comedy act, calling himself the "Intergender Wrestling Champion," and—like the shooters in the carnivals when I was growing up—offered ten thousand dollars to any woman from the audience who could beat him (none did). He also had a heel alter ego named Tony Clifton.

At some stage of every wrestler's career, he probably becomes a mark for his own gimmick, but Kaufman took it to a new level. During negotiations, he demanded that Clifton appear on two episodes of *Taxi*—along with a separate dressing room and parking space. When shooting was scheduled to begin, Kaufman showed up, acting like Clifton, decked out in jewelry and chain-smoking, with a prostitute on each arm. At first, everyone was amused, assuming that Kaufman was toying with them. But he refused to come out of character, verbally abusing the rest of the cast until security dragged him off the set. Just before he was booted outside, he hollered, "You'll never work in this town again!"

Kaufman idolized me. Whenever he heard that I was

214

appearing at the Olympic Auditorium, he tried to sneak back-stage. I remember heading to the shower after a match, and see-ing this skinny guy standing there, gazing at me strangely.

"Hey, you're not allowed back here," I shouted.

"I don't care."

"Well, *I* care. Get the hell out of here."

The next week, he was back again.

"What are *you* doing here?"

"Mr. Blassie, Mr. Blassie, I just need to . . ."

"I don't give a shit. I ran you out of here last week, you goddamn nut. Now, get lost before I beat your fuckin' brains out."

The guy left, and I turned to one of the ushers. "Who let that ding-a-ling in here?"

"Well, that's Andy Kaufman."

"Who the hell is Andy Kaufman?"

"He's a comedian."

"A comedian, huh? Well, he's not too funny to me."

A week later, I was walking to my car, around the corner from the Olympic, after the matches. Most of the fans were gone, but here was Andy Kaufman, standing on the sidewalk.

"Mr. Blassie?"

"Jesus Christ, not again." I was beginning to think that I was going to have to kill this guy to get rid of him. The man was obsessed.

"Mr. Blassie, if I can just have a few seconds of your time. . . ."

I looked him up and down. He certainly seemed harmless enough. So I gestured him over. Kaufman began talking about his life, his obsession with wrestling, his career in Hollywood. I don't know if he was trying to be funny or not, but I began laughing at the things he said. At eight years old, he told me, he began doing jokes and magic tricks at birthday parties. He refused to accept any cash, as long as the adults left the room. His routine was not for a mixed audience. In Hollywood, when he got bored, he'd occasionally take out a prostitute. He wouldn't ask for sex; he just wanted to go out on a date. Then, at the end of the night, he wouldn't pay. "Why should I?" he reasoned. "All I did was make a new friend. What's wrong with friendship?"

He seemed like such a lost soul. I wondered if he really was

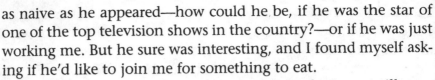

as naive as he appeared—how could he be, if he was the star of one of the top television shows in the country?—or if he was just working me. But he sure was interesting, and I found myself asking if he'd like to join me for something to eat.

We went to this bar/restaurant, where they were still serving sandwiches. After he rambled on for a little while, I said, "I can't quite figure you out. What exactly is your goal?"

"I want to be the Freddie Blassie of the entertainment world. You're one of my heroes, you know."

Well, I certainly couldn't fault him for his taste. And the longer we talked, the more I became an Andy Kaufman fan. Yeah, he was a kook. But he was really funny.

Lynn Margulies: I became Andy Kaufman's girlfriend after my brother, Johnny Legend, introduced us. Andy and my brother, of course, had a lot in common. They were both fanatical Freddie Blassie fans.

Andy liked Freddie because he was flashy like another one of his heroes, Elvis Presley. But Freddie was also smart and funny, so, to Andy, he was even more appealing. Freddie was so raucous, had perfect comic timing, and personified everything Andy loved about wrestling: the circus aspect of it, and getting people riled up over something that's maybe not real.

When Freddie was around, Andy was wide-eyed. Sometimes he'd just stand there and not say anything. That's how he acted when he was in awe of someone.

Andy based his entire career on pro wrestling. He'd point at his head and say, "I've got the brains," like "Nature Boy" Buddy Rogers. And just like wrestlers—who took what they were doing so seriously that they wouldn't admit that it was a show—Andy didn't let people in on the joke. Of course, that pissed them off even more. But Andy would say, "The more they hate you, the better you're doing," like he was a wrestling villain instead of the star of a sitcom.

One Thanksgiving, he went to Kutscher's, the big resort in the Catskills, to perform. He made this speech about how he always vacationed at Kutscher's as a kid, and asked his family to join him onstage. All these old people in the audience were charmed, seeing this Jewish kid who'd made it big and still loved his family. Then, he asked his brother and sister to reenact these shows they used to do at home when they were little. It was so dumb. He had his brother singing "La Bamba." Andy was just making fools out of his whole family. The audience was incensed: "What the hell is this? How dare he bore us with this stuff, and waste our time?"

In 1979, he went on the live TV show *Fridays,* and got into a fistfight with a couple of the crew members. The next week, he came back and apologized, saying that he was about to get kicked off the cast of *Taxi* because of the incident and his wife had left him. And he began to cry. The whole thing was a put-on, but he kept it going. A few months later, he returned and introduced Kathy Sullivan, an actress who'd been on *The Lawrence Welk Show,* as his wife. He said he was now a born again Christian, and the two began singing gospel songs. To this day, a lot of people believe that his conversion was sincere. So, like in wrestling, the people weren't sure what was real and what was a work.

Believe it or not, Andy's confidence grew after he became friends with Freddie. Freddie was someone he admired, and being accepted by him had quite an impact. And if Blassie could keep getting away with these kinds of stunts, Andy figured, so could he.

217

Even after I hung up the trunks again and returned back east, Andy kept coming around the Olympic Auditorium. In the middle of a show, he'd try to rush backstage. "I just have to talk to Roddy Piper," he'd say. "I need to talk to Chavo Guerrero." To wrestling people, it didn't matter that Kaufman was a TV star. No one was going to burst into the dressing room while the matches were going on.

Piper and Guerrero—brother of current WWE star Eddie Guerrero, and father of Chavo Guerrero, Jr.—were the two biggest names LeBell had at the time. They had some wild matches, fighting in the street and even on buses. But they couldn't duplicate the kind of business that Blassie and Tolos drew. The Los Angeles promotion was a territory in decline. Roddy and Chavo were young, talented guys, but soon they'd move on to other places, where they'd become even hotter stars. And there was no one waiting in the wings to step into their shoes. LeBell limped on for a few more years, until, in 1982, he sold his promotion to Vince McMahon, Jr., as he expanded his company across the United States.

By then, the World Wide Wrestling Federation had short-ened its name to World Wrestling Federation, and its champion was Bob Backlund. Backlund was much different than Sammar-tino and Morales. While they were ethnic heroes, he was a former amateur wrestling champion at North Dakota State University, and as American as apple pie. When he got on the stick, he was deadly serious, speaking in a low, determined voice about the importance of leading a clean lifestyle as much as his upcoming match.

You'd think that a guy like me wouldn't want anything to do with a square like Backlund, but nothing could have been fur-ther from the truth. There was no bullshit about him. He loved the sport of wrestling, didn't drink or do drugs, and was a won-derful family man. As World Wrestling Federation Champion, he believed in being a role model to fans, as well as the other boys. And he was. His parents must have been wonderful people to raise a kid like that. He was a real asset to the business.

Of course, it was my job to make a buffoon out of Backlund. The Grand Wizard came up with the name "Howdy Doody" for him because of his red hair and childlike facial fea-tures. On interviews, I'd mock both Backlund's skills and his morals. But—now that I'm no longer managing—I admit that I never meant a word of it.

Bob Backlund: Blassie would make a lot of fun of me. That was his job. But I took it very personally. I was pretty into being a role model, and took the business maybe too seriously. He said a lot of things that I didn't want to hear. To other people, it was all enter-tainment. But it had a different effect on me. I wasn't really smart to the business back then. I finally figured it all out in 1994, when I became a heel myself.

I couldn't count the number of matches Backlund had against George "The Animal" Steele. Whenever the weather got warm, Steele appeared in World Wrestling Federation—he'd been doing it for years—battling the champion throughout the sum-mer, then vanishing again in the fall.

Fans never caught on that Steele was only around in the summertime because he was supplementing his salary as a schoolteacher. Today, it would be all over the Internet. But then, how could people have figured it out? On television, Steele acted like a Neanderthal, not talking, flapping his arms around, sticking out his tongue—he'd dye it green by sucking on Clorets before his matches—and biting the turnbuckles until the stuffing poured out and stuck to his sweaty body. Steele had a bald head and a back so hairy, I understand why his wife wanted him on the road in the summer. Sleeping with him must have been the same as wearing a fur coat.

In the early 1980s, "Nature Boy" Buddy Rogers—now retired—was brought back to the World Wrestling Federation to do an interview segment called *Roger's Corner*. One week, when I was managing Steele, we both came on as guests. George didn't tell me what he was going to do beforehand, and I didn't ask. I knew that, even though his character didn't talk, Steele would give the fans something to remember.

As Rogers was making his introductions, Steele sat—his eyes vacant and bottom lip drooping—holding something to his hairy chest. Within seconds, fans realized that it was a cigarette lighter. Steele flicked it a few times, like he'd just discovered fire and wanted to ignite himself.

I jumped out of my seat and patted him down.

"This guy'll set himself on fire," Rogers protested. "Hey, this guy's some kind of nut!"

I turned to Rogers and screamed at him, "Don't call him a nut!"

"He's playing with fire, and there's hair on his chest."

"That's right. And he'll set you on fire, too."

Rogers gestured at George. "Pull this guy out of here! He's out of his mind!"

I acted outraged and offended: "Don't talk that way about George!"

I never met any of the students at the high school where Steele taught in Michigan, but I imagine that it must have been hard to keep a straight face when he blew his whistle in the gymnasium or coached football. Then again, once you got past his gimmick, George was an extremely articulate guy who commanded attention with every word he said. In fact, I envied George. He had everything I didn't have: education.

* * *

Jim Myers, a.k.a. George "The Animal" Steele: Freddie was just real special. I always thought the name "Classy" Freddie Blassie was perfect for him because that's what he was—a classy guy. When he was your manager, you felt lucky. It was never just a job for him. He wanted to entertain the people, and make his protégé look like a superstar.

I remember wrestling in Madison Square Garden, with him in my corner. He did everything to get the crowd hot, but he'd direct all their attention towards me, not him. By the time the bell rang, they were responding to whatever I did. I knew that Blassie had a long wrestling career, and was a master of crowd psychology. And I appreciated him using that wisdom to help me. After the match was over, I walked up to him in the dressing room, shook his hand, and slipped him a hundred. A hundred dollars was nothing to Freddie Blassie, but I wanted to show him I was grateful for everything he added to the match. I looked up at Freddie, and I noticed that he had a tear in his eye. He said, "No one's ever respected me like that."

Spending time with Blassie, I saw the effect he had on fans over a career of fifty or so years. After we both retired, we went out to California to do a radio show. We were walking back to the hotel, when some guy pulled up and said, "You're Freddie Blassie." He pointed at an old man in the passenger seat, and told us, "My Dad has Alzheimer's. He doesn't recognize anyone. But he just looked out the window and recognized you." We went over to the car, and Freddie had a rational conversation with the guy. The son couldn't believe it. He said, "I haven't heard him speak like that in ten years." It gives me chills just thinking about it.

Another veteran who ended up as my protégé was Ray "The Crippler" Stevens. Stevens had been wrestling since the early 1950s, when he was a teenager, and he was one of the most gifted men alive. I don't remember him putting in a hell of a lot of time into training. But when the bell rang, his instincts would take over. His old tag team partner, Nick Bockwinkle, used to talk about how Stevens would stand on the apron, flirting with a broad in the second row, not watching a thing. When Bockwinkle tagged him in, Stevens would jump right in the ring and wrestle a great match, without missing a beat. He was a natural. Unfortunately, he had no discipline—and that's what probably prevented promoters from making him into a world champion.

In World Wrestling Federation, Lou Albano and I were Stevens's co-managers. He was supposed to be a soft-spoken guy on the surface, then snap and commit acts of incredible violence. In 1982, he did an angle where he allegedly hospitalized Jimmy "Superfly" Snuka with a piledriver on the concrete floor. The fans' hearts went out to the Superfly, and—as a result of The Crippler's actions—he became a babyface and one of the biggest drawing cards in World Wrestling Federation at the time.

As convincing as Stevens could be when he was working, he could also be a complete goofball. Albano and I would be walking to the ring with him, and that son of a bitch would step on my heel.

"Don't do that, you motherfucker," I'd growl under my breath.

It was like talking to the wall. Stevens would step on my heel again and again and again—and I'd be stumbling around so much, the fans would think I was drunk.

221

When Ray died of a heart attack in 1996, I looked back at those days, and felt happy that I got to spend some time with that bastard before he retired. It was a period when World Wrestling Federation was going through a transition. There was a nice mixture of veterans and young wrestlers who watched the legends closely, then improved on what they did.

"Rowdy" Roddy Piper would soon come in, and establish himself as the company's top heel. He'd capture the fans' attention in some of the same ways I did, wrestling rugged matches, and whipping himself into a lather and spouting out entertaining gibberish on interviews.

Piper was such a good speaker that he was given his own interview segment, *Piper's Pit*. Piper—a Canadian who portrayed himself as a Scotsman—would sit there in his kilt, ripping his interview subjects to pieces with one-liners, and occasionally springing on them with his fists. Probably his most memorable exchange took place with Snuka. Piper spent most of the interview mocking Snuka's Fiji Island heritage. Then, he astonished

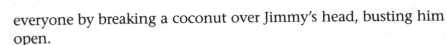

everyone by breaking a coconut over Jimmy's head, busting him open.

I remember going on *Piper's Pit* with Kamala, "The Ugandan Headhunter." Kamala was actually James Harris, a large black man from Mississippi. Harris had a wonderful sense of humor. Unfortunately, nobody could understand a fuckin' word that came out of his mouth. So he didn't say anything in interviews, and came to the ring wearing war paint and holding a spear, his big belly flopping over a loincloth. In the middle of a match, Kamala would slap his stomach, as if it was some kind of good-luck ritual brought over from darkest Africa.

"This man knows nothing about wrestling," I declared on *Piper's Pit*. "All he knows is brutality. . . . He's a cannibal, you know?"

"I don't know that," Piper replied in a quivering voice.

"He loves human flesh," I shouted, as Piper's body shook. If a lunatic like Roddy Piper feared Kamala, the fans thought, then "The Ugandan Headhunter" must really be a killer. It was a message Piper sold without ever taking a blow; it was all done with body language, and the strength of his unusual personality.

Adrian Adonis was a completely different type of character. When I managed Adonis in 1981, he wore a black leather jacket, and played a thug from Hell's Kitchen. He claimed that he'd been left on a stoop in Manhattan as a baby, earned himself a spot in the *Guinness Book of World Records* by slamming a stickball over sixty sewer caps in eleven seconds, and got his first job on the docks at age seventeen. Adonis described himself as "a kid who worked his way out of the gutter. . . . This is one mean, bad dude. I'm not just a pretty face, daddy. I am beautiful."

I thought that Adonis was an excellent worker, and a nice, decent guy. He appreciated the role that I'd played in the business, and acted very respectful towards me. It made me sad, later on, when he put on a tremendous amount of weight and was turned into "Adorable" Adrian Adonis, this clownish, chunky, gay character who wore pink trunks, makeup, and a garter belt. But even then, he remained one of the best bump takers in the business, twirling himself upside down and bouncing high while selling his opponent's moves.

His death was one of wrestling's great tragedies. In 1988, after leaving World Wrestling Federation, he had gone up to Newfoundland to wrestle. He was riding in a van with three other wrestlers—Dave "Canadian Wildman" McKigney, and Mike and Pat Kelly—and a moose stepped into the road. The van swerved to avoid it, and crashed, killing Adonis, McKigney, and Pat Kelly.

Freddie with his protégés: Adrian Adonis and Jesse "the Body" Ventura.

Adrian's name came up again after Jesse "the Body" Ventura was elected governor of Minnesota in 1998. I managed both when they were billed as the East-West Connection. Back then, Jesse never told the fans that he was from Minnesota; it wasn't as glamorous as his invented hometown, San Diego (in fact, Ventura used to call Minneapolis and St. Paul "Turkey Towns One and Two"). So Ventura claimed to be a Californian, and Adonis, of course, was the New Yorker. Because Adrian was such a stellar bump man, a lot of people said that he did all the work,

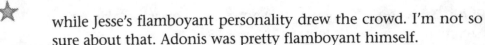

while Jesse's flamboyant personality drew the crowd. I'm not so sure about that. Adonis was pretty flamboyant himself.

After Jesse was elected, he told his opponents, "My way or the highway." He had the same attitude in World Wrestling Federation. It didn't matter to him that managers traditionally did the talking for their protégés. Jesse was good on the stick, and insisted that he could get his points across better than I could. We didn't argue about it. Like I've said before, my goal as a manager was never getting Freddie Blassie more interview time. If Ventura wanted to do the talking, he was free to try.

Because Ventura had a really impressive body, he was booked into a feud with Tony Atlas, a likable African-American man who was a former Mr. Universe. Atlas was doing a straight, babyface interview one week, when Jesse and I came out to interrupt him.

Ventura was wearing floral print tights, a feather headdress, and sunglasses. Right away, the two of us began demeaning the way Atlas won his Mr. Universe title.

"He was the only one in the contest," I said.

On the other hand, I continued, Ventura had been "Mr. Tijuana, Mr. Long Beach Pier, Mr. Cucamonga. The list is endless."

"Tony Atlas has no legs," Ventura insisted. "Mr. Atlas is thin through the center. He has no girth to his back. His arms are out of proportion to the rest of him. His neck is skinny. Where's his abdominals?"

Vince McMahon, Jr. was doing the announcing. "There's only one way to determine who has the best body," he said. "How about a posedown?"

Naturally, both parties agreed. But when they met in the ring to compare bodies, the rules stipulated that the winner would be determined by fan applause. Since Atlas was the babyface, we knew the outcome ahead of time.

"What do these idiots, these morons, know about posing?" Ventura protested after Atlas was decreed the unequivocal winner. "It's the national pastime of California. And I don't see one Californian in this crowd. These people are prejudiced against Freddie Blassie and, because I am his protégé, they are prejudiced against me."

Now, Atlas commandeered the microphone: "What's all

this jaw-jacking you doing? It was your big mouth that got us into a posedown, and the people was the judge."

"Let me tell you something, Atlas," Ventura interrupted. "You are a house with no furniture. You look good. But there's nothing in there."

We then arranged for the two to engage in an arm wrestling contest the next week. Ventura showed up with a spangly band around his right bicep, and a purple feather swinging from his ear. A table was set up in the ring. Ventura locked grips with Atlas, then jumped up and rushed over to me so we could confer. When they clamped hands together again, Jesse complained, "He's pulling on my thumb!"

Finally, the competition started. The two went back and forth, until Atlas appeared to be on the verge of victory. Then, Jesse poked him in the neck, dragged him across the table, battered him with a chair, and turned the table over on top of him.

After such an elaborate buildup—thanks largely to Ventura's performance—World Wrestling Federation fans couldn't wait to put down their money to see the two clash at their local arena.

225

I imagine that Jesse used the same skills when he was running for office, convincing the people of Minnesota that they had no choice but to cast their vote for him. As a wrestler, he knew what the people wanted to hear, and when they wanted to hear it. Still, I believe that if he was good enough to become governor, then I'm good enough to become president. I was his manager, after all. He was one of my boys.

Once in a while, I'd be given a protégé who didn't want me as his manager. Dick Murdoch was one of these guys. I understand why he thought that he was so special: he'd been a full-fledged star in the United States, Japan, and Australia. But men like Ray Stevens and Peter Maivia were accomplished veterans, too, and understood that the Blassie name only added to their allure. Certainly, Murdoch was not one of my favorites. And if you look at old tapes of us walking to the ring together, you'll see me either in front or behind him—never side by side. Of course, the fans couldn't tell that anything was going on. We kept those kinds of disagreements private.

It was a hell of a lot more pleasant managing Killer Khan. He'd grown up in Japan, watching me battle Rikidozan, and would have settled for just meeting me and getting my autograph. When he found out that I was going to be his manager, he thought he'd died and gone to heaven. He was sure that—with Blassie in his corner—he was going to become the number-one wrestler in the United States.

Killer Khan: Most of the Japanese wrestlers who'd worked in America before me were relatively short physically. I'm six-foot-five, very tall for a Japanese wrestler. And I have big hands and a big head—a very unique look. I could have billed myself as Japanese, but that would have been a throwaway. There was no "Mongolian" wrestler at that time.

You might not believe it, but Karl Gotch came up with the idea. Gotch was a great shooter from Germany, and one of my mentors, along with Antonio Inoki. He wasn't a gimmick guy at all, but

he understood that you had to sell tickets in America. He actually drew a sketch of my costume. I had a goatskin vest, and Mongolian hat—a fur hat with a little point on the top. I shaved my head, except I had a small braid hanging down the back.

In the World Wrestling Federation, I was also told to spit out this green spew, and "blind" my opponents with it. I didn't like that very much because I take a lot of pride in my wrestling technique. Winning a match with green spew is like winning a match by breaking a beer bottle over somebody's head. In my mind, even a mark could win against a wrestler with a beer bottle.

I'd always feared Freddie Blassie. I didn't know that he was any different than the guy who came to Japan when I was growing up, and bit my heroes. Then, I got to know Freddie, and he was a very gentle man. He was generous in showing me what wrestling was all about.

He said, "Don't take bumps left and right. When you do, it doesn't mean anything, and the fans don't care. Sometimes, twisting your face and groaning like you're in pain is more effective than a bump."

I listened to everything Blassie said, and was very excited

when World Wrestling Federation told me that I'd be working against Andre the Giant. When I was training in the New Japan dojo, and Andre would come on tour, I was one of the boys who'd carry Andre's bags, and run errands for him. But when we got in the ring, we had an accident. I wanted to kneedrop Andre's chest. But he started to get up, and I landed on his ankle. This wasn't an angle. Even though Andre was a big guy, I weighed three hundred pounds. If you drop that kind of weight on someone's ankle, it's going to break.

Right away, Vince McMahon, Sr. decided to take advantage of the circumstances. He said, "Let's use this injury to draw business."

World Wrestling Federation mentioned Andre's injury on every broadcast. As he recovered, the promotion began talking about a possible rematch. Pat Patterson—a great wrestler who was then semi-retired and working as a color commentator—interviewed Killer Khan and me on television. Because Khan couldn't speak English, he didn't say a word. He darted his head from side to side, twisted his face, and stared at the ceiling like a madman, while I did the talking.

227

"Mr. Blassie, I went to the hospital when Andre was there," Patterson said.

"Too bad he came out," I interrupted.

"He was in a lot of pain," Patterson continued in his French Canadian accent. "They put two steel pins in his foot. And I'll tell you one thing. Andre does have a big heart."

"And he has a big head, too," I added. "A big head with nothing in it."

A few weeks later, Andre himself came out on television on crutches, and was interviewed at ringside. He was talking about his slow road back to World Wrestling Federation when I barged in with Killer Khan. *You're all through!* I yelled.

Andre lifted his crutch and whacked me with it. When I stumbled backwards, Khan rushed forward, grabbed the crutch, and hit Andre across the back. Then, I took my walking stick and slammed it against Andre's cast. Andre reached down and moaned. Now, the fans thought, the leg wouldn't heal properly, giving Khan the advantage in their upcoming battles.

* * *

Killer Khan: When Andre and I finally got in the ring together, we worked pretty stiff. We hit each other with very hard chops, and the matches were very believable. If I went loose on Andre, he'd get mad and give me a good hard one, and say, "Come on! What are you doing? Let's go!"

There's one episode I remember where I was really exhausted and lying on the mat, flat out, straight up, looking at the ceiling. And here comes Andre with this humongous ass, and he just sat on my face. At that moment, I actually thought that I was going to die.

* * *

Hulk Hogan when he first wrestled for WWE was managed by Freddie.

Vince, Sr. saw a lot of potential in Hulk Hogan. He was a good-looking kid—blond, muscular, and tan—but very inexperienced when I began managing him in 1979. Because of his size— he was billed as six-foot-nine and 330 pounds—he was eventually matched up with Andre. In a few more years, Hogan would be the number-one babyface in the history of pro wrestling. But, for this conflict, he was still a heel.

We began the feud in a pretty typical way. Andre was being interviewed, when Hogan and I showed up and made a challenge for the next week. I did all the talking, sticking my hand in Andre's face and calling him a "monstrosity." It's hard to imagine it now, but Hogan said nothing. His days as one of wrestling's most gripping interviews were still in the future. Now, he was listening and learning from "Classy" Freddie Blassie.

When Hogan and Andre finally wrestled on TV, I played my part, getting heat on Hogan by pointing at Andre, then jamming my thumb towards the canvas before the match began. The bell rang, and the two exchanged power moves. Hogan bodyslammed his enormous opponent, a feat of strength few exhibited against "The Eighth Wonder of the World." But as the heel, Hogan had to play the coward. He retreated outside the ring, where I was waiting with a foreign object. I slipped it into Hogan's elbow pad, and he reentered the ring, flooring Andre with a clothesline. When Andre got up, his face was covered with blood, and fans knew that this war would have to be settled in a larger venue.

229

In 1987, when Hogan and Andre met in the main event at *WrestleMania III,* the confrontation was billed as some kind of dream match. Many were unaware that the two had battled on August 9, 1980, on another "supercard" at Shea Stadium. Bruno Sammartino defeated his onetime pupil, Larry Zbyszko, on the show, while World Wrestling Federation Champion Bob Backlund teamed with former titlist Pedro Morales to win the tag team belts from the Wild Samoans, Afa and Sika. In the Hogan-Andre matchup, the babyface went over, just as the fans wanted. But Hogan didn't lose any of his luster in his defeat. He was portrayed as a star on the rise, and the people only wanted to see him more.

* * *

Terry Bollea, a.k.a. Hulk Hogan: Traveling to Japan with Freddie Blassie as my manager was a real education. He told me, "Don't sell anything. When the Japanese guys hit you, act like King Kong. Don't even flinch. Keep walking towards them." And so basically, I went out and did what Freddie told me to do, and made all the wrestlers over there hate me. But it basically proved a point—that the big, American, Madison Square Garden wrestlers that Freddie brought over were impressive main-event guys.

After my first match, we went out to celebrate. Freddie said, "We never pay for food in Japan, Hogan." I said, "What do you mean, 'We never pay for food'?" And he goes, "In every restaurant, there are two or three guys who know karate or jujitsu. We'll bet that they can hit you as hard as they can in the stomach, sidekick you if they want to, and if it doesn't hurt, the deal is that we don't have to pay for food."

At the time, I was much bigger, about sixty pounds heavier than I am now. And my stomach was always big, but it had extra padding. Freddie took advantage of that. The whole time I was in Japan, we never paid for food.

Even in the 1980s, Blassie was like a god in Japan. The people were scared to death of him. I would walk to the ring with Freddie—this older gentleman whose wrestling career was over—and he would pick up his cane and give the fans a certain look, and they would spread like ants, running from him. He was something.

SIXTEEN:
"WHAT THE HELL...HAPPENED TO THE HUMAN RACE?"

I don't know when Vince McMahon, Sr. was diagnosed with cancer because nobody told us. At the arenas, he still looked healthy and distinguished. I did know that, in 1982, Vince, Jr. and his wife, Linda, had purchased the company. But that didn't seem unusual. Vince, Sr. had taken over from his father, and now another McMahon was assuming control. The old man was still very much a force behind the scenes, and we all figured that he was coaching his son on the fine points of the business.

What nobody predicted was the way that Vince, Jr. would transform professional wrestling. He'd been taking mental notes since his father first allowed him in the dressing room, and now things were about to change fast. The gentleman's agreements that divided North America into territories might have worked for the oldtime promoters, but Vince, Jr. was in a class by himself. He began using cable television to showcase World Wrestling Federation. Occasionally, he'd show matches from other organizations, too. The promoters were happy to provide the footage because they wanted the free exposure. Of course, Vince had a different agenda. He intended to go national, and steal the other guys' talent away.

Later, when he accomplished his goal, the old promoters called Vince a scumbag. Well, they were the fuckin' scumbags. If they'd paid their wrestlers what Vince was offering, they would have had loyalty. Instead, they worried about keeping their little kingdoms in place, and working together to make sure the wrestlers got screwed.

In World Wrestling Federation, you started getting paid not only for wrestling, but for merchandise sales, among other things. Vince thought of everything—World Wrestling Federation coffee mugs, pillowcases, ice cream, and video games. Eventually, there was even a "Classy" Freddie Blassie action figure, holding up a cane. And Vince had the balls to say what our business really was—"sports entertainment."

I'll tell you this: If there hadn't been a Vince McMahon, Simon & Schuster wouldn't be publishing a book about an old warhorse like me.

Before World Wrestling Federation exploded, Andy Kaufman asked me for a favor. Could I talk to Vince, Sr. and see if the company wanted to use Kaufman as a talent? I told Andy that I'd look into it, but I never did. I knew how the old man thought. The company was selling out arenas everywhere. Why did he need this nut running around? What if Kaufman got injured and sued? Or, even worse, what if Andy went back to Hollywood and told the media things that were supposed to be kay fabe?

Andy wanted to get in in the worst way, and pleaded his case to Bill Apter, a well-liked wrestling magazine writer and photographer. Apter told Kaufman to go down to Tennessee, and do something with Jerry "the King" Lawler. Lawler—the number-one babyface and part owner of the Memphis territory—wasn't as conservative as Vince, Sr., and was usually up for anything. Kaufman traveled south, called the people "hicks," and taunted them by twisting up his face and slurring out interviews in a fake southern accent. On April 5, 1982, he and Lawler wrestled at the Mid-South Coliseum. The match ended with Lawler turning his skinny opponent upside down, and driving his head towards the mat with a piledriver. Kaufman claimed that he had a broken neck, and wore a brace everywhere.

When the two appeared on David Letterman's show a few months after the incident, they got into another brawl. It was a lot like Tolos and myself on *The Steve Allen Show,* with one notable difference. Kaufman was screaming one obscenity after another, and wouldn't shut up. He and Lawler left the set in a shambles, and NBC executives had serious discussions about banning Kaufman from the network.

I'd never seen anyone so happy. Kaufman was finally a wrestling heel, just like his hero, Freddie Blassie.

Johnny Legend: In 1981, a film was released called *My Dinner with André*. For two hours, you sat there and watched two men—Wallace Shawn, a playwright, and a theater director named André Gregory—eat dinner. I suffered through the whole thing. It was so pretentious. When I left the theater, I felt motivated to take revenge.

My idea was to do the same kind of movie with Andy Kaufman and Freddie Blassie. I ran into Andy Kaufman at a World Wrestling Federation show at Madison Square Garden, and spoke to him about it.

"Will this be something like *Rocky Horror?*" he asked.

"No, this is something they'll show *instead* of *Rocky Horror*, a midnight movie, a cult classic."

Andy was being advised to stay away from wrestling at this point; his handlers thought that it had already hurt his career. But he still went out with me to see *My Dinner with André*. About thirty minutes into it, he fell into a dead sleep, then went home. After that, he started calling me at like three in the morning, saying, "When are we going to do this?"

We shot *My Breakfast with Blassie* in 1982 at Sambo's, a diner type of place, in Los Angeles. The movie was unscripted. I'd learned in the past that anytime you try to give Fred a script, you're doomed.

We had a simple three-camera setup—a master shot, and one camera on Fred, and one on Andy. When they sat down, I said, "Let's get an audio level. Why don't you guys talk to each other?" I swear, they launched into an opening scene that went seventeen to twenty minutes. It was absolutely priceless. That's why the audio is so shaky in the beginning. I couldn't yell "cut" or anything. They could have gone on forever.

I can't say that I understood the point of *My Breakfast with Blassie*. All we did was talk about bullshit. I guess there must have been a lot of Andy Kaufmans out there, if people were willing to pay for a movie ticket, just to hear my opinions about day-to-day garbage.

When the host of Sambo's led us over to the table, Andy

said, "Thank you," without even thinking about it. "What are you thanking him for?" I asked. "He didn't do anything that he wasn't supposed to do." I saw that Andy was staring at me, listening like I was God delivering the Ten Commandments to Moses. "You don't have to be that nice. *Jesus.*"

After that, I peered down at the menu, and noticed this really idiotic illustration on the cover. "This looks like a drawing thing for a little kid," I told Andy. "Doesn't look like much of a menu."

A pretty Asian woman came by to serve us. I shifted my attention away from Andy, and saw that she was pregnant. "Looks like we have two people waiting on us, you and someone else," I pointed out. "What nationality are you?"

"Thai."

"I was over in your country, Bangkok, but I never seen a pregnant Thai girl before. Come here."

The woman moved closer, and I placed a hand on her stomach. "I always like to rub," I said. "Like a Buddha. Good luck."

The waitress thanked me and returned to the kitchen. Looking back over at Andy, I said, "Don't have to tip her as much when we leave now."

As always, Andy was nervous around me. He asked me what he should order, and even wanted to know if I thought it was okay if he took off his jacket. "I mean, we're friends of good standing," I answered. "You can do anything you want. You want to get up and dance a jig, dance a jig. Do anything."

After we chatted awhile, I discovered that we both had a bit of a fixation with germs. In fact, Andy was the only guy I knew who also carried hand towels around with him. He appreciated it when I mentioned that I tried avoiding the handrail when I walked down the stairs. On airplanes, I always wiped off the armrest. "You never know what scurvy pencil neck geek was sitting there or anything," I emphasized.

"You know what I really can't stand?" Andy asked. "When people come up to me and ask for an autograph and then they shake my hand. You know, and I just went to the bathroom and I washed my hands, and I want my hands to be like a surgeon when I eat."

I couldn't have agreed more. "The reason I don't like to shake hands with nobody is because I don't know if they went to the men's room, been to the toilet, then maybe their finger went right through the tissue." I made a windmill motion with my hand, explaining my philosophy about toilet paper. "I use half a roll if I gotta go. I make damn sure my hand doesn't go through. Plus, the fact that I scrub underneath my fingernails very good and everything."

Suddenly, I realized that we were sitting in a restaurant. "What the hell are we talking about that for?" I said. "We're eating breakfast."

Boy, was I a mark. Here I was, apologizing to Kaufman for bringing up distasteful subject matter, when he and his friend, Bob Zmuda, had something really disgusting planned for later on.

As we were eating desert, Zmuda sat down at our table. I'd never seen him before, and thought he was a ding-a-ling fan. "I just wanted to ask you something real quick," he said to Andy. "I noticed that you were giving autographs out to people before. And I realize it takes a lot of time for you, with eating and everything, to give an autograph to people. So I thought that maybe I could *give* you something."

I should have realized that everything wasn't kosher when Kaufman started giggling. "I'll accept something from my fans," he said.

Zmuda covered his nose and pulled out a long piece of fake snot, before walking off. "I'm ready to puke in that asshole's face," I told Andy.

I continued eating, when suddenly Zmuda came back and spewed out some chunky substance on the table. I recoiled, sure that it was vomit.

"I did my dirt," Zmuda insisted. "I did my dirt."

Zmuda disappeared again, and Andy began selling the stunt. "Did you smell it?" he asked me. "Sour. Sour."

As he rushed to the bathroom, I began muttering to myself, so pissed off and confused that I forgot that the cameras were rolling.

"What the hell ever happened to the human race?" I wondered.

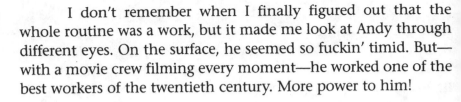

I don't remember when I finally figured out that the whole routine was a work, but it made me look at Andy through different eyes. On the surface, he seemed so fuckin' timid. But—with a movie crew filming every moment—he worked one of the best workers of the twentieth century. More power to him!

In 1983, the year *My Breakfast with Blassie* was released, the NBC show *Saturday Night Live* took a poll. Should Andy Kaufman be allowed to continue coming on the program, deviating from scripts, challenging women to wrestling matches, and causing other types of disruptions? More than 169,000 people voted yes. Unfortunately for Andy, almost 196,000 voted no. By now, *Taxi* was also off the air, and the only person in the television industry who seemed to be in Andy's corner was David Letterman. Hell, Andy could have done anything short of murder on that show, and Letterman would have thought that it was great.

Kaufman and I were both invited on the program to promote *My Breakfast with Blassie*. Andy announced that this was just the first of many Blassie-Kaufman collaborations. Next, he wanted to do a remake of the old Laurel and Hardy film, *Sons of the Desert*. When Letterman asked to see a sample of what we'd do for the cameras, Kaufman and I improvised.

"You've got us into another fine mess again," I hollered, "you pencil neck geek!"

"But, Fred . . ."

"Will you cut that out? Here you come on again, stuttering again, like you always do! I told you, when you talk to me, come out with it!"

Andy started to blubber.

"Now he's crying again!" I yelled. "You hear that pencil neck geek cry? You ever see a grown man cry?"

Suddenly, Andy simmered down, straightened out his face, and nodded at Letterman, indicating that the shtick had ended. A second later, he was on to something else, claiming that he'd chosen me to manage his Hollywood career.

Of course, Andy already had a manager, George Shapiro.

But the idea of "Classy" Freddie Blassie managing a TV star was a funny concept, so I went along with it. "As an entertainer, he's great," I told Letterman. "He can outsing Bing Crosby, Perry Como, Elvis Presley. And *dance*—he makes Fred Astaire look like he has two left feet!"

Andy kept trying to interject something.

"Keep quiet! I'm talking about you now! I'm handling you! Why don't you get over there and show the people how you can sing!"

"I don't want to do that."

I pointed at the studio band. "You know how to play 'Jambalaya,' don't you?"

As the group began tuning up, I grabbed Kaufman by the collar, and dragged him towards the microphone. "When I tell you to sing," I screamed, "you sing!"

Kaufman stood with the band for a few seconds, seemed to have second thoughts, and walked briskly away. I waved my cane and chased him back to the microphone.

It appeared that Kaufman didn't know the words, so he warbled out the tune, making ridiculous sounds—a combination between the gimmick southern accent he used to rile up the fans in Memphis, and chicken noises. The director cut away to me, sitting next to Letterman, looking disgusted. Only when Kaufman got to the chorus, did he shriek out, "Jambalaya!" before breaking into high-pitched giggles.

After the song ended, Letterman declared, "That was the stupidest thing I've ever seen in my life."

"It only goes to prove," I replied, "you don't know good talent."

Kaufman looked over at the host. "I only want to say one thing, David. David, I didn't want to sing."

"You didn't do your best," I scolded Andy.

Around Thanksgiving of 1983, Andy's family noticed that he had a cough that wouldn't go away. They urged him to go to a doctor. When he did, he was diagnosed with large-cell carcinoma. Even though he didn't smoke, he had lung cancer.

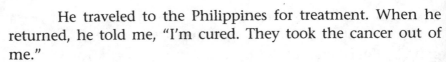
He traveled to the Philippines for treatment. When he returned, he told me, "I'm cured. They took the cancer out of me."

I said, "They must have left a hell of a scar."

"No," he answered, "there's no scar. The doctor just reached into my stomach and pulled the cancer out."

I was shocked. Andy—the man obsessed with turning everything into a work—had paid thousands of dollars to go overseas, and got scammed. But unlike a wrestling angle—or the stuff Kaufman did in his comedy show—there was nothing entertaining about this. While Andy could have been in a hospital, getting real treatment, some quack was probably holding a catgut over Andy's face, claiming that it was a cancerous tumor.

Andy also told his father, Stan, that he was cured. But Stan wasn't that gullible. He noticed that his son was dragging his leg, and said, "If you're cured, how come you're limping?"

On May 16, 1984, I got the heartbreaking news. At age thirty-five, Andy Kaufman had died at Cedars-Sinai Medical Center in Los Angeles.

Lynn Margulies: One of Andy's big regrets was that he didn't get to make that Laurel and Hardy movie with Freddie. He really wanted to do that. Oh, it would have been great.

At the funeral, Freddie was one of the few dignitaries, shall we say. No one came from *Taxi*, except [his on-screen wife] Carol Kane. I don't remember any other famous people there. They all made excuses, and said, "I didn't know about it." These guys didn't know but, somehow, Fred Blassie knew about it. He knew about it because it meant something to him. I think he really loved Andy.

I walked into the temple with Miyako, and there were three aisles in the chapel. The family was in the middle aisle, so we sat down on the left side of the building.

An usher came over to us and said, "Mr. Blassie, Stan Kaufman would like you to sit with the family." Miyako and I went right to the front. "Andy spoke about you all the time," his father told me. "He really liked you."

"That shows you he was nuts." I smiled, and he smiled back.

After the service, there were a bunch of fans outside, and a group of reporters. One fella held up a microphone and said, "Sir, could you kindly tell us about your relationship with Andy Kaufman? We know who you are, but could you please identify yourself on tape?"

"Freddie Blassie," I began. I was going to spell my name, but I just started crying. No matter how much I tried, I couldn't stop. Finally, I decided that I couldn't finish the interview, and walked away with my wife. I didn't want to think about Andy's death anymore.

In the short time I knew him, we raised holy hell together. There was nothing I couldn't do with Andy. He was my friend, but he seemed more like a son, a son who admired everything about me. At the funeral, I thought about my own children, and kind of wished that some of that quality had rubbed off on them.

I'll never meet another guy like Andy Kaufman. He was a good kid, period.

SEVENTEEN:
"WHAT CANE?"

Sometimes, when new heels came into the company, Vince, Jr. would ask me which I wanted as a protégé. "I picked one last time for you," he'd joke. "Now, it's your turn." During one of these sessions, I told Vince that I wanted to manage the Iron Sheik.

The Iron Sheik's real name was Hussein Khosrow Vaziri, and he'd been an excellent amateur wrestler in Iran—so much so that, despite his anti-American gimmick later on, he was an assistant coach for the U.S. Olympic team in both 1972 and 1976. He'd been trained for pro wrestling by amateur great Verne Gagne—owner of the American Wrestling Association (AWA)—in a camp that included former Olympians Ken Patera and Chris Taylor, as well as the man who many consider the best day-to-day wrestler of his generation, "Nature Boy" Ric Flair.

As the Iron Sheik, Vaziri shaved his head, wore boots that curled up in front, and constantly rubbed his fingers across his black handlebar mustache. When the babyface rallied in his matches, the Sheik would suddenly drop to his knees and begin bowing, like he was deep in prayer. On the road, he acted so berserk that he made Lou Albano look like a clerk at a religious bookstore.

The Sheik was fond of getting up in the middle of the night, waking another wrestler, and challenging him to a shoot in his hotel room. I guess, after all those years of playing a character, Vaziri just had to make sure that he still had it.

But you had to give him credit. He took his gimmick as seriously as he'd taken his amateur training, and tried living it as much as possible. Once, he nearly missed his flight at Los Angeles

240

The Iron Sheik.

International Airport, and went running through the terminal—in his *kaffiyeh,* or Middle Eastern headdress, and open ring robe—screaming, "*Wait!* Hold the plane for the Sheik!" During the Persian Gulf War, when he briefly played a Saddam Hussein loyalist named Colonel Mustafa, he left a match at Busch Stadium in St. Louis and walked to his hotel in an Iraqi army uniform.

No matter where the Sheik went, he got instant heat by

waving a flag decorated with an image of the Ayatollah Khomeini—in those years when Americans were still seething over the 1979 U.S. hostage crisis in Iran. I remember when *World Wrestling Federation Magazine* (now *WWE Magazine*) wanted a few shots of us standing in front of the UN in Manhattan. We were driven to the front of the building, and took a couple of pictures, pointing over our shoulders and at each other. Everything was going fine until the Sheik asked, "Is it okay to take out my flag, Mr. Blassie?"

Before I could answer, he was waving the Ayatollah's face at passing cars on First Avenue. "What the hell's the matter with you, you crazy son of a bitch?" I yelled. "Put that thing away! Do you want to get us all arrested by the FBI?"

When we were cutting a promo, the Iron Sheik wouldn't understand a lot of what I was saying, so he'd quiver, and nod his head up and down. Then, he'd shout in his thick Iranian accent, "Cam-er-a-man, *zoom* in," brush his hands over his barrel chest and abdominal muscles, and mutter, "Look at this. Look at this."

Occasionally, he'd say something to me in Farsi, and I'd pretend that I understood. "He just informed the people that, shortly, their gasoline will go up over a dollar a gallon," I said during one exchange. "See, I don't have to worry about that because I have a lot of friends in Iran. I'm a household word."

Another time, on *Piper's Pit,* Roddy told the Sheik, "The Americans don't give you the respect you deserve. They're spitting at you. They're being pigs to you. And I'm very sorry. I'd like to make a public apology myself."

I looked over at Piper approvingly. "You know, Roddy Piper," I said, "the first time I met you, I knew there was something about you. You're all class."

The Sheik and I whispered back and forth, before I continued, "Mr. Piper, I don't want you to think we're being rude by whispering in your presence. But the Sheik just informed me that you can go down and buy any car that you want, and send him the bill."

"I want a Rolls," Piper replied deviously.

"*Hah!*" I laughed. "We love to make you happy."

Probably the funniest rib I ever pulled on the Sheik was when we were doing an interview, and I revealed something that he'd told me in private. Looking into the camera, I said, "I want to speak to Ayatollah Khomeini directly. Listen, you pencil neck geek, the Iron Sheik says he likes you. Well, he hates your guts. He still likes the Shah of Iran."

The Sheik jumped in front of me and began waving his hands. "Stop that shit!" he yelled. "Stop that shit! The people in Tehran, Iran, they find out about this!"

He was in a mad panic because he still had family in Iran, and he didn't want them to get arrested, tortured, or even worse. "I was just joking," I explained.

But the Sheik wouldn't calm down. "No, no, I see the red light on the cam-e-ra," he insisted. It took a while before he realized that everybody—from Vince down to the camera crew—just wanted to have a laugh at his expense.

The Iron Sheik was one of a large collection of wrestlers who were finding a home in World Wrestling Federation, as Vince McMahon began spreading the company across the United States. No longer would guys have to jump from territory to territory, we heard. After all, Vince was going to put the territories out of business. You could sign with his company, and stay there for your entire career.

Bob Backlund had been the champion since 1978, but by the end of 1983, his days at the top were ending. There was no denying his talent. But he didn't have the same pizzazz as an Iron Sheik or Roddy Piper. There were big changes ahead, and unfortunately, they didn't seem to involve Backlund. The Iron Sheik and Freddie Blassie, however, would play key roles in Vince's plans.

Bob Backlund: I don't think I was ever really over with the people. I was over with Vince, Sr. and he wanted me to be the champion. His son took over, and made a business decision. It was a decision that broke my heart, but I can't say it was the wrong decision. He made millions of dollars with that decision.

Hulk Hogan: I never thought that I'd return to World Wrestling Federation after I left there to play Thunderlips in *Rocky III*.

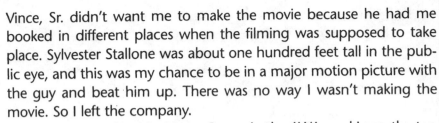

Vince, Sr. didn't want me to make the movie because he had me booked in different places when the filming was supposed to take place. Sylvester Stallone was about one hundred feet tall in the public eye, and this was my chance to be in a major motion picture with the guy and beat him up. There was no way I wasn't making the movie. So I left the company.

I was working for Verne Gagne in the AWA, and I was the top guy there. There was talk about making me their champion. Verne was trying to hook me up with his daughter. Vince, Jr. was doing this thing where he was putting stars from other promotions in *World Wrestling Federation Magazine* because he was planning to recruit them soon. Steve Taylor, the company's photographer, came to Chicago for an AWA show. As I was leaving the ring, he said, "Hulk, let me get a picture." Then, he shook my hand and slipped me a card. "Here's Vince's phone number. He wants you to call him tonight."

Vince flew out to my house, and we made a deal. I would go with him and become World Wrestling Federation Champion. But then, I got there, and Vince, Sr. said that maybe we should wait. Bob Backlund wasn't happy with the situation. He didn't think that anyone should have the belt who he didn't consider a real athlete. I said, "Well, I talked to your son and he told me something different." I had just burned a bridge, and was thinking of going back to the AWA to rebuild it. So Vince, Jr. stepped in and said, "No, Dad, I want to do things this way." And the dad passed the torch to his son.

Since Backlund and Hogan were both babyfaces, they couldn't wrestle each other. That wasn't the way things worked in 1983. So World Wrestling Federation needed a transitional champion. The Iron Sheik suddenly became very valuable because he had amateur credentials. In other words, Backlund could lose to him, and justify it.

Just before Christmas, the Sheik and I went on TV, and predicted that Backlund would be dethroned on December 26 at Madison Square Garden.

"Can we take that as a resolution for next year?" Robert Debord, the interviewer, asked me.

"You can take that for what you want—resolution, disillusion, anything. I guarantee you, this is the oil well, the Iron Sheik,

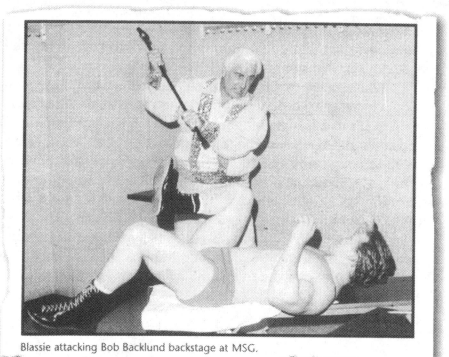

Blassie attacking Bob Backlund backstage at MSG.

next World Heavyweight Wrestling Champ*een*. Just mark that down. Mark it *dooown!* Nineteen eighty-four is the year for Blassie."

We also began setting up the circumstances for Backlund's loss. It was very rare that a heel won an important title fair and square. He had to do something treacherous beforehand to weaken the babyface. In the Sheik's case, his weapon would be his Persian exercise clubs.

When the Sheik worked out, he twirled these seventy-five-pound clubs over his shoulders. They were very difficult to handle, especially for American wrestlers unaccustomed to this type of training. Because Backlund was so well conditioned, he was one of the few who could manage these objects. So we turned that into an angle.

The Sheik was in the ring, maneuvering his clubs around his head, while I boasted that there wasn't one athlete in the dressing room strong enough or tough enough to do the same thing. This brought out Backlund, of course. He removed his suit jacket, then his vest, then his shirt. Standing bare-chested, he

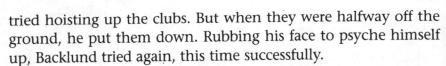
tried hoisting up the clubs. But when they were halfway off the ground, he put them down. Rubbing his face to psyche himself up, Backlund tried again, this time successfully.

I have to say that it was a pretty impressive feat. But, obviously, we weren't going to let the story end there. The Sheik clenched his hands together, raised them over his head, smashed Backlund on the back, and began stomping on him. As the Sheik and I fled, color commentator Pat Patterson told the fans that one of the clubs had landed on the champion's neck. To emphasize the point, Backlund contorted his face, grabbed his neck, and stumbled around the ring.

On the night of the match, fans believed that the champion was coming in at less than one hundred percent capacity. Just to rile up the crowd, I wore a white *kaffiyeh* for the occasion, and called myself "Ayatollah Blassie." I actually believe that I got more heat in that outfit than if Khomeini had been standing in the ring himself. See, I'm not sure that all of the fans would have recognized Khomeini; quite a few preferred wrestling magazines to newspapers. But they knew Freddie Blassie, that's for sure.

Even before Backlund left the dressing room, the Sheik pissed off the people even more by snatching the microphone and shouting, "Iran, Number One!"—triggering an angry response of "U-S-A! U-S-A!"

Backlund walked through the crowd, shaking hands, in a stars-and-stripes ring jacket. But as soon as the bell rang, he was in trouble. The Sheik wrapped his robe around the champion's neck, choking him. At one point, Backlund tried rolling up his foe for a pin. But as Bob attempted a neck bridge, he suddenly grabbed his shoulder, and flopped to the mat. A few seconds later, the Sheik squatted behind Backlund's prone body, clamped two hands under his chin, and bent him backwards in the Camel Clutch. Playing the brave warrior, Backlund refused to submit. But his manager, Arnold Skaaland—supposedly fearing for his protégé's safety—threw in a white towel, ending the reign of the company's last old-school champion.

Holding my walking stick, I hugged the Sheik in the center of the ring, and—as doctors tended to Backlund—fastened the belt around my boy's waist. The whole thing might have been predetermined, but my enthusiasm was real. As I've said before,

I grew close to my protégés, and was thrilled that, for the rest of his life, the Sheik would be remembered as a World Wrestling Federation Champion. I remembered my own WWA title reigns, and felt proud that now, I'd also achieved this honor as a manager.

The next weekend, an interview with the Sheik and I was shown on World Wrestling Federation programs. "I just called home a couple of day ago," the new titlist began. "I talked to Ayatollah Khomeini, and I talked to all the family. I heard big celebration in Tehran, Iran. Everybody happy. Everybody know I deserve to get that gold," he held up the belt, "especially I have the best manager in this country, Ayatollah Blassie. I heard the Ayatollah Khomeini and all the Iranian people, Muslim people in America, in the Middle East, in Asia, all the Muslims are happy about me. Everybody know. Intelligent people went to library, they read about the Sheik. . . . I was the best, I was the amateur. Now, I'm the best of professional wrestling, toughest, roughest sport in the world. I have to say God bless to my manager, Ayatollah Blassie, and Ayatollah Khomeini."

Hussein Khosrow Vaziri, a.k.a. the Iron Sheik: There was an Iranian newspaper in Los Angeles that put my picture on the cover, with the belt and the Ayatollah Fred Blassie. I showed the newspaper on TV, and told everybody it was the newspaper from Tehran, Iran. And I said that, if no American can stop me, I'm going to take the belt with me back to the Middle East.

I had the most heat in World Wrestling Federation history. Somebody called the office and said, "If the Sheik comes to Albany, New York, we're going to shoot him." And Vince, Sr., God bless him, said, "I want you to cancel. Don't worry. I take care of you money-wise." So I did what Mr. McMahon told me.

I knew I was supposed to lose the championship to Hulk Hogan on January 23, 1984. But then, Verne Gagne called me, and said, "Give me a favor. Don't drop the belt to that Hollywood bleached blond jibroni, Hulk Hogan. When you wrestle him, break his leg, take the belt, then come back to me in Minnesota. Remember, I was your coach. I'll give you a hundred thousand dollars. We'll book you all over our territory as the real champion."

I said, "Coach, I'll let you know after twenty-four hours."

But Mr. McMahon, Sr. was very good to me. And I believe in the Islamic religion, and I cannot cut the hand that feed me. Maybe one hour before my match with Hogan, I take Mr. McMahon, Sr. and Jr. in the private locker room of Madison Square Garden and explain everything. And they both kiss me and hug me, and then told me, "Sheik, you good man."

I went into the ring and had a fast match. When you lose a championship in a fast match, you can still keep your heat. People think it was just an accident. After the match was over, the McMahons were very happy. Vince, Sr. hug me again, and said, "Good match." Then, Hogan shakes my hand, and said, "Thank you very much. I owe you one." But then, he forgot that he owes me something. But no problem. I did not double-cross the company.

Vince, Sr. opened the curtain for Hulk Hogan as he left the dressing room to win the title from the Iron Sheik. It may have been the old man's last official act. Less than four months after the match, he died. He got to see the beginning of *Hulkamania*, but never lived to witness everything his son did to change the business. Vince, Jr. likes to say that if his father knew what the company would become, he'd turn over in his grave. But I think that the old man would have also been pleased that Vince became the greatest promoter of all time.

With the names coming into World Wrestling Federation—Paul "Mr. Wonderful" Orndorff, the Junkyard Dog, Greg "The Hammer" Valentine (Johnny's son, but a hell of a lot nicer)—Vince had an all-star team. The difference between him and the other promoters was that he understood what to do with it. For example, he knew that the Iron Sheik and Sgt. Slaughter had trained for the business together, and were good friends. That meant that, if they got into the ring, they'd trust each other and put on a great show. At the time, though, Slaughter was a heel, playing a psychotic former drill instructor. Vince looked at the situation, made a few alterations, and came up with a feud so emotional that it was able to headline Madison Square Garden even when Hogan wasn't around.

It started when the Sheik and I walked into Slaughter's path, coming and going from the ring. A couple of words were exchanged. The Sheik waved his Khomeini flag, and screamed,

"Iran Number One!" Slaughter called me a "traitor and a maggot." That was all it took. Within seconds, Slaughter became a patriotic babyface. Ronald Reagan was the president, and Americans felt more powerful than they had during the hostage crisis. If Iran, Libya, or the Soviets tried fucking with us now, we'd bury them—the way Vince was going to trample the AWA.

It was a perfect gimmick for the time.

Regis Philbin: Vince McMahon decided to have a no-holds-barred "boot camp match" between Sgt. Slaughter and the Iron Sheik at Madison Square Garden. It was great. Slaughter was the U.S. Marine. The Sheik was one of the most colorful bad guys around. He would cry and he would whine, and then he would attack from the rear.

I got to Madison Square Garden before the doors opened, went to the dressing room with my cameraman, and asked, "Where's Freddie Blassie?"

"He's not here."

"Well, where is he?"

"He and the Sheik said they wanted to be alone."

Up there on the second deck, I find Freddie Blassie. He and the Sheik are in one of these little alcoves, and the Sheik is going through his prayer. He's on his knees, praying to Allah.

We turn on the camera, and Blassie starts screaming, "Look what you did! You disturbed the Sheik! The Sheik is in holy prayer, and you came and you bothered him!"

I apologize, and Blassie tells me, "Look, the Sheik wants me to pray with him." So I said, "Go ahead. Start your prayers."

Freddie kneeled down next to the Sheik, and began doing what the Sheik was doing. I mean, you never saw a guy pray like this. Blassie's throwing his arms up in the air and screaming, and we shot it all. I showed the footage to the president of ABC because it was so good. It was wonderful, a wonderful scene.

Nikolai Volkoff: Vince decided to put me with the Iron Sheik in a tag team. It was a good idea. I was the communist. He was the Iranian terrorist.

We did this thing before every match where the ring announcer said, "Mr. Volkoff requests that you please rise and respect his singing of the Soviet National Anthem." I know the words because my mother was Russian, and I grew up in a communist country. Every time, the fans would go crazy, screaming, "U-S-A! U-S-A!" and throwing garbage. Then, the Sheik grabs the microphone and yells, "Russia, Number One! Iran, Number One! U.S.A. . . ." And he'd spit, *Paaaaatuuuu!"*

Bill Watts, the promoter in Louisiana, was the one who first had the idea for me to do the Soviet National Anthem. Except he played a tape. I had to take the tape with me everywhere. I had one copy. Grizzly Smith, the road agent—who worked backstage with the wrestlers—had another. And the office had another copy. If I come to the arena and I forgot the tape, I got fined fifty bucks.

So we go to New Orleans for a big show, and it was a sellout. And Grizzly says, "Nikolai, do you have your tape?" I said, "No, I left my tape in the office. They want to make some more copies, you know?" He said, "I forgot to bring mine. I guess we have to be fined tonight."

And I said, "No, Grizzly, I have a better idea. I'll sing the Soviet National Anthem myself." So that's what I did. When we come to the ring, I said, "Ladies and gentleman, I'm sorry we can't play my tape because the Junkyard Dog stole it." And those people cheered. They were happy as hell. Then, I said, "However, I will sing it."

The people stomp their feet and scream. Oh my God, it was unbelievable. So when I come back from Louisiana to work for World Wrestling Federation again, I told Vince about the gimmick. He said, "Okay, but sing it after the match, like in the Olympics." I explain to him that's no good. You never know what can happen in the match. He said, "Try it tonight, and see what happens."

We were doing a TV taping in Poughkeepsie. I sang the Soviet National Anthem, and Vince loved it. It got great heat. I would sing, and the Sheik would stand there and look at his biceps. And Blassie would have his hand on his heart, and a serious look on his face. The people would get so pissed off at him because he is an American, and look what he is doing. It was the best.

I enjoyed managing the Sheik and Volkoff. Volkoff had been my first protégé in the WWWF, and the Sheik was the most successful guy in my stable. Even though some fans were beginning to understand the showmanship aspect of pro wrestling, a lot more still believed. And when they saw me carousing with these two enemies of the United States, they were convinced that I was better off dead than alive.

One night, when I was walking to the ring with the Sheik and Volkoff, I heard someone yell, "Hey, Blassie!" People were hollering shit at me all the time but, for some reason, I looked over. And when I did, two teenage punks threw a hardboiled egg at my right eye. When it hit, it felt like a solid piece of stone. I was seeing moons and stars, but my boys had a match to wrestle, so I concentrated on that.

In the dressing room, I noticed that my eye was inflamed. I got some eye drops the next morning, and tried to treat it. I probably should have gone to a specialist, but, in this business, you don't run to a doctor every time you get a little scratch. Every day, the eye got worse until I realized that I could barely see out of it. And that's how it stayed. Today—after all the other shit I've gone through—I'm almost totally blind in my right eye because some asshole hit me with a fuckin' egg.

Lou Albano was very excited, when we sat down in the restaurant. "Cyndi Lauper's meeting us here tonight," he said.

Now, my musical tastes didn't really extend past the Kennedy administration. "Who's Cyndi Lauper?" I asked.

"She's a rock star. She put me in one of her videos, *Girls Just Wanna Have Fun*. I play her father."

"Yeah? Well, I never heard of her."

"Well, she's coming."

About fifteen minutes later, this girl walked in, with a thick Queens accent, made up like a clown. But she was sweet as could be, and really loved the business. Like Andy Kaufman, she wanted to get involved somehow. The difference was that she was a lot more levelheaded, and Andy wanted to make a deal with Vince McMahon, Sr. Now, his son was in charge, and it was a whole new ballgame.

Lou brought Cyndi on *Piper's Pit*, and started making fun of women. Cyndi freaked out, and smacked him. This led to Cyndi announcing her intention to become a wrestling manager.

On July 23, 1984, her protégé, Wendi Richter, defeated the Fabulous Moolah—managed by Albano—for the Women's Wrestling Championship. Newspapers from all over the world ran photos of Cyndi and Richter celebrating.

Vince's "Rock 'n' Wrestling Connection" was born. Celebrities began hanging out at Madison Square Garden, telling reporters that World Wrestling Federation was the only place to be. Since Vince was now also on the west coast, the beautiful people there began saying the same thing. Lauper brought Hogan to the Grammy Awards. Eventually, there'd be a record album—with wrestlers singing rock 'n' roll songs—and even a cartoon show called *Hulk Hogan's Rock 'n' Wrestling.*

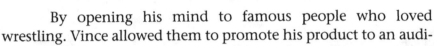

By opening his mind to famous people who loved wrestling. Vince allowed them to promote his product to an audience who'd never seen it before. And he was willing to spend money to make money, a concept that would've sent his so-called peers running for the hills. There wasn't a promoter alive who could touch McMahon's marketing genius. Still, let's not forget about Lou Albano. If he hadn't grabbed Lauper's attention with his antics on television, she might have used her celebrity to endorse something else.

On February 18, 1985, Hogan wrestled "Rowdy" Roddy Piper on MTV of all places. It was a Free-For-All. When Piper's allies, Paul "Mr. Wonderful" Orndorff and Bob Orton, Jr. got involved in the match, so did Hogan's friends, Cyndi Lauper and Mr. T. Mr. T was a rough-looking guy who was the star of the hit TV show *The A-Team,* and had appeared with Hogan in *Rocky III.* After the match, Hogan said that he wanted to team up with Mr. T against Piper and Orndorff. Now, everything was in place for Vince to promote the first *WrestleMania,* an annual event that would later be called WWE's Superbowl.

I'm convinced that every fan who attended the show in Madison Square Garden on March 31, 1985, left exhilarated. Muhammad Ali was brought in as a special referee for the main event. Liberace danced in the ring with the Rockettes. New York Yankees manager Billy Martin was a guest ring announcer.

Of course, the matches were broadcast on closed circuit—just like when I wrestled Tolos in 1971, and seconded Ali against Inoki in 1976. But now—with more and more Americans getting cable TV—the company tried a new experiment called Pay-Per-View. The orders poured in, and World Wrestling Federation became leaders in the field.

The day also had special significance for Freddie Blassie fans. How many other guys can boast about wrestling in carnivals in the 1930s, and appearing on Pay-Per-View a half century later? Not too many, I'll tell you that.

The most important title defended at the first *WrestleMania* was the Tag Team Championship (Hogan was in a Tag Team match, so his belt wasn't up for grabs). The titlists were Barry Windham—the son of my old protégé, Blackjack Mulligan—and his brother-in-law, Mike Rotundo. The challengers were the Iron Sheik and Nikolai Volkoff.

Windham and Rotundo were good-looking kids, and they fired up the crowd by leaving the dressing room to Bruce Springsteen's "Born in the USA." Their manager was none other than Captain Lou Albano, who'd united with Lauper, and was now a babyface. He and I clashed a little bit, jabbing fingers at each other outside the ring, but I did my best to stay out of the match—until the very end. As the referee argued with Rotundo over something or other, and Windham and Volkoff were punching it out in the ring, I handed my cane to the Iron Sheik. From the ring apron, he cocked back his right arm and smashed the object over Windham's head—with so much force that it snapped into pieces that flew at Volkoff and very nearly knocked him out. Windham fell to the canvas, with Nikolai on top of him, as the referee counted to three.

"A very controversial match," announcer "Mean" Gene Okerlund commented when the three of us came backstage with the titles.

I blasted him, "What do you mean, 'controversial'! He pinned him right in the center of the ring, didn't he? Did he or did he not pin him for a count of three?"

"Where's that cane of yours?"

"*What* cane?! I didn't have no cane!"

Looking back, it was an honor to play a role in a title

change on such an important card. But, if you remember, *I* wasn't the one who used the walking stick. It was the Iron Sheik. And that's the way I liked it. It was my boys' night, and I'd never want to steal the thunder from them.

Nikolai Volkoff: *WrestleMania* is when everything changed. Today, it's not the individual who draws. It's the company. It's the event. *WrestleMania* was the beginning of that.

Now, the Sheik and I traveled everywhere together. We were in St. Louis, and this beautiful girl come to me and ask, "Where's your manager, Freddie Blassie?" And I told her, "Freddie Blassie isn't here today. It's only me and the Sheik." And she started crying.

The girl told me that she was Freddie Blassie's daughter, and she didn't talk to him for years. I said, "Listen, don't cry. Just give me your phone number. And when I'm with Freddie in a couple of days, I make sure he call you."

When I saw Freddie, I told him what happened. And I said, "Please call her. Don't be ashamed. She wants to talk to you, and she's your daughter."

Freddie picked up the phone and called. And soon, he starts crying. I was in the room with the Iron Sheik and Lou Albano, and the two of them are just standing there. So I said, "Let's go. We have to give him his privacy."

When he come out of the room, I said, "Freddie, how do you feel?" And he told me, "Nikolai, thank you. I was so glad to talk to my daughter."

Nikolai is a very sensitive sort of person. He loves family life. And when he found out about my daughter, it was very important to him that I called.

After so many years, I was happy to speak to her. My greatest hope was that we would become close. But she was still upset about things that happened in the past. I understand exactly how she feels. But you can only put out your hand so many times. If someone keeps knocking it down, you're going to back away.

Still, I'll never forget what Nikolai did. In this business, people put their arm around your shoulder and call you "brother" every day. At least in his case, I knew it was true.

Andre was still up to his old tricks. And he always managed to catch me off guard. Around 1986, I was driving home with him and Arnold Skaaland, Bob Backlund's old manager who still had a backstage job with World Wrestling Federation. We pulled into my driveway, and Andre got out of the car with me.

"Freddie, I want to help you with your bags," he said.

"Thanks a lot, Andre."

We walked through the door, and Andre dropped my luggage on the floor. I looked over at him, and noticed that smile that I'd seen so many times before.

"*Andre,* don't even fuckin' . . ."

But as I was speaking, Andre let out a massive fart, and rushed out the door, his booming laughter echoing behind him. I had to run through the house, opening all the windows. Even so, the place stunk for a week.

Hercules Hernandez became my last protégé. I still had Volkoff and the Sheik, but the company believed that Hernandez,

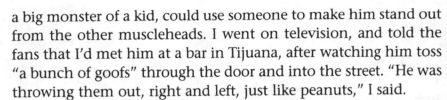

a big monster of a kid, could use someone to make him stand out from the other muscleheads. I went on television, and told the fans that I'd met him at a bar in Tijuana, after watching him toss "a bunch of goofs" through the door and into the street. "He was throwing them out, right and left, just like peanuts," I said.

Even though Hernandez had a Hispanic surname, there was nothing really ethnic about him; to the best of my knowledge, he didn't even speak Spanish. Still, I boasted, "This man, without a doubt, is the greatest Latin wrestler I've ever seen. I've been looking for a good Latin wrestler, somebody that these pencil neck geeks, these Latins, could be proud of."

Vince was doing the announcing duties, and decided to challenge me on my statement: "You've normally been managing foreign wrestlers. Why now, Hercules Hernandez, from the United States?"

"Well, he's a foreign wrestler," I insisted. "I *made* him a foreigner. With a name like Hernandez, he could be from anywhere."

I leaned over and told Hercules in a loud whisper, "Don't tell him where you're from."

World Wrestling Federation was so hot at this time that NBC was running a special wrestling program called *Saturday Night's Main Event.* They actually had scriptwriters coming up with the promos for the boys. I went along with it—hell, Vince knew what was better for the business than I did—but, on our syndicated shows, I still blurted out whatever I wanted.

"Hercules Hernandez would be a great guy to have as your son," I said one time, "especially when the Warrant Squad came looking for him. As long as you knew where he's hiding, you could always cash in on the reward."

I never got tired of speaking into a microphone. But, at nearly seventy years old, life on the road was starting to take its toll. With my old knees and bad hip and all the other injuries I had, it was getting tougher and tougher to squeeze into airplanes, get on shuttle buses in airports, and wait on line at rental car counters. There were new managers in World Wrestling Federation, like my old protégé, Mr. Fuji, Jimmy "Mouth of the

South" Hart, and Bobby "The Brain" Heenan. Sure, none of them were Freddie Blassie, but they each knew how to draw people.

The dilemma I faced was that, as tired as I was of traveling, I didn't want to leave the business. I discussed this with Vince, and he made me an offer to work in the office.

I didn't exactly have a job title. But I knew what I was expected to do. There were still a lot of gifted wrestlers working for rival promoters. If somebody else from World Wrestling Federation called them, they might have been suspicious. After all, the other promoters had them brainwashed that Vince McMahon had the same moral fiber as Joe Stalin. Vince's wife, Linda, once joked that there were so many negative things said about her husband, she was surprised that nobody ever asked him where he was on November 22, 1963—the day President Kennedy was shot. But when Freddie Blassie was on the phone, everybody took the call. So it made it a lot easier for us to poach talent.

The company was expanding so fast that there wasn't even an office for me. They had to put my desk out in the hallway. That meant that when people passed by, I could get into mischief.

There were two secretaries there, Anita and Marge, and we'd clown around all day. One time, we were standing outside of Vince's office, and I goosed Anita. She let out a big laughing shriek, *"Aaaaah."* Vince came running out with a worried look on his face. Then, he looked at me and smirked, "Oh, it's you."

Vince McMahon: I'm not sure I could write a job description for Freddie. He could have been the official-shit disturber, as far as I was concerned. It was just so wonderful to see his smiling face up and down these hallways. He was entitled to be here.

Of course, Freddie wasn't destined for an office job. He was like a time bomb, constantly fucking with people. Every day, you knew there was going to be some type of incident. Some poor bastard would be delivering the mail, and Freddie would steal his cart. The guy would turn around, and the cart would be gone. All afternoon, the cart would ride up and down on the elevator until somebody found it.

Bud Carroll (former World Wrestling Federation maintenance worker): Freddie may have pulled some ribs on us, but we got

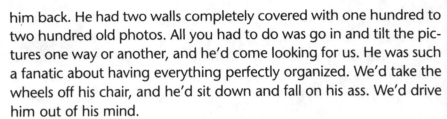

him back. He had two walls completely covered with one hundred to two hundred old photos. All you had to do was go in and tilt the pictures one way or another, and he'd come looking for us. He was such a fanatic about having everything perfectly organized. We'd take the wheels off his chair, and he'd sit down and fall on his ass. We'd drive him out of his mind.

We used to hang around with a guy, Nick Tatano, who worked in the mailroom. We had a grill on the loading dock, where we'd cook our lunch—bacon, sausage, hot dogs, hamburgers. The smoke would go up all the way through the building. Then, the phone would ring on the loading dock: "Is anyone cooking down there?" Freddie would get on and say, "No, not us."

Every day, he'd be outside with us barbecuing—until his wife found out. He was on a very strict diet, and she ruled the roost. If it wasn't for her, he would have been dead twenty years ago.

In 1987, Andre turned heel, and demanded a title shot against his "friend" Hulk Hogan. Of course, no one bothered telling the fans that the two had already had a nasty feud in 1980. So, on March 29, 1987, 93,173 spectators filled the Pontiac Silverdome—home of the NFL's Detroit Lions—to see this "battle of the century" in the main event of *WrestleMania III*. Not only did World Wrestling Federation outdraw the Pope when he appeared in the same venue, but the company took in $1.6 million at the gate—and $10.3 million in Pay-Per-View sales.

Andre did the job, but it didn't make a difference. At one point, he had Hogan pinned, and the referee counted to three, then shook his head and changed his mind, as if he'd only meant to slap the mat twice. It was a little something inserted into the match to make fans curious to see the duo battle to a decisive conclusion later on.

All in all, it was a great night for "The Eighth Wonder of the World," and something he probably needed emotionally, since he understood that, because of his condition, he didn't have much time left. There were still big days ahead—he and Haku won World Wrestling Federation Tag Team titles on December 13, 1989, and held them until *WrestleMania VI* on April 1, 1990, at Toronto's SkyDome—but I could see changes in Andre. His walking became very laborious, and he wrestled wearing a back brace under his trunks. There was a lot weighing on his mind, but he wouldn't go to the doctor. What the hell was the doctor going to tell him anyway? He knew that he had acromegaly, and people with acromegaly didn't live long.

He seemed to want to enjoy every second that he had left on earth. If there were twenty-four hours of the day, Andre tried to spend twenty-eight of them in the bar. There were many times I'm sure that he came into the ring inebriated. If an ordinary wrestler had pulled that shit, Vince would have kicked him out of the company. But we all understood that Andre was a special case. We knew that we'd miss that big fuck when he died, and didn't want to get rid of him while he was still alive.

In January 1993, Andre went to France to visit his sick father. When his father died, Andre remained in the country to spend time with relatives. But on January 27, he went to sleep in his hotel room and never woke up.

I'd always sensed that Andre stayed out so late because he didn't want to die in his sleep. Now, his premonition had come true. I can't say that I enjoyed those farts, but I certainly enjoyed Andre the Giant, even if he was a revolting bastard.

The year that he died, Andre became the first member of the WWE Hall of Fame. In 1994, it was my turn. I was inducted with Chief Jay Strongbow, "Golden Boy" Arnold Skaaland, Bobo Brazil, "Nature Boy" Buddy Rogers, Gorilla Monsoon, and James Dudley—Bobo's sometime manager, and the first black man to manage a major arena in the United States.

Once again, the company did the right thing by me. And now, I was thought of—and treated as—a genuine legend.

On March 20, 1994—shortly before my induction—I walked into the dressing room at Madison Square Garden, to greet the boys getting ready for *WrestleMania X*. Suddenly, I heard a voice boom, "O Illustrious One, where have you been?" When I turned around, I saw Burt Reynolds, one of the celebrity guests at the show. With photographers flashing their cameras, he knelt down in front of me and kissed my hand.

Jeff Krulik: In 1994, when I was working in the programming department at the Discovery Channel, I had a Freddie Blassie doll on my desk. Maybe the average person would walk by a Freddie Blassie doll in a toy store and not think anything of it. But there was something unusual about a doll of this handsome, white-haired man holding a cane to hit people. To me, it was the ultimate in outlandish pop culture.

In my opinion, Freddie Blassie transcended wrestling. I was a big fan of his from when I was involved at the radio station at the University of Maryland, and played "Pencil Neck Geek" and "Blassie—King of Men." My friend at Discovery, Brendan Conway, told me that he always thought of Blassie as wrestling's version of Fred Mertz from *I Love Lucy,* an older gentleman who was always cranky. We'd come up with different scenarios for a Freddie Blassie documentary, like, "What would happen if Freddie Blassie came to Washington, D.C., and rode around in a limo with a bunch of strippers to all the landmarks?"

The next thing you knew, we were calling the World Wrestling Federation, and saying, "How do we get Blassie to be in our movie, *Mr. Blassie Goes to Washington?*" We were told that, if we only needed him for a day, it would actually be pretty easy. All we had to do was pay a personal-appearance fee, and pick up his airfare.

We set up a date, and began arranging things. We pursued a performing dwarf from Baltimore. He was a show business veteran, who'd been in like a Three Stooges film. But he wanted SAG wages. In hindsight, it would have been one of our better investments. But money was tight, and we didn't want to spend the three hundred dollars.

We needed strippers to accompany Blassie on his journey, and actually found an agency willing to provide the girls for free. It was amazing. They did it for exposure, and twenty dollars each for lunch.

Brendan went and talked a sign company into donating these signs that said things like, WELCOME, BLASSIE—KING OF MEN for the girls to hold. And we planned to have an Elvis impersonator meet us, but—this is before everyone had cell phones—he went to the wrong location.

When Blassie arrived at the airport, and the strippers greeted him, cheering with these signs, the other passengers were slack-jawed, puzzled, and perplexed. *We* knew that this guy was so cool, but very few other people were getting it. Elliot, the cameraman, was kind of scratching his head, like, "What's so funny about this?" And the strippers didn't understand either. But Brendan and I thought it was hysterical.

The PR guy from World Wrestling Federation had set up a couple of guidelines for us. It was okay for Freddie to be on camera, doing ridiculous stuff, but when we wanted him to scream at people through a bullhorn, the idea was nixed. It seemed to be a very random decision. I guess the PR guy thought that a bullhorn wasn't dignified or something.

We started driving Freddie to the different locations. At the first one, he seemed a little confused, and asked somebody, "What's this building over here?" It was the Lincoln Memorial.

He asked another family where they were from, and they said the Bronx. And he went, "Oh, the Bronx. God's country." A lot of tourists didn't know what was going on. When they saw the camera and the commotion, they started backing away. To have someone like Freddie Blassie at the Lincoln Memorial with strippers and signs and a TV crew was totally out of context, totally weird.

It turned out that it was a year to the day that the Feds raided that compound in Waco, and you had a bunch of antigovernment, conspiracy theorists at this rally that we stumbled upon. Suddenly, Fred gets out of this limo, and descends upon them. For some reason, he decides to give a speech about how much he loves this country, and really pisses them off. Not only that, he's also stealing all their attention, subverting everything they were trying to do. So this one woman yells at him, "Thank you, thank you, Mister Blassie"—I think she may have called him "Glassie"—"go elsewhere. You're not wanted here. Good-bye."

We go outside the White House—Clinton was president then—and Freddie's screaming in that famous voice of his, "Where's Bill? Come on out here, Bill! Hillary's got you in the kitchen, making sandwiches."

One of the strippers decided to get in on the action and yells, "Bring the dog!" And Freddie looks over at her, and shouts, "He doesn't have a dog. He's got a cat."

The police sized us up pretty quickly, and decided that we weren't threatening. In fact, they were laughing at everything that Freddie did.

Freddie sees a woman with a baby, and asks her to bring it over. She's a little bit nervous and keeps walking, so he barks at her,

"Come over here! Come over here! I'm not going to hurt you!" and scares her even more.

He walks up to these two Tibetan monks and says, "You know who I am, right?" They say, "yeah, yeah," even though I'm not sure if they did, and Freddie poses for a picture with one of them. The other one is kind of hanging back, and Freddie demands that he also get in the shot, yelling, "What are you—shy?"

The whole day, we're asking each other, "When is Blassie gonna get mad at us?" We were used to seeing him lose his temper on TV, and weren't sure what would set him off.

At the end of the day, when we were heading back to the airport, the air-conditioning broke in the limo, and everyone was sweating. We get to the airport, and he's sweating and complaining about his bum knee, and, for some stupid reason, we asked him to autograph some pictures. He kind of hesitated, and we pushed the issue. Finally, he says, "I've had it," and starts cursing and yelling, and storms off. And that's how the day ended.

In 1995, World Championship Wrestling (WCW) started a show called *Nitro*, to run opposite World Wrestling Federation's *Raw* program every Monday night. On the very first episode, Lex Luger—who'd wrestled for World Wrestling Federation that weekend—appeared. Suddenly, World Wrestling Federation had a challenger on its hands. Although the NWA still existed, its members were mainly promoting in tiny arenas, and most young fans didn't know anything about them. Verne Gagne's AWA had gone out of business. But WCW was owned by billionaire Ted Turner, and had a lot of money to toss around. One by one, they started taking some of World Wrestling Federation's biggest names: Hulk Hogan, Randy "Macho Man" Savage, "Rowdy" Roddy Piper, Kevin "Diesel" Nash, Scott "Razor Ramon" Hall. Believe it or not, they even tried recruiting me.

I don't know if they wanted me as an announcer—they already had two of the best from World Wrestling Federation in Heenan and "Mean" Gene Okerlund—or manager. But they knew damn well that showing my face on their program would be the ultimate kick in the balls to Vince. From the outset, I left no question in anyone's mind about where Freddie Blassie stood on this front.

"I don't care if Vince goes out of business," I said. "I'll go down the drain with him."

For eighty-three straight weeks, *Nitro* beat *Raw* in the ratings. Then, Stone Cold Steve Austin started battling Vince in World Wrestling Federation story lines, and the company pulled ahead, and never looked back. All those guys who took Ted Turner's money were scratching their heads, going, "What the fuck did I do? How am I gonna get Vince to like me again?"

I had no such worries. My loyalties have always been with Vince because he's my friend, and because he's the best.

When I sit down and watch a WWE Pay-Per-View, I often think about the way the business has changed since I started in 1935. Despite all the differences, there are some things that have remained the same. On every Saturday night, in an armory, fairground, or high school gymnasium, some kid is getting his brains knocked out for an independent promoter, hoping to get a reputation and, one day, a push. If he's lucky, he'll be able to pay for his carfare. More likely, after he calculates in all his expenses, he's getting stiffed.

Of course, today, a wrestler can come out of the independent circuit and, within a year or two, make a small fortune in WWE. I've been asked if it pisses me off that the guys are making so much money today. Pisses me off? I'm happy for them. We're all part of the same fraternity, and their victories are my victories.

They also earn every penny they make.

When I was main eventing, no one ever delivered a moonsault from the turnbuckles to a guy on the arena floor, got thrown through a table from the top of a cage, or did a sunset flip off a ladder. On April 29, 2001, at the *Backlash* Pay-Per-View, Vince's son, Shane McMahon—who's not even an official wrestler—climbed up a truss towards the arena ceiling, and jumped off, executing a flying elbow on Paul "Big Show" Wight from something like forty feet in the air. Just before he leaped, Shane made the sign of the cross. I was watching from home, and made the sign of the cross with him.

You can't imagine how much punishment the wrestlers

endure. I don't care how well you know how to take a bump. Your body still has to absorb every blow. These guys are taking their lives in their hands every time they step into the ring, and, in some ways, this is a rougher business than it's ever been.

Just take a look at the WWE roster. Each guy is tougher than the guy before him. And almost every one of them has had to come back after crippling injuries. Steve Austin was out of action for about a year after he had two vertebrae fused. Triple H tore his quadriceps tendon in a match, and still continued the brawl, ending up on top of the announcer's table, where Chris Jericho turned him onto his stomach, and bent his legs back toward his head while applying the "Walls of Jericho." I don't know how many times I've seen Undertaker hobbling around backstage, like he could barely walk, then watched him get in the ring, push the pain out of his mind, and wrestle with his heart. That's why, behind the scenes, Undertaker is considered something of a player-coach for the other talent. He always gives you a day's work, and—just like Rikidozan, Bruno Sammartino, Bob Backlund, and The Destroyer—takes pride in being called a wrestler.

I'd love nothing more than to be with these guys all the time, telling them my old war stories, and listening to their new ones. As I got older, though, I stopped driving, and couldn't even get myself to the office. Over the past few years, whenever I've done any work for WWE, they've sent a driver and a limo for me.

Fortunately, the company's kept me pretty busy. Through WWE, I'm a "community mayor" of New York and New Jersey, meaning that I attend events with other notables—like Jackie Mason and Leslie Uggams—to raise money for disabled kids.

Every year, I play Santa Claus at the office Christmas party. The employees bring their children, and they all climb onto my lap. I hug and kiss the babies and the toddlers, and not one of them cries. I guess their parents never bothered smartening them up about the sordid history of "Classy" Freddie Blassie.

Now, when the company sends me to some other locations, it's a very different story. I regularly visit two Salvation

Army facilities—one in Long Island City, Queens, and the other in Harlem—with rehabilitation services and lodging for homeless veterans. I never forgot those women from the Salvation Army who were serving us hot coffee in the freezing cold when I was discharged from the Navy. Finally, I have the time to devote myself to an organization I'd always promised to assist.

At both locations, I always bring copies of WWE's publications—*WWE Magazine* and *WWE Raw Magazine*—and pictures to autograph. But I spend most of my time talking to my fellow vets. The majority want to discuss wrestling. A few of them, though, prefer asking me intimate questions about sex. And some of these guys—in my opinion—aren't really qualified to be having sex and making babies.

In reality, I never try to act like I'm any better than anyone else. Look, we had a lot of flakes in the service—and even more in the wrestling business—so I'm not completely out of my element. But some of these characters really push my buttons. A couple of them think I own the limo, and ask me for a job.

"It's not my car. The car belongs to World Wrestling Entertainment."

"Yeah, yeah, sure it does. We know. We know."

"You don't know shit."

Sometimes, I'll be signing autographs, and I'll notice a guy taking a wrestling magazine and walking away. "Where you going?" I'll ask.

"I'm taking a magazine."

"I see you're taking a magazine. But who the hell said you could do that? I need those magazines for the next place I'm going. And I saw you take a magazine before." See, I understand their game. They'll snatch three or four magazines, and give them out to their friends.

"Fuck you."

"Fuck you?"

"Fuck you. You wanna try to take the magazine off of me?"

"Yeah, I do, you fuckin' scumbag. I'll stuff you up one nostril and blow you out the other. You ever fight with a wrestler before? I'll break your arm. I'll snap your fuckin' neck."

"I don't have to listen to this shit."

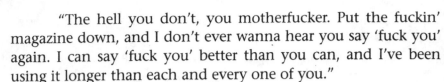

"The hell you don't, you motherfucker. Put the fuckin' magazine down, and I don't ever wanna hear you say 'fuck you' again. I can say 'fuck you' better than you can, and I've been using it longer than each and every one of you."

Now, I don't want you to get the wrong impression. Ninety-five percent of these guys are the greatest. They love when I come to visit them, and can't do enough for me. One guy at the Harlem shelter always brings me pretzels. I keep telling him, "No, no, no. I'm not supposed to have salt, and my wife is raising holy hell."

Two weeks later, he brings more pretzels. I remind him, "What did I tell you last time?" And he goes, "I forgot."

When I get home, without fail, Miyako is waiting to ask if I had any pretzels.

"This is a homeless man and he doesn't have anything else in his life, and he went out of his way to buy me pretzels," I argue. "What should I do—throw them back in his face?"

But Miyako doesn't want to hear it. Over and over again, she repeats, "No more pretzels."

In September 2002, Miyako and I celebrated our thirty-fourth wedding anniversary. If she wasn't around, I'd be a mess. She keeps track of my schedule, knows which doctors I'm supposed to visit for my various ailments, and makes sure that I take whatever pills they prescribe for me. She's been there for my knee replacement, my hip replacement, my triple bypass, nursing me back to health every time. Shit, with all the things wrong with me, I shouldn't even be walking around today. But Miyako's too tough to let me die.

Miyako Blassie: Needless to say, there are ups and down in life. When I've faced difficulties in our marriage, I was able to handle them with strenuous efforts and patience I've learned from my Japanese culture. Among Japanese people, patience is believed to be a virtue, something that helps people grow mature and tolerant. I also believe in this. That is why I don't believe in divorce.

I have watched my husband bring joy to wrestling fans all over the world. And for more than thirty years, I've known a different kind of joy as Freddie Blassie's wife. Every sacrifice I've made for him has been worth it. He's a good man, and he deserves it.

* * *

Freddie and his wife, Miyako, at a gathering of the Cauliflower Alley Club, an association of old-time wrestlers.

The biggest regret I have in my life is my relationship with my children. I know everything about them, but—with the exception of my son Ron—I've had to acquire that information from afar. Ron is a sales manager in the fabricated pipe and steel business. Gary is the horticulture supervisor for all sixty-eight parks in St. Louis County. Cheryl is a schoolteacher. I've never met my grandchildren, but know all about their academic achievements. I'm proud of them, even though I wouldn't dare take credit for their success. Whatever smarts they inherited, they got from their grandmother, not me.

No matter what anybody tells you, it hurts to be estranged from your family. I would love to meet my grandchildren, speak with them, learn about their interests and their friends, and tell them about myself—not only my accomplishments in the wrestling world, but the things I do for the Salvation Army and the community mayors of New York and New Jersey. Even though I screwed up my marriage with their grandmother, I wish that they could see the kind of life I have today with Miyako. I want them to think that I'm a decent guy, but I'm not sure if I could ever convince them.

I remember when Ron told me that Cheryl's son, Justin, was a wrestling fan. Because my daughter doesn't speak with me, I arranged for Ron to receive some tickets, and then he gave them to the boy. I heard that Justin had a great time at the arena, and told everybody that his grandfather was a champion wrestler. That made me feel so good. But imagine what we could have talked about if I'd been sitting there, next to him?

* * *

Ron Blassie: It's a shame that our family isn't closer. I think it would be great if my father called my brother or sister, or they called him. I think that, deep down, they all want to. Unfortunately, everybody's afraid of everybody else.

I'm amazed by the way that even now, people react when they hear that my last name is Blassie. It's bizarre. When I was working in Houston at this big steel company, the owner called me in one day, and said, "Ron, I want you to come back here and meet somebody." So I went into the office, and there was this Japanese guy sitting behind the desk with the owner. And the owner says, "This is Ron Blassie."

The Japanese guy goes, "Oooooh. *Brassie. Brassie.*" He couldn't control himself. In front of everybody, he started biting his own arm. And this guy's in a thousand-dollar suit.

As far as the Japanese are concerned, it might as well be 1962. I still get calls all the time from Japanese reporters who want to come over my house and visit me. No matter how many other American stars visit their country, they haven't had their fill of Freddie Blassie.

John Tolos and I still exchange letters, reminiscing about our days beating each other bloody in the Olympic Auditorium. Not too long ago, he addressed the envelope: "Mr. Fred 'Number One' Blassie." I called him up and said, "You're damn right, I'm number one. Why didn't you admit it when I was wrestling you, you son of a bitch?"

Whenever I'm out with my wife, someone comes up to me and says, "Hey, Freddie, I just wanted to thank you for the good times you gave me." I'd be lying if I said that it didn't feel good. And at least now, I'm pretty sure that nobody's going to try to throw acid on my back, or an egg in my eye.

Still, sometimes I've wondered whether today's wrestling fans would remember me. One weekend in 2001, my friend, Ed Cohen, WWE's senior vice president of live events, called me up and invited me to attend an afternoon show with him at Madison Square Garden. "Come on, Freddie," he said, "the people will be happy to see you."

"Happy to see me? Shit. I'm an old-timer."

Ed was persistent, and I hadn't been to a live event in a while, so I went along. As soon as we walked into Madison Square Garden, a group of ushers ran up to greet me. When I entered the dressing room, Undertaker came over, then Stone Cold Steve Austin, Lita, Trish Stratus, Edge, Kurt Angle, and The Rock. Ed and I took our seats and the matches started. I was talking with the people around me, when Ed nudged me.

"Freddie," he said, "they're talking about you."

Howard Finkel, the ring announcer, was telling the crowd that there was a special guest in the arena. "Allow me to introduce," he began, his voice rising, "the living legend himself, 'Classy' Freddie Blassie." The crowd lit up. I was the most surprised guy in the world.

"Stand up, Freddie," somebody yelled.

I rose to my feet, and the audience rose with me, applauding loudly. The ushers turned towards me and began clapping, too. I leaned over to Ed and smirked, "This is the only time I ever remember getting cheered in this building." Then, I applauded the people back.

The war between World Wrestling Federation and WCW came to an end in 2001 when WCW fell apart, and Vince purchased the remnants of the company. He created a story line in which his kids, Shane and Stephanie, had bought WCW and another rival promotion, Extreme Championship Wrestling (ECW), and planned to use the talent from those organizations to put World Wrestling Federation out of business.

On July 22, 2001, the *Invasion* Pay-Per-View took place, pitting World Wrestling Federation's Superstars against Shane and Stephanie's "Alliance." To entice people to watch the event, the company broadcast a vignette on *Raw* of Vince and Undertaker delivering inspirational speeches to a roomful of

World Wrestling Federation combatants. Suddenly, the door swung open, and I was brought in on a wheelchair, holding my walking stick, and wearing a purple sequin jacket.

"Gentlemen," I said, "there comes a time when every man must fight for what he believes in." I slowly rose out of the chair. "You understand? Now is the time." I gestured and barked at the talent in the same voice I used to predict the demise of Pedro Morales, or broadcast the attributes of the Iron Sheik. *"Get up! Stand up—and fight!"* I shoved my fist in the air. *"Fight!"*

As the show was going off the air, I was shown being wheeled back to a limousine. Out of nowhere, Shane and Stephanie McMahon appeared on each side of me.

"You think what you said in there had any impact at all?" Shane challenged, bending to my level and jabbing a finger at me.

Stephanie giggled in my face. "You see, Freddie, you and World Wrestling Federation have a lot in common. You're both about to *die!*"

No one had bothered to tell me about *this* part of the program. I'd known Shane and Stephanie since they were babies, and I have to admit that I was dumbfounded. I guess that's a sign of old age. It took me a couple of seconds to realize that it was all just a work—the same type of angle I'd orchestrated hundreds, if not thousands, of times in my career.

But as the limo left, I felt satisfied. My confusion only served to help sell the story line. I realized that Vince had put me on TV for a very valid reason: I'll never outlive my usefulness to professional wrestling.

Some people are cut out to do certain things. I was cut out to be a wrestler. I achieved more success in this business than I ever imagined because I loved it as much as I loved myself. That's no exaggeration. I can't think of anything else I would have rather been, except maybe the president of the United States. But I wouldn't have run. After I won by a landslide, how could I have made my bookings?

That's all I have to say, you pencil neck geeks.

270

EPILOGUE

There were times when I suspected that Freddie Blassie was keeping himself alive just to witness the publication of this book. He still had his sparkling moments, but his days were increasingly consumed by doctor's appointments and pill-taking regimens. From time to time, his friend Jerome Raguso, a pastry shop owner in the Bronx's "Little Italy," would invite Freddie to the neighborhood for a meal, and show him the things that people wrote about him on the Internet. It heartened the legend to know that fans were still obsessed with his battles. But one consistent inaccuracy drove the "King of Men" into a fury. At some stage, a myth had started that Blassie's birth name was "Blassman." Whenever he'd spot this error, Freddie would call me up in a rage, asking for reassurance that this book would tell the real story.

In May 2003 the fans began showing up at Freddie's door with copies of the book apparently procured before the official release date. Blassie signed the copies and bitched about the intrusion, but I knew he was happy. Regis Philbin wanted to put him on the air to promote the book. Miyako was worried about her husband doing anything that would aggravate his health. But when WWE offered to send a limo to take Freddie to *Raw* in Philadelphia, she couldn't say no.

Blassie's skin was unnervingly pale and he looked slightly uncomfortable in his wheelchair, but the opportunity to take part in another wrestling angle thrilled him. In a backstage vignette, Freddie and Miyako were shown getting berated by Eric Bischoff. He demanded that Blassie meet him on the entrance ramp. "What are you gonna do—hang yourself?!" Freddie shot back, exhibiting the kind of spontaneous wit that kept him on top.

But Freddie was also a little bit confused. When he got to the entrance ramp, he repeatedly stuck out his tongue. Only later did I learn that Blassie was imitating Bubba and D-Von Dudley's "Whatsssuppp!" routine—*before* the Dudleyz were introduced.

Bischoff said a few cursory things about the book, then began insulting Blassie, suggesting that he wasn't going to be alive much longer. Whatever bewilderment Freddie felt earlier instantly dissipated. When Bischoff asked the icon his age, Freddie retorted with a loud "Twenty-three!"

Within seconds, though, the levity faded, when 3-Minute Warning—the Samoan tandem of Rosey and Jamal—and their manager, Rico, rolled Blassie down the ramp, lifted his wheelchair, and made a motion to hurl him into the ring. Before they could, Stone Cold Steve Austin appeared and unleashed the Dudleyz on the thugs.

The last words a wrestling crowd ever heard Blassie shout were "D-Von, get the tables!"—a command to the Dudleyz to splinter their rivals through a slab of wood.

Backstage afterward, Blassie was mobbed by the boys. Bubba Dudley knelt before him and kissed his hand. Austin and Chris Jericho embraced him. Vince McMahon told the man he'd come to regard as a cranky but endearing uncle, "You stole the show—like you've been doing your whole life."

When I spoke to Freddie the next day, he was nearly in tears when he described the way he was celebrated by his brothers in the wrestling fraternity. As the conversation was ending, he thanked me for helping him take a lifetime of stories and shape them into his autobiography. "God bless you," he told me. "I love you."

A week later his body started to break down. He was having trouble breathing and steadying himself. Out of nowhere, he asked for Eli, his beloved stepfather. "Let's go to the hospital," a tearful Miyako told her husband. "Eli's at the hospital, waiting for you."

For two weeks, Freddie lingered. On Monday, June 2, 2003, the doctors informed Miyako that Freddie's heart was failing and he wasn't going to get better. She was with Vince McMahon's wife, Linda, and son, Shane, when she made the decision to take him off life support.

I began to hear stories about Freddie that I'd missed when we were writing the book. There was the tale of the African-American woman with the floppy hat who'd regularly taunted Blassie from ringside at the Olympic Auditorium. But when years later he returned to Los Angeles with the World Wrestling Federation and spotted her, Freddie broke character and the two rushed toward each other and hugged at the guardrail. The *Wrestling Observer Newsletter* printed an account of Freddie being interviewed about the late Rikidozan and predicting that they'd have their rematch in hell. When the reporter innocently stated that, surely, Rikidozan was in heaven, Blassie shouted, "I knew Rikidozan. He's in hell—and he's a pencil neck geek!"

The over-seventy Destroyer drove down to Freddie's funeral from outside Buffalo, slipping on his mask a few blocks from the church in order to keep up the gimmick. Former World Wrestling Federation champion Bob Backlund showed up, seating himself in front of Afa the Wild Samoan and his family. Then, in his throaty announcer's voice, a misty-eyed McMahon beseeched the crowd to give their friend a standing ovation. As Freddie left the public stage for the last time, he was once again surrounded by the familiar sounds of applause.

The only difference was that all his fans were crying.

—Keith Elliot Greenberg